CASES IN ORGANIZATION DEVELOPMENT:
FOUR PERSPECTIVES ON VALUE-GUIDED CONSULTATION

CASES IN ORGANIZATION DEVELOPMENT:
FOUR PERSPECTIVES ON VALUE-GUIDED CONSULTATION

EDITED BY

Robert T. Golembiewski
University of Georgia

Glenn H. Varney
Bowling Green State University

F.E. PEACOCK PUBLISHERS, INC.
Itasca, Illinois

Cover photo (cropped and digitally altered):
David Wasserman, Artville

Advisory Editor in Public Administration
Bernard H. Ross
School of Public Affairs
American University

Contents

PERSPECTIVE II
ODers in Unusual and Even Exotic Settings

PERSPECTIVE III
Leading Organization Change via Action Research:
An Integrative Experience with a Single Case

PERSPECTIVE IV
A Statement of Values and Ethics by Professionals in
Organization and Human Systems Development (from

Preface

We two editors have long been parallel workers—we have worked on some of the same issues, sometimes in the same ways. But we did so without really engaging as people and professionals. We plowed our own furrows, as it were, even though we often harvested the same or similar crops.

Now is the time for that parallelism to come to an end. Not only have we co-editors collaborated on *Cases in Organization Development*, but in due time we will prepare a companion book of readings to help direct and enrich the various uses of this casebook.

The related projects providing context for this too-long delayed collaboration of the two editors have a special value, we believe. No similar resource of cases is available for the present target group: ODers in early preparation. These targeted learners are perhaps primarily in our numerous Master of Science in Organization Development (MS/OD) programs scattered around the country and, increasingly, the world—at Pepperdine, Bowling Green (Ohio), and Benedictine (Illinois), among many other locations. Joining these burgeoning ranks are a growing number of doctorate OD programs, as well as such in-service certificate programs as that fielded for many years by the National Training Laboratories Institute for Applied Behavioral Science. Finally, many professional schools support the developing ODer—in public administration, business and management, nursing, social work, and so on through a long list.

So this casebook should prove to be a useful and clear complement to the existing case literature. Let us put this point in a simple but not simplified way. Several textbooks contain a number of illustrative cases, more precisely identified as vignettes; and a set of long and complex cases has been available for some time to test the mature ODer

(Glassman and Cummings, 1991).* In contrast to these two end-points, this OD casebook seeks to fill the vast middle ground, which is substantially under-resourced when it comes to collections of case studies.

Broadly, we editors take four cuts a presenting cases so as to motivate and inform. Each case in Perspective I focuses on one or a few of the range of commonplace themes and issues that ODers will encounter. Perspective II adds a baker's dozen of unusual or exotic cases, both to motivate learners to "do it one more time" as well as to stretch their sense of what OD practice can face. Perspective III offers one OD case that provides an integrative experience with the full range of OD activities. Finally, Perspective IV urges that ODers see themselves as operating in a normative context—first, last, and always.

When all is said and done, we co-editors see OD as both powerful *and* as guided. The world has seen enough of puny but precisely targeted change efforts, as well as powerful endeavors that specialize in generating unpleasant surprises.

In short, we co-editors view this casebook, and OD itself, as guided missiles. And we thank the many contributors to the OD tradition— clients, colleagues, and critics alike.

---

*Glassman, A., and Cummings, T. (Eds.) (1991). *Cases in organization development.* Homewood, IL: Irwin.

Introductory Orienting Cues

These OD cases seek to fill a specific niche in what is a large and still-burgeoning area of inquiry and application—organization development (OD) or, as it is sometimes called, organization development and change (ODC). This volume is designed to supply a missing element in the available learning resources.

Right now, the available learning resources are useful, but biased toward two extremes. On the one hand, we have available a hefty compendium of complex cases that would test all that is in the best of us (Glassman and Cummings, 1991), in relation to empirical knowledge, practical skills, and ethical sensibilities. On the other hand, ODers also have available several sets of mini-cases that underplay the relevance of contexts and circumstances, if they do not trivialize the complexities ODers encounter as well as how they respond to those complexities. There are several such sources of mini-case studies (e.g., French and Bell, 1993; Cummings and Worley, 1997).

So, this OD casebook seeks to fill an important middle ground, which can be detailed in terms of four major perspectives. Each perspective will be developed in varying detail in separate sections.

For now, a brief introduction to these four perspectives will suffice. Thus, in this introductory material we will emphasize cases that raise issues of substance, both normative and empirical, in cases of short or moderate length.

Moreover, this casebook permits users to focus on cases that raise separate issues, but it also provides an integrative case that directs users through a full "action research" cycle.

In addition, this text provides exemplars from everyday experience as well as from several less-typical (even wild!) situations that an ODer may occasionally encounter.

Finally, this collection also attempts to provide a sense of context and circumstance sufficient to inform users, but not so fulsome as to overwhelm the learners. Our purpose, after all, is to help readers gain familiarity in dealing with OD-relevant issues within manageable contexts, as contrasted with becoming expert in some specific work context that is so complex as perhaps to be unique, and hence not worth the investment necessary to master its intricacies.

FOUR PERSPECTIVES

Filling this middle-ground niche for this casebook builds on a foundation with four basic features. These major structural components can be described briefly. This introductory preview details four perspectives:

    I.   OD in conventional settings;
    II. OD in novel or even exotic settings;
    III. OD as leading change via a full action research sequence of activities; and
    IV. OD as value-loaded.

PERSPECTIVE I: ODers IN CONVENTIONAL SITUATIONS

In the largest part, the first category of cases focuses on the everyday substance of the OD intervenor's work—standard stuff, but far from humdrum. In short, we co-editors are seldom as alive as when we are involved in a consultation, with senses alert, memory banks being searched for present relevancies in past learnings, and antennae aquiver. Ideally, this casebook will have similar effects on learners, without suffocating them with local detail.

Nineteen cases illustrate the many-splendored dimensions in everyday OD activities that energize and challenge the ODer. Specifically, Exhibit 1 arrays these conventional cases in terms of two useful sets of categories: five "contexts" and 10 "activities" that generate 50 possible cells to which the 19 individual cases are assigned. Coverage here is not perfect, but it is pretty good: more than two-thirds of the cells contain one or more entries.

Let's be more specific about Exhibit 1. Thus, "contexts" are differentiated in terms of five standard categories or loci in which OD can take place: business, education, and so on. The assignments in Exhibit 1 may

Exhibit 1 Cases in Perspective I Classified in 50 Possible Cells

"Contexts" of Applications	"Activities" in Full Action Research Sequence									
	Search	Entry	Contracting	Diagnosis	Feedback to Client	Action Planning	Implementation	Evaluation	Exit	Research
1. Business	I.9, I.19		I.1, I.2, I.9, I.10, I.19	I.2, I.5, I.19	I.4, I.5, I.10, I.11, I.19	I.1, I.2, I.19	I.1, I.9, I.10	I.1		
2. Education		I.7	I.7	I.7	I.7	I.7	I.7	I.7	I.7	I.7
3. Government	I.4	I.3, I.4	I.3			I.14			I.3	
4. Nonprofit	I.12	I.12	I.12, I.17	I.12, I.16	I.16	I.16	I.17	I.17	I.16, I.17	I.12
5. Generic	I.18	I.18	I.8, I.18	I.6, I.13, I.15	I.6, I.18	I.8, I.5	I.8, I.13, I.15	I.18		

help readers in early scans of the cases. In addition, Exhibit 1 also distinguishes nine "activities" often associated with the action research approach to OD. In these nine activities, the focus is on the several steps or stages in a full OD sequence, from the search for a client, to entry into a client system, and so on, through the evaluation of an OD project and the research that may be involved.

The two ways of arraying the cases in Exhibit 1 do not exhaust all of the possibilities, of course. Thus, the following list of cases is arrayed by themes or topics, and this rough classification also might be helpful to users of this casebook.

Topics or Themes in Perspective I	Case(s)
champion or advocate	I.7
client, identification of	I.7, I.14
client, issues with	I.2, I.3, I.4, I.6, I.11, I.14, I.16
conditions for entrance	I.3, I.9
conditions for exit	I.3, I.17
confidentiality	I.10
conflicts of interest, ethical issues	I.2, I.7, I.10, I.11
culture or cross-cultures	I.1, I.3, I.5, I.16
death, organizational	I.17
designs for intervening, varieties of	I.5, I.6, I.7, I.8
diagnostic choice-points	I.5, I.6, I.7, I.9, I.13, I.15, I.17, I.19
ethical choices	I.2, I.3, I.6, I.9, I.10, I.11
family life and dynamics	I.2, I.8
groups	I.13, I.15
growth, organizational	I.5, I.19
interaction, patterns of	I.5, I.8, I.9
intervention, choice of	I.5, I.6
large systems	I.1, I.5, I.7, I.14, I.19
letting go	I.12, I.17
mischief, organizational	I.12, I.17
ODer styles	I.2, I.3, I.4, I.6, I.7, I.9, I.10, I.14, I.18
past history, historical antecedents	I.7
personal growth	I.8, I.18
personal style	I.7, I.16, I.18
phases, organizational	I.18, I.19
political features	I.3, I.7, I.9, I.14
quality of work	I.1
race or ethnicity	I.16

No doubt this list of topics or themes relevant to Perspective I could be extended. Interested users may want to do just this as they get familiar with the cases; nevertheless, the list above should help them to get acquainted with the cases.

Looked at in another way, Exhibit 1 and the list above have a direct implication, and let us put it just that way. The cases below do not exhaust the range of situations within the common reach of OD practice, but the coverage is extensive and even substantially representative.

PERSPECTIVE II: ODers IN UNUSUAL AND EVEN EXOTIC SITUATIONS

Perspective II includes cases that go beyond the ordinary, to say the least. And fascination with the bizarre is not the only reason for their inclusion in a separate section, although fascination or worse seems to your co-editors a feature of all 13 of these cases.

What is our rationale for including these cases? You can learn from more or less standard situations, which is what Perspective I attempts to facilitate. But you can also learn from situations that are "out of the box"—occurrences that are novel, challenging, exotic, or even bizarre. This second approach to learning is provided by the cases in Perspective II. Indeed, some argue that this second class of learning situations has a special relevance: all clients die, but seldom does that inevitability occur during a consultation. But death clearly can occur, and it certainly cannot be finessed. So Case II.1 deals with just such a situation, with the purpose being to add a bit of variety while raising an unusual set of challenges against which ODers can measure their values, attitudes, and skills.

Similarly, Case II.7 deals with a unique assessment of an OD consultant. Clients have different needs in this regard, this case implies. Typically, an ODer might be measured in terms of letters of recommendation or, far better still, in terms of success rates with specific classes of interventions. The client in Case II.7 went substantially beyond the ordinary. Readers may differ about whether a similar characterization applies to both client and consultant in Case II.8.

The other cases in Perspective II also deal with unusual situations that add to the present unconventional list. Thus, cases II.2 and II.13 deal with "shadow consultancies"; that is, they involve consultants who see only reflections of client systems, and even those irregularly; Case II.3 deals with an unusually defensive, but yet curiously flexible, client; Case II.4 deals with an unusual kind of crisis that ODers encounter now-and-again, that often goes unnoticed even though its recognition can inform and enrich OD practice; Case II.8 presents some common issues of "fit" of ODer to organization and to consulting team; and Case II.12 deals with exit, a common phenomenon, but in a mental health setting that makes termination an unusually tricky process.

The other cases in Perspective II also fit unusual molds, if in a range of ways. Thus, attention in Case II.5 goes to a special kind of "confidentiality"; Case II.9 may be viewed as a romp, at a superficial level, but it raises some general and tough issues; Case II.10 focuses on an intense example of the mixed relationships that can exist between client and ODer; Case II.11 relates to an exuberant and no doubt unusual way of welcoming an ODer to a consulting site, with implications that range from the mundane to the exotic; Case II.12 deals with a situation in which exiting or letting go seems especially subtle, given that exit often presents real challenges to both client and ODer; and Case II.13 extends OD's reach into organized crime, while serving to illustrate the notion of "shadow consultant."

Another way to introduce the cases in Perspective II also may aid the reader. Consider this selective list of themes that may help the user get a preliminary sense of the cases included under Perspective II:

client, qualities of	II.3, II.5, II.9, II.11, II.12
comic relief	II.9
confidentiality	II.5
conflicts of interests	II.5, II.13
consultant, qualities of	II.7
consulting style	II.10, II.11
crime	II.13
culture	II.2, II.12
death of client	II.1
diagnosis	II.4, II.5
ethical issues	II.5, II.6, II.8

PERSPECTIVE III: LEADING ORGANIZATIONAL CHANGE VIA ACTION RESEARCH: AN INTEGRATIVE EXPERIENCE WITH A SINGLE CASE*

Leading organizational change is a major responsibility of managers as well as organization development and change consultants. Developing the knowledge and skills necessary for managing systemic change requires an understanding of organizations and human behavior as well as a knowledge of how systems, technology, and people can be integrated. The dual goals are to maximize organizational performance and profitability, as well as to create a committed and satisfied workforce.

The guides to practice in Perspective III focus on the process of systemic change, again relying on the action research model, but this time in an integrative fashion as applied to several parts of a single case study involving "Jake White." This perspective provides a simple but comprehensive illustration of the steps involved in action research. Basically, it serves to complement the first two perspectives, which emphasize one or a few individual steps to action research in each separate case.

Perspectives I and II, as well as III, are based on variations of the action research model, with the basic difference being that this third perspective emphasizes integrative practice focusing on a single case study, to which all phases of the action research model are applied. Perspectives I and II thus should provide useful complements to one another, as well as to III.

The introductions to the several emphases below—beginning with "action research"—provide a template for integrative use of the case "Jake White."

*Materials in Perspective III, as well as the associated case, derive from Glenn H. Varney and James M. McFillen, *Leading Organization Change.* Class materials. Bowling Green State University, 11/19/97.

Some Details About Action Research

Action research is chosen as the model for systemic change because it provides convenient guidance about how to use our growing knowledge about organizations and human behavior to improve performance through the application of a problem-solving approach to change (e.g., Lewin, 1946). The application of action research to OD does not violate the principles of more traditional, positivistic approaches to research; nor does it negate the relevance of other approaches to problem-solving. On the contrary, the action research model serves as a guide to analyzing and diagnosing problems affecting organizations, with the goal of identifying practical solutions and thereby enlarging the reach-and-grasp of positivistic science, as by tailoring its generalizations so as to approach OD values at specific worksites. See Exhibit 2.

In sum, action research can derive guidance from "straight science" as well as contribute to its replication and validation. Put directly, action research can rest upon what we know about relationships in organizations, with the goal of achieving desired states in specific contexts. Or action research results can, in effect, test the adequacy of our existing theoretical frameworks, indicating where they suffice as well as highlighting where their gaps may complicate or inhibit attempts to achieve desired conditions.

Some Values Underlying Action Research

As emphasized at several points, OD via action research is not an unguided missile: OD often will be powerful, but it never should be indiscriminate as to ends. Exhibit 3 illustrates some elements of this normative tethering, and reflects the specific senses in which OD via action research is a technology with values. Given the same technology guided by a different set of values, one will get different effects. These effects of alternative values may be evaluated as good, bad, or indifferent, but they will not be "OD effects."

For a detailed look at the normative stance of ODers, learners can consult the "Statement" in Perspective IV below. It provides details far beyond Exhibit 3. At several points, "Instructions and Questions" attached to each case will direct learners to ways in which that "Statement" can be put to good use.

The Several Stages of Action Research

Beyond this point, the narrative provides details about the several stages of action research, seen as value-loaded. By working back and forth with

Exhibit 2   Action Research Model

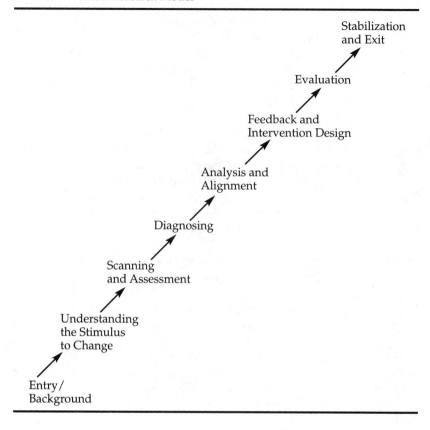

Exhibit 3   Selected Organization Development Values

✔ Service to people, organizations, and communities
✔ Teamwork and collaboration
✔ Empirically based change
✔ Freedom and autonomy
✔ Adaptability and continuous learning and improvement
✔ Accountability and responsibility

the several parts of the case study "Jake White," printed below beginning at page 215, learners will be able to mate these introductory materials into action plans sensitive to the texture of a specific work setting.

But let us hold off briefly before accessing the integrative case. Specifically, "Jake White" is divided into six parts. And the introductory materials below provide useful orientations to each, in turn, beginning with "Entry and Appreciating the Need for Change."

Specifically, also, each of the six introductions to action research will have several useful emphases. After a brief description, each introduction contains a list of "potential errors" in OD practice, as a kind of elementary warning system of what should be avoided.

In addition, each of the six introductions contains a section on "knowledge required." Again, this serves as a kind of rough but useful introductory checklist. This text does not contain details about this knowledge, which can be tapped by consulting various useful texts in OD. Our personal favorite is Robert T. Golembiewski, *Handbrook of Organizational Consultation* (New York: Marcel Dekker, 1993b, 1999).

In addition, each introduction contains a list of "skills required." Again, ODers will spend their careers adding to their inventory of skills as well as enriching their existing skills. The lists below will help alert learners to skills required, details about which will come from broad reading and experience.

Finally, each introduction to the several parts of "Jake White" contains several "reminders." These seek to emphasize important aspects of the stages of action research, by way of reinforcing important points of learning. Nothing that is important can be repeated too often, we believe.

"Jake White," Part 1: Entry and Appreciating the Need for Change

Part 1 of "Jake White" begins the task of providing a context for detailing Exhibits 2 and 3, in which task the learner will play various roles—as receptor of knowledge, as well as applier of it to the processes and dynamics of "Jake White." As with all other parts of that case, the notes below provide useful orientations for an active learner, not "answers" to be memorized. It will be the learner's job to jump back and forth between this introductory text and the several parts of the case study, whose Part 1 begins at page 215.

This jumping back and forth involves a bit of controlled schizophrenia in taking multiple roles. Doing so will help ODers build empathic skills and attitudes that are useful in all aspects of life, and perhaps nowhere more so than in OD activities.

On most occasions, the reader will be referred to as "you." At those points, be prepared to bring all of yourself—your particular bundle of values, attitudes, skills, and experiences—to the case study.

At other points, you will be observing "Pat Spritely"; and on a few occasions, you will be instructed to become Pat. So you should know a bit about Pat. To begin, Pat Spritely is relatively new to his organization, and he is openly looking for clients to test his OD skills. After all, he is a newly minted ODer—a recent graduate of Bowling Green State University's Master of Organization Development, or MOD, program.

Pat is consequently delighted with this voice-mail message from Jake White:

> "Could you drop over as soon as possible? I have an out-of-control problem with my key account reps who are not contacting potential customers, and I would like to talk to you about it."

Pat has heard a bit about Jake, who is clearly a man on the move. And Pat rubs his hands in anticipation.

But Pat first refers to notes from his MOD program at Bowling Green State University. They provide useful summary details. Organizational entry and the understanding of the need for change start with the client, and proceed to a point at which the client discloses what s/he is dissatisfied with and what s/he wants changed. Usually, the client expresses concerns about specific incidents or describes symptoms that may suggest the existence of a more complicated problem. So ODers need to be sensitive to all cues, while reserving judgment on which to include in their increasingly targeted views of the situation.

Potential Errors

1. Don't immediately accept the client's definition of the problem or her/his suggestions for solving it. Frequently, clients already have decided what actions (i.e., interventions) they wish to take to solve their "problems." Your job is to show the client the value of taking a more systematic approach to diagnosing what may well become a more nuanced issue, or a different issue, or even none at all.

   If it is a crisis, and immediate action is needed, you may want to apply "first aid." Later, you can apply a more systematic analysis (e.g., the action research model) to the situation.
2. Don't leap before you look. Make sure that the problem is something on which you are capable of working. Do not accept assignments that you are not trained to handle. For example, if the project requires

designing a customized questionnaire, and if you have no training in the techniques and statistics associated with questionnaire design, seek assistance from someone who does. A lack of skill or knowledge on your part could jeopardize the project, not to mention your job or even your career.

In short, sharpening the issues for analysis does not mean that an individual ODer has all the required skills and knowledge.

3. Don't discount the client's initial reaction to the situation. Be attentive to the client. Although you may not think that the problem is as important as the client thinks it is, at least at first, always remember whose problem it is.

4. Don't just sympathize. Be empathetic and try to show some understanding. Empathy and sympathy are not the same thing. The client is not asking for your sympathy. Clients seek your expertise. Displaying empathy may enhance your credibility with the client.

5. Don't rely on your memory. Record all information that the client shares with you. Write down dates, names, incidents, comments, and so on. Some ODers can remember almost everything, but you are probably not one of them.

Knowledge Required

1. Understanding the client's organization
2. Social and psychological aspects of human behavior within an organizational context
3. Characteristics of effective communication

Skills Required

1. Empathy
2. Interviewing techniques
3. Observation techniques
4. Interpersonal skills

Reminders

✓ Respond promptly to the client's request.
✓ Meet on the client's turf, if possible.
✓ Allow sufficient time for the meeting.
✓ Explain why you would like to take notes and ask if it is okay to do so.

With these ideas buzzing in your head, gentle reader, you can now read "Jake White," Part 1, beginning at page 215. Try to keep Pat Spritely in mind as a separate identity.

"Jake White," Part 2: Early Scanning and Beyond

Let us take a major step forward in dealing with Exhibits 2 and 3. Preliminary scanning and hypothesis development involve the ODer in acquiring enough information to be able to develop possible explanations of what is causing "the problem"—perhaps incorporating the client's early assessment, perhaps evolving a novel view. It is easy to overlook less obvious causes, and even easier to jump to attractive but spurious conclusions. Most organizational problems have multiple causes; and sometimes there are causes behind the causes.

Think of peeling an onion as you move beyond scanning. Like that vegetable, reality often comes in multiple levels, even though much of it may look the same.

Potential Errors

1. Don't jump to conclusions. Remember, problems typically have more than one cause, and some are not obvious.
2. Don't lose your objectivity. Siding with one side or another in a situation reduces your ability to be objective.
3. Don't ask the wrong questions, such as those loaded with your own interpretations, and especially early in the game. "How do you see X?" and "How do you feel about Y?" are *the* prototypic questions for the consultant to ask the client, especially at the early stages of an OD effort.
4. Don't tackle something you don't know how to handle.

Knowledge Required

1. Proper role of an OD consultant
2. Methods for contracting
3. Power and politics in organizations
4. Ethics
5. Symptoms analysis
6. Problem definition
7. Hypothesis development

Skills Required

1. Observation skills
2. Interviewing skills
3. Note-taking skills
4. Communication skills
5. Contracting skills
6. Proposal-writing skills
7. Interpersonal skills
8. Conceptualization skills

Depending on the specific context, the fields of attention can be very broad. Exhibit 4 provides one useful schema of the features that may be relevant for an ODer, and that range is clearly daunting. However, experience and reading will help potential ODers move from here to there—that is, from their present familiarity with organizations to their unfolding realities. That unfolding of the present state into the future state need never end but, fortunately, ODers do not need to "know it all" to be effective.

Everybody has to start from somewhere, but all ODers *do* need to have a real sense of the limits of what they do know. Exhibit 4 provides a useful vehicle for helping ODers make that estimate. Assessments of strengths and weaknesses at several points in time will provide a kind of moving assessment of how effectively and comprehensively one deals with the huge phenomenal realm associated with "understanding organizations" while coming to a better understanding of self.

Reminders

✓ Conduct a literature review of subjects related to the problem you think exists in Jake's situation. Summarize the information with him. This is an important way to demonstrate your knowledge, as well as to build credibility.
✓ Be sure that you don't miss anything pertinent to the situation. Use an organized method for collecting preliminary data. (See Exhibit 5.)
✓ Note the level and nature of resistance you sense from people you interview.
✓ Pay attention to the leadership style used by the client and other relevant individuals.
✓ Check the communication systems and processes used.
✓ Select a model for conducting your analysis. Have a model in mind of how you will go through the analysis phase.

Exhibit 4   Schema for Understanding Organizations

Organizational processes

Communications (What are the planned and unplanned ways in which communications take place? Are communications open or closed, accurate or inaccurate?)

Planning (What are the organization's planning procedures and how effective are they?)

Decision making (How are decisions made?)

Problem solving (How are problems resolved?)

Conflict resolution (How are conflicts resolved?)

Relationships within groups (What are the relationships within each group?)

Relationships between groups (What are the relationships between groups?)

Meetings (What types of meetings are held? How effective are they? Who attends?)

Human resource management

Management practices (What is the competency level of managers? Are they adequately trained? How effective are they? How are they perceived by employees?)

Personnel practices (How are employees recruited, oriented to the job, evaluated, rewarded, disciplined, and selected for advancement?)

Motivation (What motivators and demotivators exist in the organization? What does the organization do to motivate or demotivate people?)

Training and development (What does the organization do to train and develop individuals and groups and to learn, grow, and improve as an organization?)

Performance

Profit (How profitable is the organization?)

Productivity (What is the level of productivity?)

Work quality (What is the work quality?)

Absenteeism (What is the absenteeism rate?)

Turnover (What is the turnover rate?)

Use of supplies (How efficiently are supplies, equipment, and resources utilized?)

Goals attainment (How successful is the organization in reaching realistic and worthwhile goals?)

Innovation (How effective is the organization in initiating new ideas and ways of doing things?)

Employee utilization (How effective is the organization in fully utilizing employees?)

Employee satisfaction (What is the level of employee satisfaction?)

Work climate

Morale (What is the level of morale in the organization?)

Trust (What is the level of trust in the organization?)

Teamwork (What is the level of teamwork in the organization?)

People orientation (How people-oriented is the organization?)

Task orientation (How task-oriented is the organization?)

Commitment (What is the level of commitment in the organization?)

Attitudes (What predominant attitudes exist in the organization?)

Values (What values does the organization support?)

Norms (What predominant norms exist in the organization?)

continued

Exhibit 4   Schema for Understanding Organizations *(continued)*

External environment

Economy (What is that status of the economy in which the organization functions?)

Social climate and structure (What social values, changes, demographics, etc., influence the organization?)

Markets (Who are the organization's present or potential clients, and what is their status?)

Competitors (Who are the organization's major competitors, and what are they doing that may influence the organization?)

Political climate (What political influences may affect the organization?)

Government influences (What government influences, regulations, etc., may affect the organization?)

Technical environment (What technological conditions, advances, or changes are relevant to the organization?)

Organizational characteristics

Purpose (What does the organization do?)

History (When did the organization start? Who started it? What important events have occurred? How successful is the organization?)

Personnel (What types of people make up the organization?)

Resources (What is the status of the organization's resources—facilities, capital, equipment, etc.?)

Reputation (What is the reputation of the organization to the public, industry, and employees?)

Organizational structure

Goals (What are the goals of the organization?)

Policies (What do the policies reveal about the personality of the organization?)

Responsibilities (Are responsibilities clear and purposeful?)

Design (What is the design of the organization? Does it facilitate or inhibit the accomplishment of organizational goals and policies?)

Working conditions (What are working conditions like in terms of pay, benefits, job security, facilities, hours, staff support, supplies, equipment, safety, privacy, noise, etc.?)

Reward systems (What behaviors are rewarded formally and informally, and how are they rewarded?)

Controls (How does the organization follow up on goals and plans? How are people held accountable?)

Top management

Organization (What are the duties of top management?)

Philosophy (What are the spoken and unspoken philosophies of top management?)

Leadership style (What is the leadership style of top management?)

Member characteristics (Who are the members of top management? What are their characteristics? How much influence does each member have?)

Concerning the last point, your model should incorporate an actual state of affairs, and an ideal or better state, plus some sense of how to get from one to the other.

There are many sources of such models. You may consult such resources at several levels of analysis:

- *Overall:*   Lippitt, 1975;
- *Large system:*   Beckard and Harris, 1987;
                                                    Golembiewski, 1995;
- *Interaction between*
  individuals and in groups: Golembiewski, 1993a and b;
- *Teams:*   Dyer, 1987.

Full citations are provided on page xxxix.

As ODers gain experience, they may develop their own models—amalgams of various models, syntheses that extend the reach-and-grasp of the foundation models, or even breakthroughs or frame-breakers that provide new approaches to understanding and directing change.

After digesting these materials, you can return to the text of "Jake White," Part 3, beginning on page 218.

"Jake White," Part 3: Early Analysis and Writing an OD Contract

So back we go to providing some introductory orientation to further successive stages of action research. At some stage of scanning and assessment—and not always when the ODer is ready!—there will come a need to do one's best with what one has in summarizing early inquiry. Often, this provisional summing-up will be required for writing a contract proposal to legitimize further inquiry.

Summary of Problem Analysis

Many times, the OD game becomes: Ready or not, here goes!

Exhibit 5 illustrates one useful form of early scanning and assessment. Experienced ODers no doubt will develop their own forms for such purposes, but Exhibit 5 is not a bad place to start.

Exhibit 5 A Suggested Form for Summarizing Problem Analysis

Client's Statement of the Problem or Condition:

Other Stakeholders' Statements of the Problem or Condition:

Symptoms:

Stated Causes:

Proposed Interventions:

Writing a Proposal for an OD Contract

Preparing a contract proposal is useful for all OD projects, whether they are prepared by an internal consultant, an external consultant, or a team of internal/external consultants. Failure to write a proposal can lead to misunderstandings and a possible breakdown in the client-consultant relationship. A clearly written proposal provides a map of what the consultant will be doing, where the interventions propose to take the organization, when the work will be performed, who will be doing the work, and what costs will be involved.

The proposal follows the third step in the OD process, following the first contact (entry), preliminary scanning, and the development of a problem statement (hypothesis). This sequence of events is reflected in the schema below:

$$\text{Entry} \longrightarrow \begin{array}{c} \text{Identify} \\ \text{Stimulus} \\ \text{For} \\ \text{Change} \end{array} \longrightarrow \begin{array}{c} \text{Preliminary} \\ \text{Scan:} \\ \text{Assessment} \\ \text{Diagnosis} \\ \text{Hypothesis} \end{array} \longrightarrow \text{Proposal} \longrightarrow \text{Contract}$$

The proposal is the consultant's recommendation of a "strategy" (an approach) for solving the client's problem, for helping the client make the desired changes, and as such contains solid estimates, plans for additional learning or data, and a bit of by-guess-and-by-golly, suitably identified. Acceptance of the proposal constitutes a contract to move ahead with the project and represents agreement about the suggested strategy. Put in other words, then, the proposal sets forth a statement of the condition; what is known about it; how the problem, if any, will be verified; the ways and means of involvement of the client in the design of a corrective intervention; how much time is involved; and (last but not least) an estimate of the cost of the entire project.

Complex contracts may specify phases or stages, sometimes arrayed in probabilistic terms. For example: we will first do A, which seems most likely. If A is verified, then B will follow. If A does not yield the expected results, then we will have to decide between W and Z as the focus of stage 2.

Purposes of the Proposal

A well-designed proposal serves several purposes:

- It demonstrates to the client that the consultant understands the condition facing the client's organization;

- It provides a plan and strategy for reasonably approaching the client's problem or opportunity;
- It lays out the time frame for managing the change;
- It outlines the costs involved in the change; and
- It conveys the professional competency of the consultant.

Content of a Proposal

The innards of a proposal can take many forms. In general, however, the content of a proposal usually includes the following:

1. An introduction
2. Statement of the problem or condition
3. What's known about the problem; what unknown elements may be significant
4. A strategy for addressing the problem
5. Time frame
6. Organization of the project
7. Background of the consultant(s)
8. Costs associated with the project
9. The next step(s)

1.   *Introduction.* The purpose of the introduction is to tell the client what the proposal intends to accomplish, including a brief description of the situation leading to the writing of the proposal.

2.   *Statement of the problem or condition.* This is a central part of the proposal because the problem statement demonstrates the consultant's grasp of the client's problem. Here, the goal is to use language that the client will understand and agree to. The language of the organization—its patois, if you will—is used to support the definition of the problem. Suggested steps include citing the symptoms, stating the causes of the symptoms, and identifying how the causes interact with each other.

Clients frequently start their discussions by describing an intervention they think will guide a reasonable response to the problem. When this occurs, it is always helpful—and on most occasions, it is necessary—to include the client's ideas in the definition of the problem using diagrams, flow charts, and other visual illustrations. Including these elements not only can help the consultant, but the client may learn to conceptualize and better understand the cause-and-effect aspects of the problem or condition, which in the ideal case will generate opportunities for change.

3.   *What's known about the problem.* Observation here is critical, but no one can (or should) start from ground zero. Problems in one organi-

zation have often occurred and have been solved in other organizations. The literature also usually contains information, research, and reports on approaches used to solve similar problems or to exploit classes of opportunities. Referring to this information demonstrates a grasp of the client's problems and helps to establish the credibility of the consultant. The temptation to be avoided? There always will be fads and passing fancies. Clients may want, even demand, "this year's sheep-dip." Consultants may find it hard to resist but, nonetheless, often will profit from attempting to transcend what is convenient.

4. *Strategy for addressing the problem.* The purpose of the strategy is *not* to describe an intervention to solve the problem. Rather, the goal involves outlining a way to articulate a reasonable grasp of, and approach to, the problem before designing the intervention. For the intervention to work (absent reliance on dumb luck), it is necessary to clearly understand the problem or the underlying condition. Otherwise, improper diagnosis may lead to failure or aborted change. An effective OD strategy usually addresses the following questions:

- What questions need to be answered, and what information is needed?
- Where can answers be found to the questions—what individuals, groups, departments, records, and so on can help?
- What methods will be used to collect the needed information—interviews, questionnaires, or surveys?
- How, and to whom, will the information be fed back?
- How will the intervention be designed so as to help all stakeholders solve the problem?

5. *Time frame.* This section of the proposal describes a time line that fits the client's schedule and needs. It is important to commit only to what can be delivered within some reasonable time frame. Promises of pie in the sky, by and by, will not do.

6. *Organization of the project.* Indicate who "the client" is, and describe the client's major relationships with others in the organization. Also include plans for working with internal resources such as other OD consultants, human resource staff, or steering committees. At times, it may be necessary to identify different clients at different phases of an OD project.

7. *Background of the consultant(s).* List the name and brief background of each consultant who will be working on the project. Typically, a principal consultant serves as the contact person for the client.

8. *Costs associated with the project.* Estimate the cost of the project, usually broken down into phases or stages in the project. Costs should

be based on the amount of time and expense required to complete the project. Expenses can be included provisionally as estimates or as absolute ceilings, indicating they will be charged as incurred. It is not always necessary to provide details of how the costs are arrived at; instead, clients are usually interested in the total cost of the project. Where possible, fees/costs should be discussed before the consultant writes the final proposal. In this way you can get a sense of the client's financial boundaries, which are far better the result of prior agreement than discovered by stumbling into them, or breaching them.

9. *The next step(s).* When the client reaches this point in the proposal, the project has usually been sold and the question of any next step(s) is posed. Indicate when the project will be started and other details of start-up. A standard part of this section is establishment of the next start-up meeting.

General Guidelines for Proposal Writing

1. In preparing a proposal, a consultant usually is tempted to write too much rather than too little. Always keep the proposal brief, clear, and to the point.
2. In order to engage the client, the consultant must demonstrate a thorough awareness and understanding of the client's problems and expectations.
3. The proposal should be presented in a professional way. Use the highest-quality word-processing, paper, and binding techniques.
4. Throughout the proposal, play back expressions, words, and terms used by the client that will help demonstrate your understanding of the client's needs as well as of the local culture or ways of seeing reality and doing things.
5. Always be logical and systematic. Demonstrate to the client that you understand her/his problem.
   Now please return to case "Jake White," Part 4A, page 219.

"Jake White," Parts 4A and 4B: Later Scans and Hypothesis Testing

Determining whether a hypothesis is correct involves testing against competing explanations. A hypothesis represents, in essence, the consultant's best estimate or even belief about cause and effect. A consultant may have competing hypotheses about what is causing a problem, and thus may need to test the adequacy of these alternative explanations. To assess whether a hypothesis is true, the consultant must determine what information is needed for a good test of the hypothesis. Consultants also must decide where they can find the necessary information and have a realistic plan for collecting it.

A typical approach at this stage of the OD process is to conduct interviews of relevant members of the organization. Interviewing requires questions that probe the relevant issues and provide information for testing the hypothesis. Ideally, the process neither rests on nor reveals the consultant's beliefs about cause and effect.

Potential Errors

1. Do not ask questions that telegraph your hypothesis to the interviewees. Many times, interviewees are eager to tell you what they think you want to hear. Asking questions that reveal your beliefs about the situation may produce confirming but erroneous answers from the interviewees.
2. Don't ask too many questions. Longer interviews do not necessarily produce better information than shorter ones. Also, the longer the interview, the less may be the cooperation you receive.
3. Don't ask unrelated questions. Keep your focus on the hypothesis at hand.
4. Don't disrupt the organization's functioning with your interviews. You are supposed to help the organization, not hinder it.
5. Don't be a cause of alarm. Think carefully about how to phrase your questions to avoid sending unintended messages.
6. Don't phrase questions in a manner that would be threatening to your client. Your purpose is not to pass judgment, to criticize, or to preach. Your purpose is to collect unbiased information.
7. Don't violate confidentiality. Probing for sensitive information demands confidentiality between the interviewer and interviewee. Violating that confidentiality can be disastrous, so be careful how you define "confidential" and in delineating who can and cannot be communicated with freely.

Knowledge Required

1. Methods for defining a problem, e.g., fishbone diagrams
2. Methods for data collection and processing
3. Understanding of power and politics within organizations
4. System/process analysis: analysis of tasks, individual behavior, and environment

5. Benchmarking techniques—how others handle similar situations
6. Methods of statistical analysis

Skills Required

1. Interviewing techniques
2. Observation techniques
3. Computer skills
4. Conceptualizing skills
5. Communication skills
6. Note-taking skills
7. Content-analysis skills

Reminders

✓ Keep your client informed about what you are doing and where you are in the OD process. An "easy" issue at later stages can be threatening at early stages.
✓ Formulate your questions to ask what you really need to know. Ideally, these formulations also will be such that responses are easy to summarize and tabulate.
✓ Agree to provide feedback on the findings to participants.

Now, please return to the text of the case study "Jake White," Part 5, page 221.

"Jake White," Part 5: Diagnosis, Analysis, and Alignment: Using Data to Test Hypotheses

Diagnosis, analysis, and alignment are the general steps in the often-subtle process of understanding the data collected for the purpose of testing OD hypotheses. In other words, the data must confirm hypotheses or lead to other areas of inquiry, or both. Here, statistical analyses are useful for understanding and interpreting data.

After the OD consultant has reviewed the results and understands their meaning, the information should be made client-friendly. One useful approach is to display data in a table or graph that clearly and succinctly demonstrates the relevant issues, as viewed by the client. The presentation of the data should stimulate the client to change, often by highlighting some dilemma or presenting new information. In sum, motivational energy can be made available by such "surprises."

Potential Errors

1. Don't overlook even apparently trivial bits of information. The "devil is in the details."
2. Don't become data-bound. Sophisticated data sets have their place, but your purpose is to trigger action. So focus on the understanding of data that are operationally relevant and that also can be affected.
3. Don't focus on the data that confirm your hypothesis while overlooking data that do not. Skipping over data because they do not fit your preconceived notions is bad science and at least equally bad practice.
4. Don't surprise your client. Keep the client informed as you work through the data. Ideally, have clients participate in data assembly and interpretation.
5. Resist the temptation to collect more and more data. Data are not useful unless you can make sense of them. Avoid data overload. Your goal is to increase information, not to increase data by "counting the leaves on trees."
6. Don't make mistakes in your numbers. Clients can count, too.
7. Don't give in to the temptation to conclude what the problems are without input from your client.
8. Don't bore the client. Make sure that your data are presented in a fashion that arouses your client's interests and motivates her/him to change. A hot topic in management or behavioral sciences may have little relevance to most managers.

Knowledge Required

1. Gap analysis—e.g., concerning the need and dynamics of movement from actual to desired states
2. Systems alignment (political, cultural, and operational)
3. Networks
4. Congruencies: social and technical
5. Statistical analysis techniques
6. Modes of data presentation

Skills Required

1. Designing information and data displays
2. Presentation skills

3. Report-writing skills
4. Feedback skills
5. Conceptualization skills
6. Integrative skills

Reminders

✓ Use the computer whenever you can. Computer software makes it much easier to design and revise your report, tables, figures, etc. And some programs can do these in color, too!
✓ Design your survey for ease of scoring and processing of data.

After you use these hints about diagnosis and analysis to fine-tune your conclusions about what the data seem to say, again refer to the case study "Jake White," Part 6, page 225.

"Jake White," Part 6: Feedback and Interventions

Feedback is the process of a consultant reflecting back a visualization of the organization in such a way as to stimulate the required change. Some action-oriented types prefer the term "quick-back" as a replacement for "feedback," and that preference makes much sense.

In action research, the solution to the problem comes from the client, with the OD consultant playing less the role of substantive expert and far more the role of facilitator. Facilitation does not exclude the offering of expert ideas. However, a high level of skill often is required to guide the client in the design of interventions, and this skill is central because the client typically will have to implement the action plan. In short, client involvement can reduce resistance and heighten commitment.

Potential Errors

1. Don't fail to encourage the client to take responsibility for the change process. Even insist on it, early as well as late. The ODer's job is to help prepare the client and the organization to operate on their own, especially after the ODer is gone.
2. Don't pick a solution "off the shelf." Use your knowledge and skill to help the client tailor a solution to fit the organization's specific needs.

Knowledge Required

1. Resources
2. Intervention design for ad hoc purposes
3. Feedback process and skills
4. Awareness of types of interventions used by others
5. Learning theory
6. Experience-based techniques and tools
7. Evaluation and measurement techniques
8. Needs analysis

Skills Required

1. Persuasion skills
2. Presentation skills
3. Personal feedback skills
4. Group problem-solving skills
5. Teaching skills
6. Facilitation skills
7. Visioning skills

Reminders

✓ Review some of the group problem-solving techniques that promote participation and creativity among group members.
✓ Review some of the different techniques for delivering feedback.
✓ Consider using some candid, but anonymous, quotes from the survey or interviews to illustrate issues to the audience. This is often an effective device for inducing a sense of face-validity.

After finishing these notes, please refer to "Jake White," Part 7, page 227.

"Jake White," Part 7: Intervention, Implementation, and Evaluation

Interventions are actions designed to exploit perceived opportunities or to correct identified problems. The implementation of an intervention requires careful monitoring and evaluation to assure that the intervention "works." Success of the change process may be claimed when valid and reliable effectiveness measures indicate that the original condition or problem no longer exists and that the change goals have been met.

Potential Errors

1. Don't make your client dependent upon you. Conduct yourself in such a way during the change process that the client becomes able to carry on the change process independently. A continuing dependency on the part of the client spells trouble for the host organization, if not disaster.
2. Don't disengage from the client until the change is stabilized in the organization. If you separate too quickly, the organization is likely to revert to its original methods of operation or even become worse.

Knowledge Required

1. Facilitating change
2. Transitioning
3. Reinforcement theory
4. Group dynamics
5. Motivation to change
6. Measurement and evaluation
7. Costs/value added; cost/benefit analysis
8. Interventions and their fine-tuning
9. Disengagement
10. Organization design

Skills Required

1. Coaching skills
2. Teaching skills
3. Facilitation skills
4. Team-building skills
5. Personal growth
6. Feedback skills
7. Integrative skills
8. Interpreting evaluation data

Reminders

✓ Review the situation and identify the relevant independent, moderating, intervening, and dependent variables, if you can.
✓ Review various types of measures, both process and end result.

✓ Select effectiveness measures that are relevant to the intervention, that are sensitive to the potential impact of the changes being made, and that are practical given the situation.

✓ Review motivation theories, such as expectancy theory and reinforcement theory, to identify issues and techniques relevant to stabilizing change.

PERSPECTIVE IV: A STATEMENT OF VALUES AND ETHICS

This section will conclude our introduction to the four orienting perspectives to this casebook, in effect, saving for last the most essential elements. This concluding Perspective IV provides normative guidance—a set of values or normative crosswalks that apply to all of the cases, both commonplace and exotic.

Why are such guidelines essential? To put it in a revealing way, OD is value-loaded in specific senses. Hence, OD cannot serve just any old set of values.

The "Statement" reprinted in Perspective IV reflects a broad (if incomplete) consensus about the overt as well as nuanced character of this value-loadedness, of this need to give direction to OD approaches and techniques by infusing them with specific values. A bit more specifically, the most salient values are related to three questions:

• Why OD?
• OD for which particular purposes?
• What should ODers do, and why?

Here, the "Statement" provides guidance—at times, specific directions, and at other times, insights about what directions ODers should lean as they act. Thus, the "Statement" sometimes details, at other times sketches or suggests, the value or ethical limits of what can be done, as well as orients the reader to how and why. This is not everything of normative or ethical relevance, but it helps a great deal.

The compound goal only requires stating. How far can the ODer stretch in response to specific contextual or situational features and still retain the label "OD" by respecting normative limits? The related judgments can be tough ones, but the general point nonetheless obtains. Going "too far" results in something other than OD, as does "not far enough."

The "Statement" does not imply that other value-loaded approaches to consultation have no usefulness. Far from it, in fact. Rather, the

"Statement" circumscribes OD and permits a judgment about whether or not some action-taking falls within OD's orbit. There are some who would stretch this definition of OD's turf in extreme ways, but pushed far enough, the position here is that the added territory will become something other than OD.

Let the basic point be repeated, lest it be misinterpreted. OD should not be static. Ideally, indeed, OD should contain a viable core as well as an expanding periphery. Lacking either such a core or a periphery, OD's life chances would not be bright. Put in simple terms, the "Statement" provides a set of value tethers on what is the core as well as on what constitutes an expanding periphery without such over-expansionism as to justify a label "other than OD."

ONE CONCLUDING NOTE: WHAT IS A "CASE"?

The text above keeps referring to "case study" or "case," but the truth is that the exemplars below at times stretch the sense of common usage. More accurately, the focus here is on what might better be called "stimuli for learning." But that is a clumsy usage, so "cases" it will be, if the reader will please give the editors a bit of definitional slack.

Whatever the label, other questions—for example, did *that* incident actually happen?—are secondary to the learning potential in a "case" or a "stimulus." To be direct, all but a few of the "cases" describe "actual situations," or portions of them, but some qualifications are relevant.

Let us be brief about some of these qualifications. Some cases below purport to a full statement of some action-setting, as far as that is possible for human minds and hands. Other cases tell the variously varnished truth, as is true when names are disguised or when the generic term "ODer" is utilized. For their own reasons, some real-life participants prefer it that way. Or case incidentals may be simplified or even disguised for similar reasons. A few of the learning stimuli are best seen as "type cases"—that is, an ODer with reasonable experience is likely to run into related situations, but the "case" reported is a conflation of several honest-to-God incidences. Such "cases" seek to increase the learning potential rather than to report "what happened" in a discrete situation, even as essential issues are highlighted by variously conflated contexts.

References

Beckhard, R., and Harris, R. T. (1987). *Organizational transitions*. Reading, MA: Addison-Wesley.

Cummings, T. C., and Worley, C. G. (1997). *Organization development and change*. Cincinnati, OH: South-Western College Publishing.

Dyer, W. (1987). *Team building*. Reading, MA: Addison-Wesley.

French, W., and Bell, C. (1993). *Organization development*. Englewood Cliffs, NJ: Prentice-Hall.

Glassman, A., and Cummings, T. C. (Eds.) (1991). *Cases in organization development*. Homewood, IL: Irwin.

Golembiewski, R. T. (1993a). *Approaches to planned change*. New Brunswick, NJ: Transaction Publishers.

Golembiewski, R. T. (1993b). *Handbook of organizational consultation*. New York: Marcel Dekker.

Golembiewski, R. T. (1995). *Practical public management*. New York: Marcel Dekker.

Golembiewski, R. T. (1999). *Handbook of organizational consultation*. 2nd ed. New York: Marcel Dekker.

Lewin, K. (1946). Action research and minority problems. *Journal of Social Issues*, 2: 34–36.

Lippitt, G. (1975). Models of organization change. In R. T. Golembiewski, *Handbook of organizational consultation*, pp. 501–507. New York: Marcel Dekker.

PERSPECTIVE I

OD and ODers in Conventional Settings

I.1

Creating a High-Performance Work Culture: The Boeing Duluth Story

Ralph DeKemper

During the mid 1980s, the Tactical Missiles Division of Rockwell International Corporation had trouble fulfilling defense contracts for the U.S. Army. The contracts involved the Hellfire missile product line.

The Hellfire missile was designed by engineers at a Columbus, Ohio, facility, with the intention of transitioning the design into production in a new high-volume, low-cost facility in Duluth, Georgia. Most of the engineers involved in the design process elected to stay in Ohio rather than join the new start-up project in Georgia. This separation of design from implementation created numerous problems related to procurement, test equipment, production planning, drawing interpretation, engineering design changes, inexperienced management staff, and an untrained workforce.

These problems hampered the plant's performance with regard to quality, cost, and delivery of product within contractual constraints. The customer, the U.S. Army Missile Command, set up processes and personnel at the Duluth site to oversee contract compliance and to audit compliance to specifications. An unfavorable score on a large-scale audit in 1984 resulted in Rockwell's decision to bring in a new leadership team to enhance the plant's infrastructure and to establish and implement a corrective action plan designed to improve customer confidence in the company's ability to perform.

By 1987, the new management team had implemented many improvements; performance issues related to documentation, cost and schedule continued. The customer chose to conduct a second audit. The results were unsatisfactory. The business received notification that it would be expected to institute significant and substantial improvements in performance.

With this critical performance feedback, the leadership team had its back to the wall. Meanwhile, competitors were standing in the wings eagerly awaiting cancellation of the lucrative Hellfire missile contract and its subsequent award to one of them.

At this important juncture in the evolution of the Rockwell International Corporation, the company's human resource directors embarked on an experiment to inject into the organization several bright practitioners of the emerging organization development field. While OD principles had become well known in many commercial businesses such as Proctor and Gamble and Hewlett-Packard, little exposure to this new way of thinking existed in the defense contractor community, which mirrored its military customer in having a highly controlled stovepipe bureaucratic organization structure and business orientation.

In an effort to address the plant's problems, the leadership team at the Duluth site had eagerly attempted to apply many of the fads of the day, implementing a "program of the month" approach to getting the problems under control. A popular national magazine featured a cover with the terms of many of the day's hot problem-solving approaches. This became a banner for the business. These efforts included Integrated Product Development, Gainsharing, Statistical Process Control, Total Quality Management, Cycle Time, Core Competencies, Employee Empowerment, Just-In-Time Delivery, and Quality Circles.

A key influence on the leadership team was the teachings of William Conway, one of the first U.S. executives to adopt the Edward Deming quality principles and teachings and implement a fairly simple approach to improving business performance and reducing waste.

During the leadership team's scramble to find the "silver bullet" that would save the business, an opportunity presented itself. As has occurred in many similar situations—when the going gets tough, in the eleventh hour—creativity prevailed and an answer presented itself.

The leadership team, primarily drawn from the ranks of engineering, business development, finance, program management, manufacturing, quality control, and human resources, was detail-oriented. A pattern began to emerge from the chaos created by the programs of the month, none of which had made significant inroads on the performance problems of the business. The approaches could be placed in four large groupings:

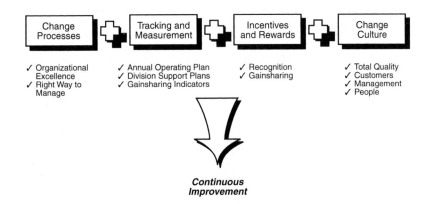

Continuous
Improvement

Utilizing the basic framework of the McKinsey Model, the leadership team modified the formula to include eight key factors that when aligned, would enable an organization to move from its current operating state to a future desired state in a systematic and disciplined process that would take into account the social or "people" aspects of the transformation.

Following is the Rockwell version of the model:

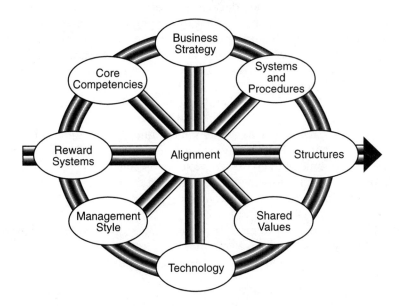

It soon became clear that several conditions were needed to ensure successful culture transformation:

- Avoid being overcome by pressure to meet schedules
- Ensure clear communication of expectations throughout the organization
- Garner support from middle management as well as senior management
- Develop a clear case for change based on business rationale
- Supply key resources to support change efforts

During the subsequent days and months, the Duluth plant made considerable progress toward its stated vision of becoming a high-performance work culture that produces high-quality products and is recognized as a leader in industry.

ORGANIZATION REDESIGN

The executive leadership team determined that to achieve improvements in quality, cost containment, and schedule, the company needed to make some drastic changes. They decided to reorganize Hellfire production operations and related support areas into high-performance teams.

Initially, a design team was established and met over a period of approximately two years to learn about high-performance organizations. The team also targeted specific systems and processes for change and gained consensus from the leadership team that change was essential for the company's survival and that all departments would support the redesign effort.

A formal agreement was written and signed by all 30 members of the design team. The document outlined the boundaries and the expected outcome of the redesign project. Also included was a description of what the employees would gain from the redesign effort.

The agreement included the following objectives:

- To provide an environment that encourages open communication, group participation in decision making, and teamwork
- To provide an environment that encourages a positive attitude toward constructive change
- To enhance job satisfaction through recognition of progress toward, and the achievement of, mutually established and realistic individual and team goals

- To provide a productive, caring, safe, and healthful working environment
- To establish an environment that fosters cooperation with mutual trust and respect, and in which people take pride in their work, demonstrate an enthusiastic "can-do" attitude, and are motivated to strive for continuous improvement
- To provide programs for compensation and rewards for individual and team performance
- To provide opportunities for personal and professional growth
- To achieve the common goal of producing a high-quality product and becoming recognized as a leader in our industry
- To empower, with full accountability, all teams to be innovative designers of their own job tasks

During the early stages of the project, effectiveness teams focused on key elements of the organization effectiveness wheel. Each team compared the current state of the business practices with a desired future state. This exercise brought to light key issues and processes that required change or realignment in a Team Charter to support business goals:

- Review and improve information systems
- Overhaul business procedures and management system
- Create a high-performance work culture
- Improve internal and external customer relationships
- Incorporate cycle time into existing total quality system
- Access markets and align business strategy
- Establish advanced factory modernization strategy
- Define individual and organizational accountability
- Broaden employee ownership of the strategic business and planning process
- Develop and implement program execution process

PRODUCTION REDESIGN

As a direct result of the activities of the effectiveness teams, production redesign began. Many issues surfaced, including the following:

1. Management style would have to change in the new organization. An organization effectiveness team that was charged with creating a high-performance work culture tackled this initiative. A set of desired

behaviors and competencies evolved. Then a peer, subordinate, and leader survey instrument was designed to measure the managers' performance. When deficiencies were noted, the design team generated action plans to foster improvement.

2. The plant's general manager held weekly meetings to review progress with managers and teams. The teams discussed progress on issues, emphasizing use of data and quality tools such as statistical process control and flow-charting. The leadership team sat in the back rows and the other teams sat in the executive seating around the huge table, thus reinforcing the idea of honoring the teams and their work.

3. In line with components of the Total Quality Systems model, tracking and measurement became the next key component. A process developed by one of the organization effectiveness teams to use an MBO (management by objectives) approach identified goals at the business level and followed them out to the organization and teams. Progress on goals was reviewed regularly by teams, and leadership at the business level was evaluated by the general manager and his staff.

4. Recognition and rewards constituted the final component of the Total Quality Systems model. A Gainsharing program was developed to track business performance and to reward employees for gains above and beyond the annual business plan.

5. Finally, training aids and programs evolved to support changes in corporate culture, to empower employees, and to aid managers in becoming coaches and leaders of their people. Courses focused on team processes and dynamics, team leader responsibilities, team member responsibilities, problem solving, and quality tools. With these tools, teams of employees could solve problems and work to improve systems, processes, and reduce waste in those systems. Key accomplishments included:
   - Improved asset utilization
   - Reduced scrap and rework
   - Reduced budget expenses
   - Reduced hours to produce product
   - Dramatically improved sales per employee
   - Improved engineering development cycle time, cost, and schedule
   - Substantially improved quality of product
   - Improved employee morale
   - Improved customer satisfaction
   - Improved performance on deliveries and costs

INSTRUCTIONS AND QUESTIONS

1. System designers sought "to empower" employees. Identify actions that supported this goal, as well as any actions that seem to have been counter-productive.
2. In what ways did the "Rockwell model" influence the new design?

I.2

This Matter Needs Attention, Now!

Bradford Jones was relaxing in his hotel room after a couple of intense days of team building, with nothing more demanding in view than an evening of watching Monday Night Football. He was staying at his favorite home-away-from-home, a hotel that Brad and his confidantes liked to call "Our Place." It was out-of-the-way, but not very far, with a small but great restaurant, a dark place with many nooks and crannies. Just the kind of place to go when there were important things to discuss over good food, and when one had a desire to avoid prying eyes. Brad's organization development cohorts called this restaurant "The Cabal," since so many projects were hatched there.

It was just about kick-off time when the phone rang.

"Hey, Brad, this is Shelly. I see by your phone number that you are at Our Place."

"Well, compadre, how clever you are. Long time, no see," Brad chirped. That was not the literal truth, for a week ago Brad and Shelly had spent several days together helping to develop a work plan for her internal staff group. Brad knew that Shelly had recently returned from a "due diligence" trip; and for the two of them, a week could be a very long time between meetings.

"No time for chit-chat, my friend," Shelly replied. "This matter needs attention, now! Can I have a piece of you, soon? *Real* soon?"

"My plane leaves at 10:00 tomorrow morning," Brad noted. "I planned to sleep in."

"Great," she replied, "how about 6:30 tomorrow morning? In 'The Cabal.'" She added, "Oh, by the way, this has to be a freebie, at least for now."

"Triple affirmative," Brad shot back. Shelly said a quick goodbye and hung up.

"Well, I'll be dipped," Brad thought to himself. "No rest for the wicked. But I owe a lot to her, and I wasn't going anywhere tomorrow morning anyhow."

So Brad forgot the TV game and began doing what had to be done. Most pressing, Brad had to make some investment decisions and then place several phone calls. In 18 hours or so, Brad could be in possession of insider knowledge, good or bad, which could inhibit taking actions that he had concluded were prudent. Now might be the only time to get these things decided in time to take action.

After 90 minutes or so of such stewardship, Brad slipped off to sleep, wondering, "Just what matter needs attention, now, and as a freebie?"

No advanced degrees were necessary to resolve that question when, at 6:25 AM sharp, Brad entered "The Cabal." In the deepest recess was Shelly, holding hands with a fellow executive, Steve, who also had been on that "due diligence" trip.

"We've been seeing one another a lot recently," Shelly announced with evident relish. "And we thought you ought to know, given our shared projects."

"Well, you guys aren't hiding that fact very well, I'd say," Brad noted. "The stars in your eyes really light up 'The Cabal.'" Brad's tone reflected his pleasant surprise. He knew that both Shelly and Steve had a brief fling a while back, that they were both unhappy in their marriages, and that they were both attractive and shared many values and interests.

"Don't be flip, Brad," cautioned Steve. He added, "This is serious stuff for both of us. This is no casual thing. We intend to live together as soon as we can, and then to marry. But that will take time, and until then we'll see each other as much as is humanly possible, without causing real trouble."

What would "take time?" There were separations and then divorces to arrange, and most of all there were two clusters of children that both Shelly and Steve wanted to nurture as well as cushion from the dislocations both anticipated and feared. And there were issues associated with religious affiliations that were not fully supportive of either their relationships or their short-run plans.

Brad's mind went into overdrive, with an organizational focus. Some points of fact:

- Both of their spouses worked for the same firm as did Shelly and Steve. That could be awkward.
- Both Shelly and Steve were prominent actors in the firm, and tabbed by most observers to become more so. Organization politics could complicate an already difficult situation.
- Brad was involved with both Shelly and Steve in crucial projects moving toward the "firm of the future"; all three could well be major

actors in cascading events, and any personal matters could have organizational implications and consequences.

- Both Shelly and Steve seemed "swept up" by recent surges of their shared emotions and passions. Neither struck Brad as being very cautious, in sharp contrast to their usual work behaviors and styles. Brad caught himself several times referring to them as "you kids"—meant affectionately, but also subject to more than one interpretation.

To Brad, such factors implied a high potential for personal and organizational trouble. For example, he learned that the couple not only had shared a single suite during their recent trip, but had registered as "Mr. and Mrs." Their separate company expense accounts contained only a single charge for lodging, which could well serve as grist for the rumor mill if noted by an inquisitive reviewer or auditor.

"We didn't plan on staying there together, or anything like that," Steve explained. "It just happened."

"No kidding," Brad observed aloud. "That's just what has to be done differently from now on—we need to better plan our common futures, as long as they last."

Brad added, "For openers, we have to avoid doing any work together for which I charge the company, at least until we get your immediate futures in a sharper focus."

INSTRUCTIONS AND QUESTIONS

1. As Brad, what would you do immediately? At successive points down the track, if any?
2. What seems to be Brad's opening strategy?
3. If you were Brad, how would you react to being taken into confidence in this way?
4. Should it be part of Brad's concern to determine how sincere the couple is about a long-run relationship, as well as about marriage? If so, how can Brad test that sincerity?
5. Seek access to some business or public agency. How would its policies apply in this case?
6. Can you find anything in the "Statement of Values and Ethics by Professionals...", in Part IV of this text, that applies to this case?

I.3

A Troubled Transit Line

PART 1

Bill Jackson was feeling good about the world. He had just made all the preliminary arrangements with Regional Transportation Property, or RTP, for finalizing a probable consulting venture that had multiple attractions. The project would get "the old team" together again: two advanced and very promising graduate students from Missouri as well as a colleague from out of state for whom Bill had been major professor with whom he had worked on several consulting and research ventures. Moreover, a labor union was involved in the project, and Bill had a special zest for doing work that other organization development consultants finessed or neglected, such as projects involving labor unions. Moreover, the contract would be for a sum in the mid-five figures, and Bill's university would be delighted with the overhead charges associated with such a sum.

This much being the case, Bill with relative confidence arranged for a "finalizing session" with representatives of labor and management at RTP. Management officials had resisted the joint session, in part because they wanted to authorize the project themselves. In response to broad hints from the home office, "getting started yesterday" was their initial preference. In fact, due to an apparent misunderstanding, RTP officials had already sent a large check to Bill's university to facilitate an early start.

But the RTP management team soon changed its collective mind. Its four members accepted the view that it was best to test for willingness early in the game, thus possibly saving their money and everyone's time. Besides, Bill refused to do it any other way. "I'm not partial to probable failures," he explained.

Union officials had consulted with their international union and quickly agreed to participate in a joint session to outline the "rules of the game" for a possible survey/feedback effort at RTP.

Thus it came about that the four consultants assembled in Columbia, Missouri, late on a warm Tuesday afternoon, to drive to the site for a meeting with the principals: the management team of an urban transportation property and five elected union officials. The consulting team would have a get-together dinner that night, meet with management and union officials the next day, and then return to Columbia on the third day, where they would wrestle with several research tasks.

The OD team knew only a little about their potential clients, but enough to engage their interests, if not defenses. RTP had recently become part of a national corporation, which had a philosophy of substantial decentralization to local officials. Previously, RTP had been locally owned and managed. In this case, the new national managers were pushing for a survey/feedback effort to improve relationships between the new local management team and the unionized employees. Labor/management relationships definitely had not been placid.

Moreover, the OD team knew a union election was about six months in the future, and the "old boys" and "young Turks" in the union were scuffling for dominance, but with a long lead time. Indeed, "Big Red," an old-timer and the present union president, had announced he would retire about two years after this election, and he wanted a "good send-off into retirement." The young Turks had not yet fully declared themselves. They saw Big Red as something of a throw-back to earlier days of adversarial unionization, and as being too confrontational for their tastes or for the needs of the day. The cautious heirs-apparent preferred to improve the "quality of working life" via collaborative ventures between labor and management, but they moved deliberately. If nothing else, the new local management was a largely unknown quantity, and few employees were predisposed to give them the benefit of the doubt. Moreover, Big Red still had a large following, and there was no certainty that challenging him in the upcoming election would be successful.

So, the conversation during the drive to meet with the OD team's potential clients had a direct focus: What constitutes a valid, and early, test of the probability that RTP management and union officials would ultimately agree on a successful intervention?

INSTRUCTIONS AND QUESTIONS: PART 1

Imagine you are one of the members of the consulting team en route to the session with your possible clients. What would constitute a valid test of the probability that RTP will be able to achieve more collaborative relationships between management and labor?

PART 2

The conversation during the trip had two major themes. First, it had been difficult for all consulting team members to schedule this short visit with the client, and matters were not likely to improve much in the near future. Hence the shared need to test the "cultural readiness" of the client. Unanimously, the OD team members did not need "just another client."

Second, in addition to the anticipated reconnoitering that would characterize this short visit, the team decided a reasonable test of RTP's "cultural readiness" would be any indication of labor/management willingness to work together, if only on a narrow issue.

Consistently, after some introductions and bantering, the agenda for the next day was set: to choose a test acceptable to labor, management, and the OD team; and, depending on the results, to negotiate contract details.

The participants accepted the agenda. The managers seemed anxious to get on with it. The five union officials attending had thought the consultants would be outlining the survey, but they accepted the "consultants' foreplay" with good humor.

Choosing a Test

The criteria for the choice of a test were direct: something that rankled labor and/or management; something that fell within the competence of people in the room; and something that would reasonably signal to others that the RTP project was not just "this year's sheep dip."

These criteria were barely articulated when the union contingent whooped with delight, with the exception of Big Red, who missed no occasion to reflect on how and why the charge was a "mission impossible." Neither side would "give in," he predicted, to avoid "showing weakness before the election."

The union's near-consensus choice for a test case had a modest scope, but it spoke worlds about the grudging—if not vengeful—state of local labor/management relationships. Basically, the issue affected only a small number of employees: those working the graveyard shift who ended their morning shift at 5:59 AM Friday, but could not get their paychecks until 9:00 AM that day. Drivers on other shifts had several opportunities to pick up their checks, but the graveyarders faced some unattractive choices. They could kill time for four hours; they could leave and then return to the bus barn after 9:00 AM on Friday; or they could come back to get their checks later, maybe as late as the following Monday if they had no weekend work.

All of these options were unattractive, especially since many bus drivers lived from one paycheck to the next. Even a short delay in getting and cashing a check might cause an inconvenience, if not worse, for some union members.

Typically, all checks had been processed by late afternoon Thursday. So no technical problems precluded getting checks to the night supervisors for distribution to the drivers at the end of the graveyard runs at 6:00 AM or thereabouts.

An Abortive Test

For more than seven hours, the union and management attendees debated the issue. Basically, under the general manager's lead, management approached the issue in conventional adversarial terms: they would not "give away" any "managerial prerogative" unless union officials first "gave up" something.

Unionists responded derisively. "See what hard heads they are!" consultants were told.

The consultants did not try to be "unbiased." They were unimpressed by various management rationales for the check-availability procedure, which seemed only a remnant of a time when "sticking it to" the union and employees had dominated management thought. One practical concern reinforced management's reactionary posturing. Local management did not want to appear "soft on unions," as headquarters was making funds available for improvements in "quality of working life" via a possible survey/feedback design.

The position of the union officials was more complicated but similar. One or two of the union officials on occasion seemed to soften a bit, but Big Red worked hard to project a united front. Given the upcoming election, this was not the best time for him to be seen by union members as "playing footsie" with management, especially given the past history and such surviving irritations as the check-availability issue. Moreover, the international headquarters of the union was not overly enthusiastic about labor/management "collaboration," having warned the local union representatives that consultants might be overresponsive to management, which, as in the RTP case, was to pay the consultants' fees. Even worse, several unionists noted, the new initiative could prove to be the opening wedge of a union-busting effort.

The union officials asked the consultants, "What would you think if management would not bend enough to make a piddling change like the one we've been fussing about for hours?"

The OD team did not evade the challenge. "I would guess we would not be hopeful, maybe even suspicious," was the OD team's response.

During the rest of the meeting, the union officials had very mixed reactions. At least two of them complained of serious stomach pains as the hours wore on, and several breaks were called. A Gelusil bottle appeared, and much of the afternoon saw one or more union officials flat on their backs as they struggled with their gastric juices.

Basically, the consultants saw such symptomatology as a sign of the significant forces-in-opposition among union leaders. Big Red was not one of the overt sufferers. As he said, more than once, "I give ulcers, not get them."

Almost at the stroke of 5:00 PM, all union officials disengaged—quite dramatically so, in fact.

Before the session broke up, Bill called for a brief follow-up meeting the next morning at 8:00. Both sides agreed.

The consultants were the last ones to leave the room, and one of the younger unionists held back a little. "Sorry to do that to you guys. You seem OK. You see, we had to stay until 5:00 PM to get paid for a full day, according to the contract. But not a minute longer!"

INSTRUCTIONS AND QUESTIONS: PART 2

The consulting team had a convivial evening, a short portion of which was devoted to outlining immediate next steps. What should the consulting team say at 8:00 the next morning?

PART 3

Bill opened the morning meeting by summarizing the previous day's session and asking for any second thoughts. "We're ready to go on like yesterday, indefinitely," Big Red summarized the general sense of things. Management expressed similar feelings.

After testing such a hard line several times, Bill concluded with a summary of the consultants' view of the situation:

> "Well, the bottom line seems clear enough. This does not seem to be a good time for getting into a survey/feedback mode, let alone the action planning that should follow it. Perhaps things will be better after the election.
>
> "If you couldn't deal with the check-availability issue, we can't see how we could design and implement a balanced survey. There isn't enough Gelusil in the world.
>
> "Please feel free to call on us at any time, especially if things change for you. Right now, we cannot be remotely optimistic that the required time, costs, and energies have a reasonable chance of being well spent.
>
> "So, we'll close the RTP file, *after* we bill the bus property for fees and expenses. The substantial remaining management prepayment will be returned by the university."

Only a few contacts followed. The CEO of the transit property sent a fulsome letter to Bill's university, extolling the competencies and integrity of the consulting team.

INSTRUCTIONS AND QUESTIONS: PART 3

1. What is your reaction to the closing session?
2. Does the consultants' position give an advantage to management? To the union?
3. Would you have done things differently? And if so, why?

I.4

Be Sure to Bring Along Plenty of Shells!

Jack Sims did not believe in meeting the broad range of his personal needs through a client, so it was with some reluctance that he accepted an invitation to be flown to the CEO's ranch to take part in a quail hunt. Jack reminded himself that he and the CEO had just completed a very successful OD venture. A personalized fiesta was not out of the question, and perhaps was even appropriate.

At the same time, Sims was not inclined to be the CEO's hunting and social buddy. If nothing else, becoming too chummy with the CEO might create doubts within the corporation about his third-party and independent status as an "honest broker," and much important work remained to be done back home. Sims did not relish the prospect of having to demonstrate, once again, his "independence"—that although the CEO "paid the consulting bills," Sims nonetheless tried both hard and successfully to avoid any extensions of that reality into diagnoses or interpretations.

The CEO had been uncharacteristically insistent about acceptance of his invitation, even suggesting at one point that "we might find some consulting work to be done," in an attempt to counter Sims' obvious reservations. Sims had long ago noted that the CEO's subordinates kept their distance from their boss, typically (even desperately) inserting Sims between themselves and the CEO at meals or meetings.

Perhaps most significantly, Sims was not certain that *this* CEO would be the one to lead the corporation into tomorrow's vision.

So, there was much "unfinished business" percolating in Sims's brain. Ultimately he accepted the invitation to hunt, but—as the French idiom that so aptly expressed his general motivational state would have it—his acceptance was made "with one buttock."

As the departure date approached, Sims gradually became more comfortable with his decision. He no doubt would enjoy the hunt, and the day would be a short one, because both the CEO and Sims were leaving on "the evening plane," which would drop off Sims near his home and then transport the CEO to corporate headquarters.

Moreover, without doubt, this was to be a hunt, not a long walk. The state limit on birds per day was 12, the CEO reported after prodding, even on "personal preserves" such as the CEO's ranch. And from all reports, including that of the CEO, there were so many coveys on the ranch that a short walk would fill the daily bag limit, even for a poor shooter.

Uncharacteristically, Sims used this interim period to call the state fish and game commission to check on the daily bag limit. Twelve birds it was—no more, but it could be less.

So, in good time, Sims was off in the wild blue yonder in the CEO's Lear jet. He was dressed in light hunting gear, per the CEO's instructions that "we get right on with the shooting." He had brought a small bag with a change of clothes, "should we [in the CEO's words] decide to do something a little formal for early dinner."

The plane had barely stopped rolling when the CEO drove up with an entourage: several Jeep-like vehicles with enclosures for the dogs, a vehicle for two guides, and one for the CEO and Sims.

Introductions were made all around by the CEO, who urged Sims to "be sure to bring along plenty of shells" from the guides' Jeep. "You never know where the vehicles will be when you need more," the CEO advised. "I always carry a bunch." He was true to his words: two bellows pockets of his hunting jacket bulged with shells, perhaps as many as 40 or 50.

Sims accepted some shells from a guide and quickly joined the CEO.

"Well, that didn't take very long," the CEO observed. "You couldn't have picked up many shells in that time! Sure you don't need more?"

"I've got enough," Sims replied.

"How many is that?" the CEO asked.

"Well, 13 to be exact," said Sims. "One for each legal bird, and one extra."

"Pretty confident," said the CEO. "Why not just leave the thirteenth shotgun shell with the guides?"

"You never know," Sims noted in a measured tone, "when you might have to protect yourself or the dogs against a snake."

INSTRUCTIONS AND QUESTIONS

1. What's going on here?
2. Why did Sims hesitate to accept the CEO's invitation? And why did he verify the daily bag limit with the CEO's state fish and game commission?
3. Do you suppose the men did something "a little formal" after the hunt?
4. What agenda would you propose for the two men when they had both returned to the corporate setting?
5. How many birds, do you guess, were bagged by Sims? By the CEO?

I.5

A Grumble or a Meta-Grumble?
A Fateful Targeting

Patricia Rankin had recently been recruited as part of a team of specialists in large system change, and that team was about to expand from three members to six. The client was a large multinational firm that mined bauxite and processed the resulting alumina, and its pattern of growth had resulted in a veritable United Nations of a work force. This diversity extended into the upper levels of middle management, although the executive levels still were largely populated by a single nationality.

The overall goal of the team was to move the company toward a single dominant corporate culture, built into and around ethnic and national diversities. The general approach could be described as "seeding" the organization. On a voluntary basis, individual managers could elect to undergo a modified sensitivity training experience designed to introduce people to the corporate culture—values, attitudes, and skills—thereby undergirding subsequent emphasis on team building with a dominant interpersonal orientation. As conditions permitted, and this time in a mandatory mode, many teams involving all employers would be "built" or "developed" around the world to meet emerging needs.

Rankin enjoyed this consultancy and the many associations it brought. As a facilitator of groups in several iterations of the opening design, she was given much leeway for design details. The several facilitators met periodically as a team—to get a sense of their evolving selves; to benchmark each other with the results of a standard evaluation form; and to get filled in on extensions into the field of the central training in values and skills.

Typically, during these group sessions, Rankin used a simple model to provide participants with a handle on their experiences. That model compared degenerative to regenerative systems, based on four variables.

- *openness,* or the tendency to "tell it like it is";
- *owning,* or the tendency to acknowledge ideas and reactions as one's own;
- *risk,* or the degree of threat in a situation; and
- *trust,* or the degree of confidence that a group of associates can cope successfully with challenges.

Figure I.5.1 depicts this model, outlining the negative consequences of degenerative interaction.

Most of the participants in the group sessions could generate convincing lists of the consequences or covariants of regenerative interaction at their work sites. Moreover, participants were able to generate examples to illustrate the four variables, e.g., "People who send valentines signed 'guess who' are being open but they do not own their feelings." Participants were able to apply the model to their common realities, e.g., "You bet, that's us. Not only here when we first met, but at work, all over the world. We definitely tilt toward the degenerative." Participants clearly understood the desirability of moving people and systems from degenerative to regenerative, e.g., "We did that here, so why can't we do that at work?"

It was during one of these discussions that Rankin made a fateful distinction. A bit cryptically, she observed, "Degenerative interaction often is the source of many grumbles, for sure; but the meta-grumbles often inhere in structural problems."

The group erupted. In effect, they complained, "We thought English was *the* language here. And there you go talking academese again."

So Rankin began to explain, voicing a concern about the team's tendency to intellectualize during group sessions as a way to limit emotional impact. Basically, and quickly, Rankin compared the typical bureaucratic structure with a "flow of work" model. The basic distinctions were simple, but the effects were profound. See Figure I.5.2 where activities A + B + C yield some product or service.

The participants caught on quickly. "We're like Model A back home," most participants observed, in effect. "And what does that imply for the dominant pattern of interaction?" Rankin prompted. "Well, that structure typically will be centralized, because in Model A only M_{ABC} can make reasonable decisions about an entire flow of work. And participants in activities A, B, and C typically will have fragmented self-interests, which could well decrease openness and owning."

Figure I.5.1   Two Models for Interaction

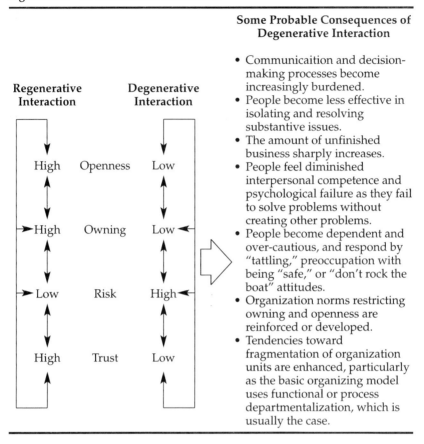

Some Probable Consequences of Degenerative Interaction

Regenerative Interaction — High Openness High Owning Low Risk High Trust

Degenerative Interaction — Low Openness Low Owning High Risk Low Trust

- Communicaition and decision-making processes become increasingly burdened.
- People become less effective in isolating and resolving substantive issues.
- The amount of unfinished business sharply increases.
- People feel diminished interpersonal competence and psychological failure as they fail to solve problems without creating other problems.
- People become dependent and over-cautious, and respond by "tattling," preoccupation with being "safe," or "don't rock the boat" attitudes.
- Organization norms restricting owning and openness are reinforced or developed.
- Tendencies toward fragmentation of organization units are enhanced, particularly as the basic organizing model uses functional or process departmentalization, which is usually the case.

And so the mini-analysis went, with citations for those who wished a fuller treatment (e.g., Golembiewski, 1995). The bottom line was clear enough to most participants: Model A, *their* model for structuring work, tended toward degenerative interaction.

The group hummed with energy. Participants had a major conceptual handle to help transfer learning from their offsite group experience, which almost all relished; and they saw a clear approach toward applications at work, which most saw as variously problematic.

Rankin was at peace with the world, feeling pleased with a job well done. A real grumble—degenerative interaction—had been tied to one of

Figure I.5.2   Two Contrasting Models for Organizing Work

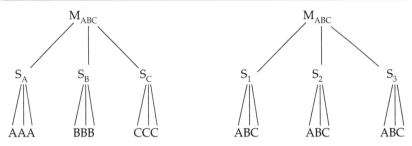

- Departmentalization is by separate functions or processes: structure aggregates the *same or similar* activities.
- Authority is basically vertical.
- Span of control is narrow: few subordinates report to a superior.

Model A: Bureaucratic Model

- Departmentalization is by flows of work—products or discrete sub-assemblies: structure aggregates *related* activities.
- Authority has horizontal as well as vertical components.
- Span of control can be broad: many subordinates can report to a single superior.

Model B: Flow of Work Model

its common causes. In short, structure often would be the meta-grumble underlying a common grumble.

Suddenly, however, Rankin found herself on the outside, looking in. Her next scheduled iterations of the offsite T-group experience were cancelled, including one that had been scheduled to occur so soon that the client paid in full, as was the practice when cancellations occurred less than three weeks before the scheduled date.

INSTRUCTIONS AND QUESTIONS

Rankin finds herself a bit richer for no work, but with holes in her schedule.

1. What's going on? All of Rankin's group sessions were highly rated by participants, and her grumble/meta-grumble session had blown the top off the rating scale.
2. How do you go about isolating a workable view of what's going on?
3. And what do you do with your speculations about what's going on?

Reference

Golembiewski, R. T. (1995). *Practical public management*. New York: Marcel Dekker.

I.6

Choosing Your Degree of Risk

A powerful staff executive, Ernst, and an ODer got into an animated debate about leadership styles. This clash of views occurred in the very early stages of a mutual consideration of the usefulness of team building for Ernst and his immediate subordinates.

In the heat of the moment, Ernst jerked a marker from the ODer's hand and sallied forth to cover several pages of newsprint, lecturing his own subordinates as well as the ODer. The eyes of several attendees rolled upwards, giving the clear signal, "Here we go again!"

The ODer grew restive after about 15 minutes. He inwardly debated these alternatives for intervening:

1. "Now, Ernst, it might be helpful at this point for us to review people's reactions to the last few minutes to see if they're getting what they expected from this meeting."
2. "Ernst, it's clear to me that either you have not understood what I tried to say earlier, or that I did a very bad job of it. And your knowledge of the research literature on leadership styles seems very weak to me. Give me the marker, Ernst, and I'll start again, if the misunderstanding is general."
3. "Ernst, I may be getting ahead of myself, but it occurs to me that what you're doing right now is a basic reason why we should be considering a team-building experience for you and your subordinates. Can we return to our main agenda item?"

∞

INSTRUCTIONS AND QUESTIONS

Should the ODer serve as a facilitator, a point-man for making things happen, or something in between? Does the very early stage of the group influence your choice of a leading intervention?

Now, become more specific:

1. Generate the piece of feedback you believe Ernst should receive.
2. Next, revise that piece of feedback, this time relying on guidelines for giving effective feedback. Many sources for such guidelines exist, but you could consult the work of Golembiewski (1993a, Vol. 1, pp. 37–72 and 163–169). He elaborates the same guidelines in several places (1993b, pp. 331–334). See also Schein (1988, Vol. 1, pp. 159–166).

References

Golembiewski, R. T. (1993a). *Approaches to planned change.* New Brunswick, NJ: Transaction Publishers.

Golembiewski, R. T. (1993b). *Handbook of organizational consultation.* New York: Marcel Dekker.

Golembiewski, R. T. (1999). *Handbook of organizational consultation.* 2nd ed. New York: Marcel Dekker.

Schein, E. (1988). *Process consultation,* Vol. 1. Reading, MA: Addison-Wesley.

I.7

Evaluating a Dean's Performance: One Intervenor's Perspective*

The academic year 1996–97 held great promise for Bob G, research professor at New University. Several projects were in their final stages, and others were in the early conceptual stages that he relished. Perhaps most important was the fact that September 1996 was the beginning of Bob G's last term as a member of the Arts and Sciences Senate.

A brief look backward provides context for the promise of 1996–97, as well as for several surprises.

PART 1

Bob G had been a now-and-again critic of the Arts and Sciences Senate over the years, especially in connection with its 1986 pseudo-survey of Dean P's performance, which required only a "yes" or "no" response by faculty. Bob G saw imprudent or incompetent polling as the modern analog of polluting a waterhole in the Old West. The latter was a hanging offense, for obvious reasons. And here was the 1986 Senate challenging Dean P with a one-item "survey."

Definitely, there were no tactical reasons for Bob's criticism of the 1986 survey: It was seen widely as a postscript, for one thing. Most observers agreed that Dean P soon would be gone, along with the president often seen as allied with him. So why waste energy or political capital on a lost cause?

*All descriptions are selective, and this case is perhaps more so than most. The focus is on one intervenor. Many tests of his perspectives were attempted—from archival records as well as from notes and interviews—but several cases could have been written by various stakeholders who would have differed in notable regards.

However, there were reasons for concern among good University citizens. Basically, the times were a-changin', and one could speak out or accept what came down the road. Indeed, the University had changed substantially over the past decade, and the end was nowhere in sight (Calbos, 1984).

Bob G had a good view of this decade-long transition. He had been department head during the final throes of what may be called Old University. Bob had resigned as head in 1972 because of his prediction that a period of institutional stabilization was in the cards, and Bob G saw himself as no steady-state manager. He had also served as internal consultant of a review at the presidential level which led to major changes in roles and personnel (Golembiewski, 1993, pp. 308–314).

With a swiftness that surprised many, and even jolted some, New University had emerged under the impetus of some resignations and a number of reassignments. Also prominent in this transition was the burgeoning of the New University administrative infrastructure in most sectors. Several efforts at university-wide centralization also were attempted—as by a vigorous and rigorous review of promotions.

Prominent in the Arts and Sciences version of the broader realignment were several "young Turks," especially in Senate roles. Their influence increased, perhaps especially because of a major University embarrassment about the education of athletes that got into the courts. This exposure weakened the then-president, as well as Dean P.

Certainly, Bob G had no hidden personal agenda concerning the 1986 poll. He felt that he already had the "best job in the University," and he was convinced that both the president and the dean would soon be gone. Other aspects of Bob G's motivation were direct. He had been doing survey/feedback designs in industry and government, and he had co-authored a book on the subject (Golembiewski and Hilles, 1979). Broadly, he was more convinced than ever of the usefulness of a well-conducted survey, and he was not willing to watch the forfeit of what could have been a valuable learning process for all parties.

In addition, Bob G was active in various helping roles among a coalition of change agents who were at that time crafting and testing the framework for practice that became "A Statement of Values and Ethics for Professionals in Organizations and Human Systems Development" (Gellermann, Frankel, and Ladenson, 1990, pp. 394–409). So his professional and ethical defenses also were on full alert.

Moreover, Bob G and his family were making a decision about leaving New University, and the survey might set unfortunate precedents if the family opted to stay. To be more precise, in fall 1986, Bob was negotiating for a compound role: three-quarters' time as vice president for human resources of a research-oriented firm; and one-quarter service on a business faculty near the firm's headquarters. The early odds favored the move—perhaps by 70 to 30—on the G family betting line.

INSTRUCTIONS AND QUESTIONS: PART 1

You are Bob G. You have just returned from four months as a visiting professor in Canada, and you have had little time to assimilate data about the nuances of the 1986 Senate survey. What would you do as a self-avowed professional intervenor in large system change?

PART 2

Bob G acted quickly, after belatedly learning of the proposed 1986 survey on his return from a stay at the University of Calgary, Canada. He sent a letter to all known specialists in surveys at New University—24 of them. The letter solicited their open-ended opinions about the usefulness of a one-item survey for any purpose, especially in a university community that should try to energize learning even under extreme conditions.

Twenty-three of the recipients of this letter responded quickly, by return mail in many cases. None supported the use of a one-item poll, and several expressed concerns about professional codes or practices.

Reports about this response were quick to filter into informal communication networks, and then into the media. The Senate also was quick to respond. A close acquaintance who was a senator dropped by to make sure Bob G was aware of Dean P's all-but-certain replacement, and the visitor pressed two points: that some downplaying of the responses to the survey letter not only would be reasonable, but also would be helpful to the Senate.

Bob G agreed about the probable fate of Dean P, and added that the president also seemed likely to move on. But Bob G let the correspondence about the survey stand on its own.

At about the same time, Bob G was being painted as a lackey of the threatened president and dean. For example, Senator S had excoriated Bob G at a public Senate meeting, which Bob G attended on the friendly warning of several senators that his letter of concern about the survey would be on the agenda. Significantly, this senator read a written statement because, as the speaker explained, that reduced the chances of a law suit.

Bob G was incensed during the reading, but his anger soon dissolved into amusement. Why had not Bob G come forward earlier, to help guide the Senate rather than becoming a critic late in the game? This only proved his complicity, some senators urged. "I was out of the country from September to January," Bob G chortled in delight, "and I was out of most loops." "Oh...," his attacker responded.

The string of events soon played itself out. First, the media ignored the senator's prepared presentation. Second, very soon thereafter the critical Senator S wrote Bob G proposing to bury the hatchet. Third, the president and dean were soon gone. Fourth, life went on at New University, under the gentle stimulus of a very long interval in seating a replacement for the departed president. The new president survived a decade, and four Arts and Sciences deans appeared over the same interval. Fifth, as part taunt and part a request for help, a Senate coalition in 1986 and 1988 asked Bob G to participate in designing a useful survey, if any dean would remain in office long enough to qualify for a survey.

INSTRUCTIONS AND QUESTIONS: PART 2

What should Bob G do, if anything, in response to these post-survey events? (See Perspective IV in this book for some professional guidelines for ODers.)

PART 3

Somewhere in the flurry of late 1986 events, Bob G and his family chose to remain at New University in his research professorship. Bob G's potential employer was uneasy about the 75/25 split of duties Bob G proposed, with so much that needed doing in the firm. Bob G's heart was in academia, and he preferred to maintain a solid university connection, ideally one that expanded over time. Negotiations stalled, and family opinion became more conflicted about moving.

Beyond this big decision for Bob G's family, he made definite but restricted responses to 1986's end-of-game play. First, he acknowledged Senator S's letter, asked for a copy of the prepared address, and received it. Bob G also noted that if the senator really wanted to "bury the hatchet," he needed only to renounce his statement where he made it.

On reading the statement, Bob G could not regenerate the high dudgeon he had experienced during the Senate reading.

Second, Bob G developed a satisfying relationship with the ex-dean. In part, this was a matter of old things to be talked about, and often laughed over. In far larger part, Bob G respected the dignity and resolution with which Dean P completed his administrative term and then went on to teach for several years before retirement.

Third, concerning a role in crafting a future Senate survey, Bob G responded casually. "Sure," he said in 1986, "call on me in about four-and-a-half years. We can mount a real action-planning survey for you." The review of the dean's stewardship was scheduled for every five years of service according to A & S Senate Bylaws.

Fourth, Bob G decided to learn more about the Senate, if only to become a more informed critic. Later he was elected to the Senate, serving a three-year term from 1994 through 1997.

INSTRUCTIONS AND QUESTIONS: PART 3

1. Evaluate Bob G's reactions to the events of 1986. What kind of guy does he seem to be? Does he fit your view of an OD intervenor?
2. Is Bob G making trouble for himself in the years to come?

PART 4

In due course, the academic year 1996–97 opened, and unexpected events changed Bob G's expectations about it. He had spent two easy years on the Senate Admissions Committee, and in September 1996 was peremptorily appointed to the Professional Concerns (PC) Committee, which usually was a hot spot. Among other duties, the PC Committee was empowered (Section VI, Bylaws, Arts and Sciences) in these terms:

1. To recommend to the Senate, to the Dean, and to the administrators and staff personnel of the University ways to improve conditions of employment for the Faculty of the College.
2. To poll the entire Faculty of the College, during the spring term of every fifth calendar year following the incumbent's appointment as Dean, concerning the Faculty's assessment of the effectiveness and

success of the incumbent Dean in carrying out the charge to "administer the rules and regulations enacted by the Faculty" and in performing the other duties and functions assigned to the Dean by the *Statutes of The University*....The Committee shall conduct additional polls when the Senate so requests by a majority vote at a regular or special meeting or when 100 Faculty members of the College sign a request and submit it to the Committee.

3. To provide the equitable and timely resolution of grievances and other conflicts that may arise in the operation of the A & S College...the Committee shall follow the guidelines and procedures set forth below and such other procedures as it may deem appropriate. The Committee may appoint *ad hoc* faculty panels to assist it.

   The Committee shall consider issues of professional concern presented to it by individual faculty members. Issues of professional concern include (but are not limited to) these: the assignment of professional responsibilities such as teaching loads and allocation of time for research or administration; remuneration; and issues relating to termination....

   [Mediation or a full-scale hearing may follow.]

Bob G was elected chair of the PC Committee in recognition of his interest in human resources. Ironically, also, Senate leadership saw Spring 1997 as the time for reviewing the present dean's activities. There had been several acting and permanent deans since 1986, but the incumbent was the only one who had lasted long enough to be reviewed by the Senate.

These occurrences may have happened by accident, but who could be sure? Sprinkled among major 1996–97 actors were several who had played key roles in 1986 events. These included Senator S, as well as another senator who with a grin told Bob G on the day of his surprise appointment to the PC Committee and election as its chair: "Now you have a chance to show us how it's done!"

Not only were Bob G's plans for 1996–97 threatened, but he soon saw several complications. He knew well only one PC Committee member. Moreover, Bob G was far from convinced that a firm-but-fair survey would do anything more than get the messenger shot. Also a soft spot, Bob G's department and the dean had been arguing for some time over a major issue of resources. As chair of the committee doing the survey of the dean's stewardship, Bob G might well be seen as having a conflict of interests, whatever the survey results.

In addition, most other members of the PC Committee were not, by their own recognition, in the strongest position either to devote large chunks of time to Committee work or to absorb organizational heat. That is, a full majority of members were either untenured or had not yet been promoted to full professional rank, or both. Committee members identified such vulnerabilities (and others) to one another in get-acquainted sessions during October 1996, but they did not dwell on them. Also prominent was the fact that only a single PC Committee member, Bob G, had strong organizational development interests.

INSTRUCTIONS AND QUESTIONS: PART 4

You are Bob G, and your plate has suddenly become very full. What do you do? The situation calls for a clear action plan, with contingencies for both political and technical concerns.

PART 5

Bob G decided on a simple approach with two features. First, both the Senate and the dean were to be given a meaningful opportunity to reprogram, with two possible outcomes:

- If the two decision-makers decided to change arrangements, Bob G and the PC Committee were substantially out from under what seems a sticky situation, if not an unredemptive one.
- If the dean and the Senate decided to retain present arrangements, in effect, that constituted a special legitimation that increased the probability of later support and reduced possible contention about conflicts of interest.

Second, if the latter alternative were to come to pass, Bob G was prepared to take the leading role. It required striking a balance between playing the role of initiator in survey matters and being a shock absorber with respect to PC Committee and Senate processes.

How to provide such a reasonable opportunity for public choice to affirm the PC Committee's mandate or to reprogram? Bob G began where he always does—with the formal statements of missions and roles—and he hit paydirt quickly. In summary, Bob G:

- Learned that 1997 was not clearly the fifth year of the current dean's service but, arguably, the fourth. The points at issue are whether to count his period as acting dean, and how much to count it.
- Discovered that the vice president for academic affairs had scheduled his own review of the Dean for fall 1997, which without question would be the end of the Dean's five years of service. If so, a new PC Committee in 1997–98 could handle that review.
- Found language in the Senate Bylaws that suggested that Bob G, and perhaps one or two other PC Committee members, were not clearly eligible for the PC Committee appointments. The key issue was delicate. The Bylaws read, in part, that PC Committee members "shall be [elected from among Arts and Sciences Senators and] shall serve staggered two year terms..." (Bylaws, Section VI).

  The rationale underlying this stipulation was that PC Committee membership is a tough assignment, with a learning curve long enough to require two-year stints.

  Since 1996–97 was to be the third and last year in Bob G's Senate term, and given that he had no intention to seek re-election, Bob G reasonably could be viewed as ineligible to serve on the PC Committee or to be its chair. Simply, Bob G could *not* serve a two-year term.

Quickly, letters were dispatched to the Dean and to the Presiding Officer of the Senate, raising the issues sketched above. Both sources acted to re-legitimate the status quo, which in effect strengthened the mandate of the PC Committee by direct action of the two major immediate stakeholders. Two features added detail to this re-legitimation:

- The Senate had a useful discussion about the Bylaws, as well as about current practices, and clarified its criteria for committee appointments.
- The Dean was agreeable to a review in spring 1997. PC Committee members speculated that a presidential search at New University was in its early stages, and plans called for the announcement of several finalists in early June, with a final selection to be made several weeks later. (The issue was never raised with the Dean, however, and he later noted after reading a draft of this case that no such connection had existed.)

INSTRUCTIONS AND QUESTIONS: PART 5

So re-legitimation has been gained, but now what:

1. Design some next steps for the PC Committee's review of the Dean's first five years in office.
2. What style seems appropriate for Bob G in his role as chair? Does he seem to have the appropriate skills and attitudes for this position?

PART 6

The PC Committee soon decided on a direct course of action. The game plan evolved during frequent PC Committee meetings in October through December. (The records do not permit an exact count, but an estimate of 20 to 25 PC Committee meetings would not be far off.) Typically, Bob G issued proposals, and detailed massaging of proposals by PC Committee members led to a unanimous or at least a consensual buy-in.

Early PC Committee dynamics were reflected in an extended discussion about a grievance that might be raised by a faculty member against an A & S departmental colleague. Members were predisposed to be openly accommodating to the petitioner, with strong leadership from an experienced member. PC Committee members emphasized collegial responsibilities and keeping alternative lines of communication open. Bob G did not disagree, but he suggested that PC Committee involvement would have been reasonable at far earlier stages if other ongoing actions had not pre-empted this role. Moreover, PC Committee members would be very busy with the survey, in ways they would have to experience to appreciate fully.

On several polls of the members, the balance was maintained: all others but Bob G were in favor of accommodating the petitioner.

After about an hour of discussion, Bob G served as his own process observer: "OK, so be it. Everybody has been heard, the differences are clear enough, and reasonable people can always accommodate such differences, if trust is there." Priority went to responding to the petition.

Via similar give-and-take dynamics, with Bob G typically initiating details and the other committee members evaluating and tailoring, the survey process began to evolve. Beyond the PC Committee, major elements of the approach were reviewed in several Senate monthly meetings, and particularly in a December 10 meeting with the Dean.

Four emphases dominated. First, the focus of the survey was to be on action research, or AR—how to learn from survey results. This obviously required the Dean's consent, which he extended soon after having been given a short description of AR to read (Golembiewski and Hilles, 1979, pp. 23–30), which was part of the materials that PC Committee members had reviewed.

The primer on AR also contained an example of an authorizing letter from a CEO, and the Committee asked the Dean to prepare a similar letter for distribution to all Arts and Sciences faculty.

By mutual agreement, the Dean's office forwarded a copy of the Dean's letter announcing the survey to each of the 25-plus department heads and they, in turn, were to send copies of the letter to all eligible faculty. See Exhibit I.7.1. This obvious convenience encouraged only minor concerns within the PC Committee and the Senate.

Second, the Committee asked the Dean in the December 10 meeting to prepare an outline of the major achievements of his administration. This would help the Committee draft its survey, and the Dean might also use the product as an informational piece for distribution to all A & S faculty.

The Dean agreed.

Third, the Committee agreed unanimously to follow a tight schedule, concurred on by both the Dean and Senate. See Exhibit I.7.2. Senate discussion of the milestones occurred several times, beginning with the December monthly meeting. Updates occurred in each of the next several monthly Senate meetings. Paramountly, the schedule reserved more than a month for action planning after the Senate's formal consideration of the results and before the Senate's last meeting of the 1996–97 academic year. In the interim, a full summary of results would be made available to all interested faculty through their departmental representatives on the Faculty Senate, or through the members of the PC Committee. This was considered preferable to either an unprecedented reliance on e-mail or a flood of hard copies of a substantial report to each of the 700-plus faculty members. The first round of action planning also could begin during that interim, with possible follow-up during the summer of 1997, should the Dean see value in that.

One factor underlying the schedule in Exhibit I.7.2 was both unobtrusive and potentially consequential. A presidential search was underway at New University, and it planned on releasing a short list of candidates in early April. The schedule sought the best of all worlds: the schedule avoided entanglement with any dynamics associated with the long list of candidates, while survey results and action planning followed the public announcement of the short list of candidates, when no internal candidates might still be in the running.

Fourth, the Dean provided support for the survey. Bob G had expected to take some resources out of his budget to supplement any costs beyond the Dean's contribution. This was Bob G's way to get others to allow the participation of graduate students eager to have a

Exhibit I.7.1   Letter from the Dean to A & S Faculty Encouraging
Support of Survey and Action Planning

February 5, 1997

Faculty in Arts and Sciences
New University

Dear Colleague:

Our College Bylaws require the Faculty Senate to undertake a review of my
performance as dean during my fifth year of service. Dr. G, Chair of the
Professional Concerns Committee, is a specialist in reviewing the performance
of organizations and their administrators. He has proposed that a survey
would be a more meaningful way to review my performance than would the
usual "yes or no" ballot. I am in full agreement with his proposal and feel that
the results of this sort of survey would help me understand what aspects of
my performance as dean you have found satisfactory and what aspects of my
performance you feel could be improved. I would like to encourage you to
complete the questionnaire developed by Dr. G and the Professional Concerns
Committee. I can assure you I will take seriously the information you provide
and do my best to respond constructively to your ideas and opinions.

Information about my responsibilities as dean and my activities as a faculty
member may be found on the College's Web site.

Exhibit I.7.2   Major Milestones for Dean's Survey

—First week in February	Review survey with Dean
—February 10	Dean's letter to faculty (see Exhibit I.7.1)
—February 20	Questionnaires distributed
—March 5	Final date for receipt of completed surveys
—April 9	Report to A & S Senate Presiding Officer; to Dean, shortly thereafter
—April 16	Survey results reviewed with Dean
—April 24	Final report due to all senators
—until May 29, or last Senate meeting for 1996–97	Early rounds of action planning

hands-on experience in an AR application. As it turned out, volunteers were more than willing to gain some experience in a planned change application. At various stages, three graduate students provided help.

One hitch occurred due to the tight schedule when the Dean was out of town. As the Dean's office was preparing to mail to department heads the letter announcing the survey, Bob G received a call about whether it was OK if the Dean's summary of accomplishments was attached to the letter announcing the survey. "No," he replied. "The PC Committee discussed that point and unanimously believed that any such informational materials should be sent separately by the Dean's Office and under his own letterhead." The rationale was direct: as much as possible, PC Committee members sought both the reality and perception of an "independent, professional survey." At the same time, the PC Committee encouraged the Dean to summarize his accomplishments as well as to disseminate that summary for several reasons, including the probable heightening of response rates to the survey from a faculty without a history as active respondents.

The Dean's accomplishments were posted on the A & S Web site, along with a legend to the effect that the PC Committee had requested the statement and its publication. See Exhibit I.7.3 for the "Dean's Statement of Five-Year Accomplishments."

Some PC Committee members noted that this legend was correct in one sense, but misleading in the sense that the PC Committee always sought to distance itself from any informational activities by the Dean's office.

INSTRUCTIONS AND QUESTIONS: PART 6

If you were Bob G, how would you react to the legend on the Web site? Would you:

- Consider the matter a misunderstanding, and let it go at that?
- Raise the issue at the next meeting of the PC Committee?
- Call a special PC meeting?
- Call the Dean to complain?

As an alternative, you could instigate informal efforts to try to track down the source of the incorrect legend. For example, ex-Senator S, who headed the 1986 survey, might be helpful. He was now an associate dean.

Exhibit I.7.3   Dean's Statement of Five-Year Accomplishments

January 9, 1997

Dear Bob:

Please find enclosed the information you requested for the Faculty Senate's review of my performance as dean during the past five years. It has taken me a little longer than I expected to put this material together, but it has been a useful exercise for me to think about what I have done since becoming dean.

1. Past Five Years
   - Faculty Development: built faculty travel budget; adjusted faculty teaching loads to provide more time for scholarship; provided additional College support for faculty leaves; set aside portion of salary raises to adjust inequities and began adjustment of salary inequities between departments.
   - Management: developed planning and analysis for all College operations; appointed and reappointed heads on the basis of faculty input; opened College finances and operations to faculty scrutiny; worked to make administration responsive and supportive; encouraged and utilized faculty governance at department and Faculty Senate levels in setting policies and administrative procedures; utilized Dean's Student Advisory Board to obtain regular feedback from students.
   - Instruction: obtained significant additional funding to support instruction and systematized how it is allocated; focussed equipment budget on instructional needs.
   - College Infrastructure: increased operating expenses to departments by 50%; built annual budget for networking; provided support for departmental computer-support personnel.
   - Program Development: provided additional faculty positions and other support to strengthen instruction and research in Music, Drama, Languages and Linguistics, Anthropology, Geography, Criminal Justice Studies, Ecology, Marine Sciences, and Computer Sciences; restructured and strengthened international programs.
   - Recruitment: revised recruitment policy and provided resources to hire faculty in top group of candidates; obtained funding for start-up equipment and renovations needed by new faculty; stressed proactive recruitment of minorities and women.
   - Professional Activities: continued to teach each year (although at a reduced level); maintained research program, currently supported by two National Science Foundation grants; continued to supervise graduate students.
2. Coming Years
   - Continue and expand planning and analysis of College operations, with the goal of providing additional funds to departments from any savings identified.
   - Continue strengthening of computing and networking infrastructure of College.

continued

Exhibit I.7.3   Dean's Statement of Five-Year Accomplishments
(continued)

- Continue program development with goal of building research and teaching programs across the College.
- Stress value of excellence in teaching and see that good teaching is rewarded.
- Manage problem areas of semester conversion and enrollment increases as smoothly as possible.
- Strengthen international programs and cross-disciplinary studies.

PART 7

Bob G decided to wait for the next PC meeting. The survey might well prove trying for all, and the members of the PC Committee had developed a shared norm about personal ownership of the associated processes. Thus, typically, all PC members attended meetings with the Dean.

Although there was some concern at the PC meeting about being "snookered," there were reasonable explanations of what had occurred, and why. Moreover, the Dean "seemed to be buying the program" of AR. So why protest too much on an issue that was clearly not essential?

"Let's get back to designing the survey instrument," soon became the call of PC Committee members. And several rounds of review followed.

The development of the survey was accomplished in about six PC meetings, lasting over two hours each, on average. Typically, Bob G took the initiative in drafting alternative forms, often responsive to the knowledge of Committee members or to input from A & S faculty. PC members briefly contemplated sensing groups, but tabled this topic. *The problem became the development of a serviceable form that would inform AR without demanding so much effort that it would induce response rates below the moderate-to-low levels expected.*

Basically, the survey went through three developmental forms, with the successors being shorter and lighter on behavioral science interests. For example, faculty's "intent to turnover" was seen as an issue worthy of attention, but the usual operational definition was seen as respondent-unfriendly. The items were eliminated, in substantial part because PC members were concerned that the response rate would "be low enough, at best." The same concern was expressed in several Senate reviews of progress, typically with the Committee's urging that senators "talk up the survey" among their colleagues. The issue of a "satisfactory" response rate was never raised with the Dean.

The final form of the questionnaire, shown in Exhibit I.7.4, sought to assess many aspects of the Dean's performance. To outline a few major foci,

- Items 3 and 4 are central. These open-ended items seek to elicit what's going well and what needs improvement, to assess the "working balance in Arts and Sciences." PC Committee members expected that many "needs improvement" suggestions might motivate and even guide AR.
- Items 8 and 11 contrast espoused vs. action theories—"talking the walk" vs. "walking the talk," in today's managerial argot.
- Item 10 overviews 11 aspects of A & S administration.
- Item 12 relates to the Dean's reappointment.
- Items 13 and 14 solicit expectations about the survey and the uses to which survey results will be put.

Significantly, also, the survey sought to accommodate a major feature of A & S life: some faculty members might have little experience on which to base reactions to the Dean. Hence, the 11 items under Question 10 did not force a choice. The survey noted: "If you have no experience relevant to an aspect, CIRCLE NOT RELEVANT (NR)." In addition, Question 6 would permit breakouts of data based on self-rated differences in the ability of respondents "to arrive at a solid conclusion," rated on a 5-point scale.

Beyond these elements, Bob G's intent was dual: he drafted working versions of the survey that would provide data useful for AR, but not at the expense of putting PC members in positions with which they were uncomfortable. Hence, discussions of the survey were long, with some positions being tested and retested. All final judgments were unanimous.

On schedule, a survey form was available for the Dean on February 11, with the Dean having about a week to review the form.

Per their forceful preference, all Committee members wanted to attend the meeting with the Dean for a review of the survey form; and all did so. Bob G was delighted.

Just before the Dean received his copy of the survey for the review with PC Committee members, the usual Senate pattern of updates was expanded in the monthly meeting of January 30. Bob G reviewed the

Exhibit I.7.4   Final Survey Form

1. My faculty employment status is best described as (Check One)
   ☐ tenured
   ☐ tenure track
   ☐ non-tenure track, full-time member of corps of instruction

2. I have been employed at New University for (Check One)
   ☐ 2 years or less
   ☐ more than 2 and less than 6 years
   ☐ 6–10 years
   ☐ 11–20 years
   ☐ 21 years or more

3. In my opinion, the most positive things about [the Dean's] administration include:
   1. _____
   2. _____
   3. _____
   4. _____
   5. _____
   6. _____

4. In my opinion, the things needing most improvement in [the Dean's] administration include:
   1. _____
   2. _____
   3. _____
   4. _____
   5. _____
   6. _____

5. I am actively searching for an employer alternative to New University. (Circle One)

1	2	3	4	5
Strongly Disagree	Disagree	?	Agree	Strongly Agree

6. I have had excellent opportunities to arrive at solid conclusions about [the Dean's] stewardship and A & S operations—e.g., as department head, as administrator, via committee or other New University assignments. (Circle One)

5	4	3	2	1
Strongly Agree	Agree	?	Disagree	Strongly Disagree

7. My reactions to headship search(es) in New University departments in the past five years have been very positive. (Circle One)

5	4	3	2	1	Not
Strongly Agree	Agree	?	Disagree	Strongly Disagree	Applicable

Exhibit I.7.4 Final Survey Form *(continued)*

8. [The Dean's] *professed* style is (Check One)
   ☐ equal treatment for all departments
   ☐ preference for one or a few departments
   ☐ treatment of each department relative to its status/productivity among counterparts at comparable schools
   ☐ no clear *professed* tendency, overall
   ☐ I have insufficient basis for judgment.

9. As soon as it is possible, I will retire from New University. (Circle One)

1	2	3	4	5
Strongly Disagree	Disagree	?	Agree	Strongly Agree

10. Please appraise each of the following aspects of A & S administration.

    CIRCLE ONE RATING if you have relevant experience.

    If you have no experience relevant to an aspect, CIRCLE NOT RELEVANT (NR).

		Lowest Rating				Highest Rating	
a.	equitable distribution of resources	1	2	3	4	5	NR
b.	clear sense of mission	1	2	3	4	5	NR
c.	keeps you informed	1	2	3	4	5	NR
d.	competent and caring regard for students	1	2	3	4	5	NR
e.	promptness and efficiency	1	2	3	4	5	NR
f.	clear policy guidance, across the board	1	2	3	4	5	NR
g.	encourages your inputs of information and perspectives	1	2	3	4	5	NR
h.	curriculum responsiveness, as in environmental literacy or multiculturalism	1	2	3	4	5	NR
i.	inspires confidence that your inputs will be taken into account	1	2	3	4	5	NR
j.	funds for travel	1	2	3	4	5	NR
k.	appointments to administrative positions and committee appointments	1	2	3	4	5	NR

Exhibit I.7.4   Final Survey Form *(continued)*

11. [The Dean's] basic style *in action* is (Check One)
    ☐ preference for one or a few departments
    ☐ treatment of each department relative to status/productivity among
       counterparts at comparable schools
    ☐ equal treatment for all departments
    ☐ I have insufficient basis for judgment
    ☐ no clear tendency, *in action*, overall

12. In my opinion, the overall record justifies a second five-year term for [the
    Dean]. (Circle One)

1	2	3	4	5
Strongly Agree	Agree	Not Sure or Abstain	Disagree	Strongly Disagree

13. As a next-to-last step in completing this survey, do you have anything to
    add relevant to this survey?

    _____
    _____
    _____
    _____

14. After completing all the items, it is my opinion that the information from
    this survey will be responded to constructively. (Circle One)

1	2	3	4	5
Strongly Disagree	Disagree	?	Agree	Strongly Agree

Thank you for your help.

Please return the completed questionnaire to:
Professor Robert T. G
Chair,
Professional Concerns Committee
211 Baldwin Hall

---

on-schedule process: the survey would be reviewed with the Dean on
February 11, the questionnaires would go out on the planned date, and
a report would be made to the Senate on April 24. Moreover, as had
been emphasized earlier in several settings, the PC Committee would
report the survey results, and the Senate would then reject or accept the
report and go on to interpret the results.

However, a senatorial hot button required special attention. Something very much like the following exchange took place on Thursday, January 30:

Senator: Can we see the questionnaire?

Bob G: Why not? That was *not* the Committee's original intent to show the questionnaire to senators, as was noted more than one time. The only question is a practical one: Can you review the document in time for the Committee to keep its appointment with the Dean?

Senator: If you get it to us on the e-mail by Friday noon, we'll respond by Monday noon.

Bob G: Great, but don't count on the Committee to do that job.

Senator: I can get the stuff on the server if you get a final copy to me by 6:00 PM.

Bob G: Done!

Senator: Will this review limit your Committee?

Bob G: I hope not! Ideally, we'll learn something. And in any case the Senate certainly has every right to follow the process, in whatever detail. You have known for months of our intent to involve the Dean as deeply as possible in all survey phases, and especially in subsequent action planning. And the dates as well.

An appropriate Senate motion passed unanimously. By the February 3 deadline, four senators had responded to Bob G via e-mail; no substantive concerns had surfaced; and, indeed, several overt supporters of the Dean had gone out of their way to say nice things about the survey.

A copy of the survey was hand-delivered to the Dean's office on Monday afternoon, leaving the Dean about a week to review it before the scheduled meeting with the Professional Concerns Committee on February 11.

INSTRUCTIONS AND QUESTIONS: PART 7

There remains only a short time before the Committee meets with the Dean for his review of the questionnaire.

1. What do you expect from him, given his reading of Exhibit I.7.4? Remember, AR is new to the Dean and much of the University.

2. Do you see any items on the survey about which the Dean might feel special concern?
3. What do you make of the Senate's review of the questionnaire? Why did some senators, especially those supportive of the Dean, urge this review of the survey form at the time they did?
4. How would you go about assessing the Dean's degree of buy-in—not only with respect to the questionnaire, but also with respect to the AR process?
5. Do you see anything missing in this welter of detail? For openers, how about the treatment of the issue of "satisfactory" response rate?

PART 8

The meeting with the Dean in his office ran long, and the tone was relaxed and positive. The Dean suggested not a single change to the survey, and expressed several times that he needed the Committee's best judgment. Hence, he went along with the survey, as long as Committee members were comfortable with it. All PC Committee members attended the meeting and affirmed their ownership of the survey.

As to AR, the Dean agreed with the hope that all this effort should lead to constructive action, if indicated. He reiterated his commitment to a more efficient and effective Dean's Office.

All in all, the members of the Professional Concerns Committee saw an appropriate level of buy-in. The Dean was supportive enough, within the boundary of the elemental reality that the "votes were not yet in." Helpfully, also, the Dean solicited the Committee's position about whether he should attend the Senate meeting at which survey results would be presented and discussed. The Dean was inclined to be absent, in the interests of full and free discussion. "It's your call," was the unanimous Committee opinion, "but we encourage you to be there." The Dean was noncommittal, adding that the Committee should "feel free to revisit the recommendation."

Committee spirits were high, and Bob G scheduled a "final review" of the questionnaire in time to meet the release date that had long ago been announced to the Senate and the faculty. Bob G noted, "We'll go through the survey section by section—Do we touch all the big issues? And then we'll do it item by item—Do we have items that provide a good chance of getting the information that will both motivate and guide AR?"

INSTRUCTIONS AND QUESTIONS: PART 8

You are a PC Committee member.

1. Keeping Bob G's charge in mind, go through Exhibit I.7.4 and isolate any sections that you see as promising useful data for action planning. Does the questionnaire contain items that seem to you to get at relevant A & S features? Do you see items that should be eliminated?
2. How do you evaluate the Dean's reactions?
3. Do PC members seem to have a realistic assessment of the situation?
4. How do you interpret the Dean's final comment about the Committee revisiting the members' strong view that the Dean should attend the Senate review session scheduled for April 24? How would you act upon your interpretation?
5. Is there anything missing?

PART 9

The Committee's unanimous decision: Do it! They made no changes in the questionnaire, for the first time in three major reviews of the survey form.

As agreed, the Dean's Office was to send a single form to each department head, who would then distribute copies to all eligible faculty. This is a standard distribution procedure, but Bob G raised the obvious question of whether more distance from the Dean's Office would be preferable, if only for symbolic purposes. All other members of the Committee observed, in effect: The procedure works, and it's easy on us. The Senate was twice informed of the procedure, and senators accepted it with little comment.

Three features characterized the survey. First, early response rates encouraged attention, suggesting a response rate of about 30 percent, with almost all returns coming from the tenured faculty. A few responses came from those on the tenure track, and "other faculty" were virtually unrepresented.

Discussion before the Senate was unanimous about the goal of a "high" response rate, but no one had the answer to what constitutes "high" in A & S. Bob G reported on several recent A & S faculty-wide elections to committees, which had response rates in the 10 to 15 percent range. On the crucial issue of whether "low" rates reflect faculty satisfaction or disaffection, opinions differed.

Discussion elaborated a similar point regarding the Senate's interpretation of survey results, broadly viewed. Basically, the Committee could report, but only the Senate should interpret. No technical answers existed to questions such as the following:

- What distribution of opinion urges interventions concerning specific aspects of A & S management and quality of life?
- What proportion of respondents reporting positively on survey question 12 would justify a second five-year term for the Dean?

University sources such as the A & S Bylaws provided no specific guidance. A & S experience contained only a single distant clue: A Department head being reviewed for another term could be reappointed if 70 percent of the faculty cast a secret ballot in favor of reappointment. Otherwise, a full-scale search is required, in which the incumbent head might be a candidate.

The Senate was the basic vehicle employed to promote the survey, especially via grassroots efforts by individual senators urging participation in the academic department each represented. In addition, perhaps 15 to 20 phone calls were made to various influential persons to seek their help.

No media involvement was solicited, perhaps because an earlier survey had become the subject of a "media circus." PC Committee members expressed only minor interest in aggressively involving media, which might raise response rates but had its costs, as in portraying PC as an adversary with a special interest. In any case, local media opinion tended toward three views: the survey was "internal faculty business"; the local newspapers were vigorously embarked on campaigns to be "regional papers" in which University stories did not have the high priority of even a few years ago; and the student newspaper focused its interest on the upcoming conversion to a semester calendar. All media had access to all Senate meetings, but coverage was not extensive.

Late in the polling period, Bob G heard from a reputable source that faculty in one large department had not received surveys, and it was a department in which pro-Dean opinion was expected to be especially strong.

Bob G extended the polling period for 10 days, after unsuccessfully trying to contact most PC Committee members. He acted on the information that an illness in the department's mail office may have caused a delay in distributing the surveys. In any case, Bob G saw no other alternative, and was confident of Committee support, if after the fact.

Notice of the extension went out to all A & S faculty, again using the department heads as conduits. Few additional returns came in.

In this impromptu interregnum, several members of the PC Committee—including Bob G—gave renewed attention to the interpretive problems highlighted by recent discussion in the Senate about interpreting the survey. The most obvious issue was whether a majority of positive votes for the Dean should justify the recommendation of a reappointment. The interpretation of other survey items posed even more subtle issues about standards.

The most extreme approach was for the PC Committee to recommend throwing all interpretive issues back to the Senate for judgment *before* data were available, and in a hardball version with the Committee suspending survey operations until such guidance was made available by the Senate. Committee discussion raised several objections to this course of action:

- The Senate might well relegate the issues of interpretation to the Committee, but most members considered interpretation in principle to be the Senate's prerogative and problem.
- In practice, the Committee agenda was already full, and probably would get worse in several pending cases of mediation.
- Senate discussion reflected little or no enthusiasm for prior consideration of interpretive conventions, no doubt in part due to an optimism by some that the survey would be "a landslide." Some predicted the Dean might receive 70 percent of the direct preferences favoring reappointment.
- The items most relevant for action planning presented issues other than the direct "vote" for the Dean's reappointment, and various distributions of opinion would be encountered, each presenting interpretive problems that were better faced in specific cases than in general principle.
- Above all, we do nothing to deflect attention from the survey results and action planning—and insisting on prior Senate interpretive criteria might do just that.

INSTRUCTIONS AND QUESTIONS: PART 9

1. Would you recommend changes in the PC Committee's orientation to the media?
2. How do you evaluate Bob G's action in extending the survey? As a PC

Committee member? As a senator?
3. What about the criteria for interpreting the survey? Should the related issues be forced with the Senate at an early date?
4. Who is the client? Or are there different clients for different purposes?

PART 10

The extended polling period resulted in no flood of returns, and the extension left the Committee with a somewhat tighter schedule. Four major tasks faced the Committee:

1. Compiling two forms of the open-ended questions "What's gone well in the Dean's tenure?" and "What needs improvement?"

    The total responses filled about 120 pages of single-spaced comments, with about two-thirds dealing with suggested improvements.

    This compilation of direct quotations was for selective distribution: full copies would go to the Dean, a VP, the President, and the Senate's presiding officer.

    A few items were lightly edited, largely to mask identities.

    All responses were sorted by PC Committee members into themes, with frequencies giving approximate but useful indications of the salience of themes.

    This abridged set of themes ran to six pages. See Appendix A.

    This set of materials was to be made available to the four major stakeholders listed above, as well as to all senators. Distribution to interested faculty and others then could occur through individual senators.
2. Processing data from all other items on the questionnaire.
    Aggregate data would be made widely available—first to the three major stakeholders, to all senators, and then to all interested faculty and others, through individual senators.
3. Preparing a short summary of findings that would serve as an orientation to all sets of detailed materials described above.
4. Running various break-out analyses as interests developed and as data permitted.

    For example, the survey asked who was planning to leave University employ, and it might be interesting to see if those planning to leave had attitudes different from those staying. There were no plans to share broadly such break-out analyses, but they could potentially enrich action research.

Appendix A contains the materials made available to most stakeholders. This package lacks only the short summary of survey results mentioned above, which is in Appendix B.

The period of completing and analyzing surveys had one notable feature. Various individuals among the senators became frequent callers, especially one senator openly identified with the Dean. Several senators had been anxious about the results, for several weeks, even as surveys were still being distributed. Bob G always shared the latest response rates with them, along with a message to try to encourage their colleagues to respond to the survey. Beyond that, Bob G's two basic responses were: "It's too early to say"; and, later when data processing was substantially advanced, "It is no slam-dunk for the Dean."

INSTRUCTIONS AND QUESTIONS: PART 10

1. Consult Appendix A. You might find it instructive to prepare a short summary of the findings for distribution to target populations you consider relevant.
2. Take the role of Bob G. What is your strategy in preparing this draft, given the nature of the findings?
3. As Bob G, do you decide on a single summary, or different ones for the several stakeholders—the Dean, his superiors (the President and a VP), the Senate, the faculty, and other interested publics?

PART 11

The PC Committee decided on a single-page summary of results that by design was "plain vanilla." See Appendix B. To permit more facile comparisons with the aggregated results on the survey form reported in Exhibit I.7.4, the summary followed the order of the survey items. As was characteristic of Committee dynamics, Bob G prepared a first draft of the summary of highlights, which was considered line-by-line in Committee session. No formal votes were taken, but unanimity or something approaching it characterized 9 of the 10 highlights.

The "Survey Highlights" in Appendix B, that is to say, are generally consistent with the PC Committee's oft-stated view that it would report but not interpret survey data. Hence, the highlights do not intend to be a "report" in the conventional sense, but rather seek to aid understanding of the survey data so as to facilitate interpretation.

One exception to this generalization about Committee unanimity exists: point 9 in the highlights refers to "One reasonable interpretation of Q12." PC members seriously debated that wording, and two positions emerged. A determined minority was intent on noting that the survey emphasized senior faculty views, and preferred a harsher summary than appears in the highlights, but accepted the wording that point 9 constituted only "one reasonable interpretation" of the survey responses to Q12. A non-interpretive version of point 9 would note: Approximately 55 percent of the respondents favor reappointing the Dean. A full copy of the whole package of the PC Committee's survey processing first went to the presiding officer of the Senate, as a matter of protocol. The expectation was that the Senate's Steering Committee soon would see the report.

About two weeks prior to the date of formal Senate consideration, Bob G carried to the Dean one copy of the full Committee report, headed by the short summary, for his information. Schedules were tight, and Bob G only got to highlight the 55 percent positive vote supporting reappointment of the Dean. The Dean responded in a modulated way: "I would have liked to have done better."

An early morning session between the Dean and the PC Committee was scheduled for the day before the Senate's consideration of the Committee's report. The Dean had the report for about 10 days.

INSTRUCTIONS AND QUESTIONS: PART 11

Appendix B contains the short summary statement that headed the Committee's report.

1. How does it compare to the draft you prepared for Part 10, question 1?
2. What reactions do you expect from the Dean? From the senators? From other interested parties?

PART 12

The Dean was not pleased with the results of the survey. That conclusion seemed obvious to the PC Committee members, who were redirected from what had become the normal site for meetings with him—his main office, near numerous work areas, on the top floor. Committee members were directed to a room on the lowest floor which, during the early morning hours, was quite isolated.

Overall, the Dean announced, the survey was "unprofessional." Specifically, it developed, he was referring to several things for which he considered the Committee, and especially Bob G, responsible:

- The response rate was troubling low.
- The summaries emphasized the negative, especially in the sense that fewer pages were devoted to "things going well" than to "things needing improvement."
- Bob G had undue influence on the Committee.
- The wording of item 9 in Appendix B concerning respondents' preferences regarding a second term for the Dean—i.e., the item beginning "One reasonable interpretation"—was seen as slanted and insufficiently positive.

The climate in the meeting was argumentative, if not belligerent. One PC Committee member served as mediator, while all other members addressed aspects of the Dean's main points.

A brief review of the 90-minute-plus meeting summarizes Committee responses to the Dean's emphases. First, a higher response rate clearly would have been desirable, but there was no benign or definite interpretation of the present rate. Committee policies and procedures might be faulted; faculty apathy might be alleged; fear of the Dean could be emphasized; or combinations of such elements might explain the low turnout. But there was no way of assigning causality with certainty.

Two conclusions were clear to the Committee members: the survey encompassed the opinions of many tenured faculty, and they could not be neglected; and the turnout rate was similar to, or higher than, turnout in other areas, such as the several yearly votes of A & S faculty on assignments to college committees.

Second, the Committee's position concerning attractive elements in the Dean's performance vs. those that needed improvement was twofold. True enough, the latter outnumbered the former in the summarized themes (see last pages of Appendix A), but that was because of the far larger number of "needs improvement" comments. Such an over-representation was not surprising in the context of a lack of similar public opportunities, and might even be generic to the basic survey design.

Third, Committee members unanimously noted that the survey and its products had been generated by the full Committee and released only after extensive discussions and revisions by PC members.

Fourth, the Dean had identified one compromise expression of a major point in the Committee's internal debate about survey results: i.e., "One reasonable interpretation of Q12 approximates 55 percent favoring reappointment of Dean" (see item 9 in Appendix B). This was clearly the majority view, but a minority had urged a stronger interpretation of the response to Q12. As Senate discussion had earlier emphasized, no consistent guides existed for interpreting the results of surveys relevant to administrative reappointments. However, A & S policy did provide that heads of departments could be reappointed directly if they received 70 or more percent of the relevant faculty's votes. Less than that, and a formal search would be required. The same explicitness is not extended to the deanship, but an insistent minority of Committee members had seen value in interpreting the survey in such terms.

After some discussion, the PC Committee had selected the less contentions of what members saw as the two major possibilities. The Dean objected to the choice made, but "one reasonable interpretation" was intended to imply that other interpretations not only were considered but also could be viewed as reasonable. This compromise language satisfied all Committee members. The wording kept the faith with the Senate by being honest about events, while remaining respectful of basic Senate responsibility for interpreting the survey and avoiding more inflammatory wording.

When the Dean left the room, all Committee members remained to review the process, and especially to consider strategy for the next day's formal report to the Senate.

INSTRUCTIONS AND QUESTIONS: PART 12

1. How do you characterize the tone of this session? Do those dynamics suggest that the Committee was a highly cohesive group?
2. As a PC Committee member, how would you react privately in the review after the Dean's departure?
3. How do you evaluate the Committee's choice of wording in Q12? Would it have been better to use words that were less revealing about the dynamics of the Committee's internal debate?

PART 13

Reactions of surprise dominated in the review. Most Committee members had been optimistic that the Dean had "bought into" the action research design, based on various clues gathered during two extensive sessions with the Dean; none of the Committee had ever seen the Dean flushed and angry; and Committee members also remembered Bob G's recollection of the Dean's initial response to the 55 percent positive vote he had achieved.

The Committee held its position, after review of the process, and with no apparent dissent. The next day's Senate session would feature a Q-and-A session, with Bob G as the point. No changes were considered in the style or details of Committee products.

INSTRUCTIONS AND QUESTIONS: PART 13

You are Bob G, now sitting alone in your office a couple of hours after the morning's session with the Dean. You "had been there before," but you were concerned nonetheless. Paramountly, the Committee had remained firm under unexpected pressure, but you hoped that the earlier attention to PC processes and relationships in consensual decision-making would pay dividends, given the cross-pressures.

As Bob G, do a bit of ruminating:

1. How do you read the members of the PC Committee?
2. Do you have any expectations about what the Dean will say in the next day's open session?
3. How do you intend to represent yourself in that open Senate session?
4. Are there any things that you need to do in the next 26 hours or so—contacting senators about the morning's meeting, for example?
5. How about reminding the media of the next day's meeting with the Senate?

PART 14

Bob G came to several decisions in the hours after returning to his office following the heated meeting with the Dean. First, he decided to call only the Senate's presiding officer, who had long been aware of the planned meeting with the Dean and had received a full set of survey results to share with his own Steering Committee. "The Dean was not pleased," Bob G reported; and the presiding officer expressed his thanks for the information.

The presiding officer then asked whether the Dean should attend the scheduled open session with the senators. The Dean had raised that possibility earlier, in the interest of an open discussion. The Committee proposed that it was clearly the Dean's call, but that the upside possibilities of attendance were substantial, with no great downside potential, as viewed even after the high-energy meeting with the Dean. Bob G reiterated that Committee position to the Senate's presiding officer.

As for anticipating the Dean's approach before the Senate, the decision was to be as technical as possible in presenting the results. Let the survey results speak for themselves, and (at least) avoid easy charges either of "mounting a political campaign" or "running scared." Bob G did not invite representatives of the media, and none appeared on their own. It also would have been possible to try to orchestrate some moderating efforts, as with senators supportive of the Dean but available to Bob G as sounding boards and possible go-betweens. Members of the PC Committee made no such attempt, although several were aware of suggested coalition formations of one persuasion or the other.

No contacts were initiated with any senators before the open session. This was not beside the point. Overtures to do so were made to Bob G and to other Committee members.

After the review of the morning's meeting with the Dean, Bob G went back to his other work, and his mind was at peace. At home that evening, Bob G asked his wife to pick him up after the next day's Senate meeting so they could go on to a quiet dinner. The night before the Senate session, right or wrong, Bob G monitored his internal processes in the usual way. Things seemed OK: he slept straight through the night for more than eight hours.

Nonetheless, Bob G was edgy before the Senate meeting. He arrived early, and in fact was the second person to arrive, preceding everyone but the secretary of the Senate. Bob G also went for a cool-down walk, and returned to sit in the second-row center, just as the Dean took his usual place in the front row, right.

The Dean opened the session, and he proved both brief and moderate. Procedurally, the results would become part of the Dean's evaluation by the VP of Academic Affairs that would be held during Fall Quarter 1997. Substantively, the Dean did not characterize the survey in any detail. But he expressed concern about the response rate, and clearly withheld any enthusiasm for the survey results, while noting that he always gave attention to "solid" faculty views and opinions.

Bob G followed with some background to put matters in perspective. He emphasized three points. The public quality of the A & S's survey was unique at the University, and perhaps the state, and he lauded the Dean's openness. Moreover, the survey reported the opinions of many tenured faculty members, and thus the data required respect. There was "no benign explanation" of the low response rates for the two other classes of faculty participating in the survey, and senators could come to reasonable and different interpretations. In sum, no technical answer existed as to what pattern of survey results would support a resolution endorsing the Dean for a second term. That was the Senate's call.

Paramountly, Bob G emphasized that the survey was designed to facilitate action research, and the survey contained much data that could be put to such a use to make A & S a more efficient and effective system for the large investment that taxpayers made every year in the University. Bob G encouraged the Dean to make use of those opportunities in the data, especially concerning Q10a–10k.

A question-and-answer session followed, and overall, Bob G felt his treatment was gentle. For example, perhaps most attention centered on the fact that one department, a very big one, had not received its ballots in a timely fashion. True enough, Bob G noted; but the Dean's Office had distributed the questionnaire form to department heads, and this had put the issue beyond the Committee's control, even if it had possessed malevolent intent. Moreover, a member of that department— himself a senator, and even now in the room—had explained to Bob G that a mailroom illness underlay the tardy distribution. Finally, Bob G observed, the survey period had been extended by 10 days, without any prodding.

That did not settle this issue: indeed, one senator denied the view that a mailroom illness explained the delay. However, at a minimum, no substantial support developed for the proposition that a further extension of the survey would have substantially changed either the response rate or the pro-Dean vote. Bob G emphasized that "only a handful" of completed surveys were received in the substantial interval the survey had been extended.

Several other features further illustrate the coverage and tone of the Senate Q-and-A. First, what explained the very low response rates for both the not-yet-tenured faculty and those in non-tenure-track positions? Both might lack information about the Dean's activities, various discussants noted. Was one or the other the dominant explanation? Bob G simply described the several survey features accommodating those with inadequate information. He added that those faculty reporting high vs. low adequacy to observe the Dean's actions did not differ much in their opinions as to the desirability of a second five-year term for the Dean.

Second, another faculty member asked whether the Dean's critics might not have been more motivated to respond than his supporters. Again, Bob G said there was no precise answer to the question, but he did mention a separate analysis showing that critical respondents submitted their questionnaires no earlier than supportive ones.

Third, one senator tried to reframe the response rate issue, noting that a "reliable source" informed him that the President and relevant vice president "had already decided to disregard the survey because of the low response rate." The senator suggested that this view, if true, was myopic: "The issue is not whether the Dean's critics outnumber his admirers but which of their assessments was valid." The "reliable source" was not identified.

And so it went, until one prominent senator noted he had heard enough. "Let's accept the survey" he proposed, and this was done unanimously. About an hour had passed.

Now, only the issue of using the data for action planning remained, and the Senate's presiding officer drew attention to that point. Bob G reiterated his earlier pitch in two sentences, with an emphasis on the cost of failure to take some action as an inhibitor of future "upward feedback."

No clear response followed, and the Senate's presiding officer scanned the Senate for a way to take a next step.

INSTRUCTIONS AND QUESTIONS: PART 14

You are Bob G. Things could have gone much worse, in your view; but now is a crucial time. What do you do? Whatever you do, it must be done quickly.

1. You can seek a delay, which also would permit caucusing with your Committee but only by risking a slow death. This is the next-to-last Senate meeting for the academic year, and any new business might well carry the subject over until late September. Then, you and several members of the PC Committee would be ex-senators.

2. Do you adopt a strong advocacy role—pro-survey and hence (in many people's eyes) anti-Dean? You are pro-survey but, neither by Committee role or personal persuasion, are you anti-Dean. You are pro-action research.

2. Or do you settle for what the moment seems to offer, the Senate's perhaps surprising acceptance of the report, which contains useful data for action planning?

PART 15

"Our Committee has had a good chance to develop an agenda." Bob G offered, "and now perhaps the Senate leadership can try its hand at action planning with the Dean. I'll be happy to serve as consultant to the leadership, if they want."

A deal was soon struck. The Senate's Steering Committee would within 10 days draft a letter to the Dean concerning what might be done to begin working with some of the specific survey results. And the Dean promised a reply to the letter during the course of the next Senate meeting—the last regularly scheduled meeting of the academic year.

The Senate's presiding officer added a brief valedictory. The Dean's evaluation was a tough one, which no one solicited or relished. And the Professional Concerns Committee, he concluded, had "done a truly professional job."

Bob G took two further actions. On the way out of the meeting room, he paused beside the seated Dean, extended his hand, and noted, "I admire what you have just done." And then he went to dinner with his wife, who was then just beginning to simmer in her parked car on an unusually warm April afternoon.

INSTRUCTIONS AND QUESTIONS: PART 15

You are Bob G, again. Do you do anything during the month-long interval? Or do you just let well enough alone?

PART 16

In the next several days, Bob G made brief contacts with all available Committee members, for several purposes. Primarily, he wanted to thank them for hanging in there. "I'm proud to have been on the Committee with you," he said to every member he could contact. In addition, Committee members were asked whether or not Bob G should attempt to provide guidance for the Steering Committee's letter to the Dean. On balance, members supported a brief letter to supplement the survey results by highlighting for Steering Committee members a few areas for action planning. Exhibit I.7.5 reproduces a copy of that letter.

During this interval, no media coverage occurred, although several callers inquired whether "there would be a fight." "I hope not," Bob G

Exhibit I.7.5

Date: April 30, 1997
To: Presiding Officer, A & S Senate
From: Bob G
Re: Suggestions for Steering Committee about Possibilities for Action
           Planning

Feel free to use any or all, in any combination.

Note these come off-the-top. The themes in the 1997 survey also could be winnowed for other targets for action planning.

Thanks for the level playing field.

Possibilities for Action Planning
I. Policy Clarifications
1. Spousal hires
2. Conflicts of interest when a department faculty takes action against a faculty member with some years of service—as in not recommending for promotion—does a department of necessity get to hire only a freshly minted assistant professor?

   This outcome could encourage conflicts of interest in retention/promotion votes, with more serious consequences when post-tenure evaluation gets going.

II. Management Initiatives by Dean
1. Develop mission statement.
2. Publish a list of goals and accomplishments, once a year, on the model of the 1997 summary the Dean put on the Web.
3. New upward and downward feedback links—e.g., a yearly "State of the College" presentation to increase visibility of Dean's programs/performance.
4. Diversify A & S officials [by gender and race].
5. Program follow-up on 1997 Survey items [concerning] retirements and relocations.
6. Clarification of Dean's orientation to decision making (see 1997 survey, especially Q8 and Q11).

III. Major Redesign Issues
1. Review/change processes for reappointing heads (see 1997 survey, several locations).
2. Target one or more of the "aspects" (Q10 of 1997 survey) for enhancement and possible redirection.

IV. A & S Senate Changes
1. Change review of Dean
   —More frequent than five years—e.g., every sixth semester, with the first iteration in a dean's five-year term to fine-tune objectives, and the second iteration to focus on evaluation for reappointment.
   —Make resources available to Senate to promote as well as implement review.
   —Specify criterion(ia) for reappointment in Bylaws, on the model of existing requirements for heads of departments.
   —Accommodate possible changes, such as II 2.

---

responded. "We are out to improve A & S, not to raise the collective blood pressure." This general opinion seems to have been broadly shared. In any case, the Committee's report had been widely available for more than a month—all senators had received a copy of the report about the survey, as had all faculty members who expressed an interest. In some departments, senators made individual copies available to interested parties; in others, a copy of the Committee's report was posted in some public space; and perhaps other variations were utilized.

The final meeting of the Senate occurred on May 29, and the Dean responded to the letter from the Steering Committee. That letter had been delivered to the Dean in sufficient time to permit him to formulate a response; and all senators received a copy just as the final meeting for that academic year had begun. Exhibit I.7.6 reprints that letter in full.

At the Senate meeting on May 29, the Dean expressed pleasure with the positive tone of the Steering Committee's letter, and he confined his remarks to that letter. The minutes of the Senate meeting reflect some give-and-take with senators, but no substantive changes were reported to the Senate. Exhibit I.7.7 provides an overview of the Dean's remarks concerning the Steering Committee's letter.

The Dean also publicly turned to the issues of his relationships with A & S faculty on June 2, during the annual report on the College's state. The Dean reviewed a substantial record of accomplishments over the past year, the scope and nature of which are suggested by Exhibit I.7.3.

The Dean did not mention the survey directly, but two parts of his presentation seemed relevant to it. First, the Dean drew concerted attention to various improvements in budget and policy that over the last year or so had advantaged the historically less-influential departments in A & S. These benefits were real enough, but had in part been paid for by the Dean's initiatives that negatively affected several of the larger and more prestigious departments. In part, the Dean observed, the dynamics associated with this necessary redistribution could have induced some discontent. For example, a reduced teaching schedule was extended throughout A & S, whereas reductions had taken place in several departments for some years, in some cases even before the present Dean's term of office had begun.

To compensate for these and other changes, the Dean had over the years increased the number of available teaching hours. Thus, the Dean fully implemented an action about which he had alerted departments some time before: the transformation of research assistantships in a few prestigious departments into teaching assistantships because "state money should not go into research assistantships." Rather, the Dean and other University officials agreed, research assistantships should be

Exhibit I.7.6   Letter from A & S Senate Steering Committee
                        to Dean

May 12, 1997

Dear Dean:

At the request of both the Professional Concerns Committee and you, the Steering Committee of the Faculty Senate met on Tuesday, April 29, to discuss the recent survey of your five years in office conducted by the Professional Concerns Committee. Our goal was to isolate and articulate a few key themes that you might like to address in your remarks to the Senate at our May 29 meeting, the last of this academic year. In our discussion, we frequently noted both the thoroughness of the review and the generally positive tone of faculty response and comments. As Bob G, Chair of the Professional Concerns Committee, noted several times, no dean in living memory has experienced such a thorough review.

We thought it right, therefore, to begin by acknowledging and summarizing the substantially positive response from faculty that the survey elicited. Based on our reading of the survey items and the summary of specific comments, the faculty feels strongly that you have a great deal of personal and professional integrity. You are an eminent scholar and a dedicated teacher, qualities that we consider important in the Dean of Arts and Sciences. As a result, you have provided members of the College with strong support for both teaching and research; the fact that a substantial number of respondents noted the improvements to teaching load and travel budgets suggests as much. Your commitment to environmental literacy and multicultural education was also noted with appreciation. Furthermore, you are perceived as caring about students, their academic progress, and their general welfare. As for your administrative style, the faculty sees you as approachable, open, and receptive to faculty opinion. As an administrator, you are sincere in your effort to treat all departments equitably. You are efficient and hard-working, and you encourage and reward these virtues in your faculty.

Having been specifically charged to identify a few common themes on the subject of "areas of improvement," we sifted through the comments collated by the Professional Concerns Committee, and came up with two broad sets of concerns: one is "Communication and the Formation of College Policy" and the other is "Micromanagement and the Implementation of College Policy."

1. "Communication and the Formulation of College Policy"
   Fifty-six respondents noted the "strong, decisive leadership" of your administration; only your approachable style and efficiency were praised more highly. Some of the more critical remarks contested this assessment, suggesting that the administration's general "vision" of the College and its goals could be sharpened. (On question 10b, 37.8 percent of faculty perceived a clear sense of mission in the college, giving a rating of "4" and "5.") Some faculty were unclear or unhappy about the relationship between projected problems in the College and concrete policies for

Exhibit I.7.6   Letter from A & S Senate Steering Committee
to Dean *(continued)*

---

remedying those problems. Lack of "real" faculty input in policy-making
and the transfer of policy-making from departments to the Dean's Office
were cited as areas of discontent. Sometimes, it was suggested, the faculty
were presented with "solutions in search of a problem." Some faculty
questioned or disliked the role played by the associate deans in a perceived
"centralization" of policy decision-making. Finally, there was a perception
that the formation of policies neglected real differences between
departments, disciplines, and areas of research.

The Steering Committee, in an effort to focus these observations in a
concrete manner, identified some possible ways of addressing faculty
concerns about the formulation of College policy.

- A new mission statement.
- An annual report from the Dean about College achievements, policies,
  shortcomings, and long-range goals, perhaps modeled after the 1997
  summary put on the Web.
- A Dean's Advisory Committee, composed of some Senate members and
  some faculty members from the College at large, to insure equitable
  representation according to race, gender, rank, discipline, etc. This idea
  has been discussed in both the Professional Concerns Committee and
  the Steering Committee over the past two years, and in a previous
  meeting, you expressed willingness—and eagerness—to consult with
  the Senate in this way.
- A more regular, perhaps annual, survey of faculty opinion regarding
  College goals and policies, to address the feeling of some faculty that
  although input from faculty is encouraged, it is often ignored.
- A structured and complete study of how the College's system of
  instruction is working, on both the undergraduate and graduate level,
  before policies are changed or implemented. How do we know what
  needs to be changed until we know what is working and what is not
  working well?

2. "Micromanagement and the Implementation of College Policy"
   A number of respondents expressed frustration at their perception of how the
   Dean's Office implemented policy on a practical basis. While some faculty
   perceived the administration to be biased in favor of the sciences, we could
   not tell exactly how many of the 130 respondents who cited "lack of respect of
   faculty differences" as a problem actually expressed this specific opinion. On
   question 10a of the survey proper, 47.8 percent felt that resources were
   distributed equitably. Many faculty therefore agreed, at least in the abstract,
   that the Dean's commitment to fairness expressed itself in practice.

   Some faculty, however, feel that departments are losing control of their
   own governance, that departments are losing control over their own
   budgets, and that an increasing number of decisions that were and ought to
   be the province of departments are being transferred to the Dean's office.
   Perhaps in the name of efficiency, perhaps in the name of fairness, real and
   important differences among departments are ignored in an attempt to
   make administrative "templates" that govern all departments. As a result,

continued

Exhibit I.7.6   Letter from A & S Senate Steering Committee
                 to Dean *(continued)*

there is a perceived discrepancy between the Dean's personal style—open
and fair—and the practical implementation of policies, which can seem
"autocratic" and "rigid."

Some concrete topics that might be addressed in the implementation of
College policy include:

- Advising
- The use of teaching assistants and temporary instructors
- Departmental control over budgetary issues
- Selection of department heads
- Administrative release units

Please consider these thoughts as our committee's best effort at
interpreting the survey and the faculty's responses to it. The members of
Steering Committee and of the Senate appreciate very much this opportunity
to work with you toward improving the College of Arts and Sciences. Thank
you again, and we look forward to hearing from you.

Exhibit I.7.7   Senate Minutes Concerning the Dean's Responses to the Letter
                 of the Steering Committee

1. *Mission Statement.* On the matter of a mission statement for the College,
the Dean indicated that his goal, the strengthening of the College's research
and teaching capacities, has always been explicit.

2. *Dean's Annual Report.* The Dean will discuss his policies, achievements,
and long-range goals at the June 2 meeting of the College of Arts and Sciences.
He added that this annual report to the faculty, like the president's annual
report in the fall, is a convention he hopes will continue.

3. *Dean's Advisory Committee.* The Dean does not object to an advisory
committee that would represent the College's race, gender, rank, and
disciplinary makeup. The Senate, however, already acts as such a committee.
Furthermore, the Dean meets regularly with department heads and a Student
Advisory Board. He urges the Senate to deliberate further on this proposal to
ensure that yet another advisory committee will be in the College's interest.

4. *Annual Survey of Faculty Opinion.* An annual survey, according to the
Steering Committee's letter, would address faculty concerns that the Dean
ignores the advice and criticism whose expression he encourages. The Dean
believes such a survey might be useful but that it is the Senate, not his office,
that should conduct it.

5. *Instructional Policy.* The Steering Committee's letter recommends that the
Dean determine the current effects of instruction before changing instructional
policy. The Dean responded that such an investigation is the Senate's
responsibility, not his. He reminded the Senate that his policies have led to major
instructional advances, including freshman seminars, mathematics and English
Web sites, and an intensive-writing pilot program. Freshman complaints about
the negative aspects of their experience have contributed to these new initiatives.

continued

6. *Micromanagement and Implementation of College Policy.* The Dean believes that complaints about his administrative style, which also appear in the Steering Committee letter, stem mainly from his efforts to gain better control of the College's budget and finances. Pooling salary savings, to take one example, enables the College to redress inequities and strengthen its weaker departments; yet some departmental representatives claim that this measure centralizes decision-making. He fully understands these and other legitimate conflicts of interest but cannot hesitate to make hard decisions. On the other hand, he has never refused to entertain reactions to these decisions.

7. *Selection of Department Heads.* The Dean cannot understand why his supervision of department heads selection should be problematic. He has never imposed on a department a head whom it had rejected.

8. *Student Advising.* Despite some strong faculty opposition, the Dean is convinced that juniors and seniors are entitled to faculty advising. Efforts to bring upper-level faculty into closer contact with students are being undertaken nationwide, and his policy does no more than bring the University in line with this desirable trend.

9. *Structure of the College Administration.* The Dean believes that the Franklin College, which composes approximately half the university's faculty and students, is administratively lean. No superfluous administrative positions exist.

Having commented on all the concerns raised in the Steering Committee's letter, the Dean invited comments and questions from the floor.

Barry Schwartz commented on the use of graduate assistantships. The Dean, in Schwartz's view, emphasizes the benefits of his policies but is silent about their costs. In particular, the restriction of graduate student activity to teaching severely limits opportunities to collaborate with faculty on research projects that add publications to the dossiers students take to the job market. In the labor-intensive social sciences this condition devastates students' job prospects.

The Dean responded that the function of the graduate assistant is to support teaching. The exceptions are the 12 assistantships devoted exclusively to research and the university-wide assistantships, whose recipients may perform research. It is unclear how assistants came to be diverted from teaching to research in the first place. Neither the Dean nor any other administrator can find formal justification for using assistants for research. New research assistantships may be created, but it is impossible to assign them to one department without doing so for another. And there is the additional problem of providing the weaker departments with a greater share of assistantships of all types in order to enhance their traditionally low level of resources.

Some departments, including Art and Music, have a significant shortage of graduate assistants to staff their courses and the Dean has gone to the higher administration on their behalf for teaching assistant lines. He has succeeded in adding a half million dollars to the assistantship budget.

Dino Lorenzini asked the Dean whether the College budget is holding its own in relation to the remainder of the University. The Dean responded by saying that he has brought in five million additional dollars to the College over the past five years, and is proud of the fact that administrators of other schools and colleges complain that Arts and Sciences receives too much money.

[The minutes go on for a half-page or less]

funded out of grants. Some of these applications of state funds to RAs had been in place for several decades, including a substantial number of RAs in Bob G's home department.

Second, the Dean noted in response to a general question that his administration was more open than some acknowledged. Thus, he had earlier "opened all files in the Dean's Office" to interested faculty, and took this opportunity to reiterate that policy, which was not widely known. The Dean observed that certain parts of those files—e.g., letters solicited from external referees about the promotion of University faculty—might not be available for perusal because they had been solicited as closed or confidential inputs, and hence would be released only with the specific agreement of those providing such information.

INSTRUCTIONS AND QUESTIONS: PART 16

After the May 29 meeting, virtually all Senate work ceased. Bob G, as well as several members of the 1996–97 Professional Concerns Committee, in late September 1997 would see their successors sworn-in to the A & S Senate, with the first meeting for 1997–98 now scheduled for late September.

You are Bob G. What do you do, if anything, during the post-survey period?

1. The new President was announced, to take office on September 1, 1997.
2. You learn only about a few points of possible relevance to the survey. Thus, immediately after delivery of the survey results the Dean carried them over to his immediate superior, the VP for Academic Affairs, whose own review of the Dean would occur in Fall 1997, 4 to 6 months later. In addition, in the interim between the Dean's initial receipt of the report and the stormy meeting with the Dean described above, the short list of candidates for the open presidency became publicly available. Only outsiders survived.

References

Calbos, D. P. (1984) *Information system implementation: PPBS at New South University*. Unpublished doctoral dissertation, University of Georgia, Athens, GA.

Gellermann, W., Frankel, M. S., and Ladenson, R. F. (1990). *Values and ethics in organization and human systems development*. San Francisco: Jossey-Bass.

Golembiewski, R. T. (1993). *Approaches to planned change*, Vol. 1. New York: Transaction Publishers.

Golembiewski, R. T., and Hilles, R. (1979). *Toward the responsive organization*. Salt Lake City, UT: Brighton Publishing.

Appendix A   Materials Distributed to Major Stakeholders

Re: Survey of the Dean's Five Years in Office

To: Senators, Various Officials, and Publics

From: Professional Concerns Committee, Robert G, Chairperson

Attached find an 11-page enclosure reviewing the survey of the Dean's five-year stewardship mandated by the Bylaws of the A & S Senate. Please excuse the convenience of this format.

The two main goals of the survey are:

—improving the information available concerning the Dean's five-year term
—providing targets for action planning to improve A & S functioning, via isolating what to continue, what should be started, and what is better stopped

The enclosures provide an introduction to five approaches to these two goals. In turn, the enclosures present:

—highlights of the survey (1 page)*
—a summary of responses to the survey on the questionnaire form used as the primary means of gathering information (4 pages)
—a thematic overview of the "most positive things" about the Dean's tenure (1 page, labeled Q3-1), abstracted from respondents' own words*
—a thematic overview of "things needing most improvement" (labeled Q4-1 through Q4-4) emphasized by respondents
—a thematic overview of "anything to add relevant to the survey" (labeled Q13-1) by respondents*

Note that the Dean will receive a copy of the respondent comments summarized in these thematic overviews. These are typed from the questionnaires to preserve the exact character of the respondents' reactions, and approximate 120 pages.

Any questions about the survey will be addressed at the Senate's regularly scheduled meeting, April 24.

continued

*See Appendix B.

THEMES, WITH EXAMPLES, OF "MOST POSITIVE THINGS"	Q3-1 Mentions[†] (Approx.)
DEMEANOR AND ADMINISTRATIVE STYLE —approachability —communication —openness —support for faculty input	102
EFFICIENT/WELL ORGANIZED/WELL-INFORMED/FAIR	83
STRONG, DECISIVE LEADERSHIP —clear goals and policies	56
INCREASED TRAVEL FUNDS	43
GOOD BUDGET MANAGEMENT	36
THE DEAN'S STRONG ACADEMIC STANDING AND HIS HIGH ACADEMIC STANDARDS	29
THE HIGH QUALITY OF THE A & S ADMINISTRATIVE "TEAM" (INCLUDING ASSOCIATE DEANS)/HARD WORKING	23
ENCOURAGES GOOD TEACHING/RESEARCH/SERVICE AND REWARDS THESE ACCORDINGLY	23
SUPPORTS PROGRAMS IN THE COLLEGE —multicultural —environmental literacy, etc.	20
MINORITY-RELATED EFFORTS	12
IMPROVED TEACHING LOADS	11
UPGRADING COMPUTERS/OFFICE EQUIPMENT/TECHNOLOGY	10
GOOD RELATIONS WITH THE UNIVERSITY ADMINISTRATION	2

THEMES, WITH EXAMPLES, OF "ANYTHING TO ADD"	Q13-1 Mentions[†] (Approx.)
NEGATIVE REACTIONS ABOUT DEAN —opinions of respondents about style, connectedness to faculty, etc. —policy/handling of particular department issues —comparison to other deans —lack of A & S mission statement	45

[†]Themes are listed in order of number of mentions. Examples are *not* listed in order.

POSITIVE REACTIONS TO DEAN   26
   —opinions of respondents about style, connectedness to faculty, etc.
   —comparisons to other deans

SUGGESTIONS FOR DEAN AND HIGHER ADMINISTRATION   16

COMMENTS ABOUT THIS SURVEY   14
   —positive
   —negative
   —clarification of earlier response
   —confidentiality

REMARKS DIRECTED TO PROFESSIONAL CONCERNS   14
COMMITTEE
   —about effectiveness and management of survey
   —departmental issues unrelated to Dean
   —travel and salary
   —about academia, broadly defined
   —temporary instructors

	Q4-1 Mentions[†] (Approx.)
THEMES, WITH EXAMPLES, "NEEDS MOST IMPROVEMENT"	
TOO LITTLE RESPECT OF DEPT./FACULTY DIFFERENCES IN NEEDS, INTERESTS, PROBLEMS FACED	130

   —infrequently seek faculty opinions early enough to take into
    serious account
   —grant money too much a guiding criterion, and especially
    where generally unavailable
   —limited applicability of "hard sciences" or "genetics" models to
    all A & S (e.g., departmental advising, class sizes, etc.)
   —favoritism to biological sciences: "need affirmative action for
    humanities and social sciences"
   —salary compression
   —ceiling on summer salaries
   —lack of opportunities for professional development

TOO MUCH "LEVELING DOWN"   82

   —solid departments disadvantaged to benefit weak ones, or to
    serve other needs (RAs converted to TAs)
   —decline in standards due to financial pressure: huge sections,
    erosion of climate for teaching/research, etc.
   —replacing senior faculty losses with junior faculty
   —too little emphasis on quality differences between departments
    in budget allocations

[†]Themes are listed in order of number of mentions. Examples are *not* listed in order.

LACK OF A & S "VISION" TO GET TO THE "NEXT LEVEL"   69

—A & S reactive vs. proactive
—ad hoc nature of decision-making
—a new vision will guide needed redirection of A & S budget

Q4-2

CONCERNS ABOUT HEADSHIPS/DEPARTMENT GOVERNANCE   62

—too little "real" faculty input in selections
—incumbents often seen as "weak"
—often "yes people"
—they get supported by [Dean] even in questionable cases
—departments declining as centers of governance as decision-
   making centralized

TOO MUCH EMPHASIS ON "NARROW EFFICIENCY" OR   55
"FACTORY-LIKE" APPROACHES TO PEDAGOGICAL ISSUES
—"doing wrong things more efficiently"
—lacks respect for non-science values, needs, problems
—excessive and often redundant flow of paper, awkward or
   impractical deadlines
—decisions: not clearly associated with a guiding "vision"; seem
   reactive vs. pro-active; often seem merely ad hoc or convenient
—replacing retiring senior faculty losses with juniors

ENHANCE DEAN'S "CONNECTIONS" TO FACULTY   49

—budget used as substitute for in-depth contacts with
   departments, faculty
—perhaps could use A & S ombudsman or elected advisory
   committee to surface issues early
—relegates, delegates too much to associate deans
—Dean "too aloof," distant

TOO LITTLE A & S ADVOCACY   48

—[Dean] too compliant to higher administration
—A & S needs/deserves "bigger piece of pie," but does not get it
   and Dean's "honeymoon now over"
—[Dean] reactive vs. pro-active

Q4-3

LIMITS OF DEAN'S PERSONAL STYLE   47

—[Dean is] autocratic, rigid, hierarchical, brings pre-formed
   opinions/conclusions to too many decision-making
   situations
—lacks listening skills/attitudes
—lacks presentation skills
—"mechanistic approach to pedagogical issues"

TOO MUCH MICROMANAGEMENT   43

   —departments lack autonomy, especially regarding budgets and
     headships
   —"no real governance" at departmental level as decision-making
     is increasingly centralized
   —too many associate deans; too much reliance on them

DECISION-MAKING RE: PERSONNEL/FUNDS PERCEIVED AS   40
ARBITRARY, PUNISHING, INEFFECTIVE

   —entomology reassignments
   —headship searches
   —needs to "catch somebody doing something right"; greater
     reliance on positive reinforcers
   —RA conversions to TAs

POLICY UNCLARITIES OR INADEQUACIES   35

   —unequal teaching loads across campus
   —A & S use of "faculty lines" for administrative hires
   —guidelines about replacing faculty against whom departments
     take adverse actions (e.g., about tenure)
   —relative values of research/teaching need readjustment favoring
     the latter

                                                          Q4-4

ASSOCIATE DEANS   25

   —lackluster, "undergunned," short on leadership (e.g., semester
     conversion)
   —major downsizing needed, "overstaffed"
   —target of too much relegation as well as delegation
   —NB: balanced by a few positive opinions

GREATER REPRESENTATION OF SENSITIVITY TO GENDER/   20
RACE AMONG DECISION-MAKERS

CONCERNS ABOUT DECLINING OR STABILIZING STATUS OF   15
PROGRAMS, AS IN PERCEPTIONS OF:

   —diminished research missions
   —too great responsiveness to "narrow efficiency" or various
     conveniences (e.g., spousal hires)
   —"status quo or convenience at the cost of excellence"

                                                       SUMMARY

1. My faculty employment status is best described as (Check One)
    84.7% tenured
    11.6% tenure track
     2.0% non-tenure track, full-time member of corps of instruction
     1.6% missing cases

2. I have been employed at [New University] for (Check One)
    <u>2.4%</u>   2 years or less
    <u>10.4%</u>   more than 2 and less than 6 years
    <u>22.5%</u>   6–10 years
    <u>35.3%</u>   11–20 years
    <u>27.7%</u>   21 years or more
    <u>1.6%</u>   missing cases

3. In my opinion, the most positive things about [the Dean's] administration
    include:
    1.   82% of survey respondents provide an average of 2.2 exemplars per
         respondent
    2.
    3.
    4.
    5.   For summary themes, see attached pages Q3-1 through Q3.2.

4. In my opinion, the things needing most improvement in [the Dean's]
    administration include:
    1.   78% of survey respondents provide an average of 2.9 examples per
         respondent.
    2.
    3.
    4.
    5.
    6.   For summary themes, see attached pages Q4-1 through Q4-4.

5. I am actively searching for an employer alternative to [New University]
    (Circle One)

1	2	3	4	5	
Strongly Disagree	Disagree	?	Agree	Strongly Agree	Missing Data
40.7%	26.8%	15.9%	11.0%	5.7%	3 cases

6. I have had excellent opportunities to arrive at solid conclusions about
    Dean Anderson's stewardship and A & S operations—e.g., as department
    head, as administrator, via committee or other UGA assignments. (Circle
    One)

5	4	3	2	1	
Strongly Agree	Agree	?	Disagree	Strongly Disagree	Missing Data
34.4%	30.4%	15.4%	14.2%	5.7%	2 cases

7. My reactions to headship search(es) in A & S departments in the past
    years have been very positive. (Circle One)

5	4	3	2	1	
Strongly Agree	Agree	?	Disagree	Strongly Disagree	Missing Data
16.7%	27.9%	17.1%	20.7%	16.7%	27 cases

8. [The Dean's] *professed* style is (Check One)
   48.0%   equal treatment for all departments
   7.0%   preference for one or a few departments
   15.6%   treatment of each department relative to its status/productivity
           among counterparts at comparable schools
   10.2%   no clear *professed* tendency, overall
   19.3%   I have insufficient basis for judgment.
   5 cases missing data

9. As soon as it is possible, I will retire from [A & S]. (Circle One)

1	2	3	4	5	
Strongly	Disagree	?	Agree	Strongly	Missing
Disagree				Agree	Data
33.2%	25.4%	19.3%	9.7%	12.6%	11 cases

10. Please appraise each of the following aspects of A & S administration.
    CIRCLE ONE RATING if you have relevant experience.
    If you have no experience relevant to an aspect, CIRCLE NOT RELEVANT
    (NR).

		Lowest Rating				Highest Rating	NR
a.	equitable distribution of resources	1 13.8%	2 23.6%	3 14.8%	4 29.6%	5 18.2%	46 cases
b.	clear sense of mission	1 15.8%	2 24.1%	3 22.4%	4 21.1%	5 16.7%	21 cases
c.	keeps you informed	1 9.8%	2 16.7%	3 20.9%	4 26.9%	5 25.6%	15 cases
d.	competent and caring regard for students	1 10.6%	2 11.2%	3 23.4%	4 28.7%	5 26.1%	61 cases
e.	promptness and efficiency	1 4.1%	2 5.9%	3 20.4%	4 37.6%	5 32.1%	28 cases
f.	clear policy guidance, across the board	1 12.8%	2 22.2%	3 17.7%	4 27.1%	5 20.2%	46 cases
g.	encourages your inputs of information and perspectives	1 25.6%	2 17.1%	3 13.7%	4 23.9%	5 19.7%	15 cases
h.	curriculum responsiveness, as in environmental literacy or multiculturalism	1 4.4%	2 10.0%	3 26.7%	4 30.6%	5 28.3%	69 cases
i.	inspires confidence that your inputs will be taken into account	1 32.9%	2 20.1%	3 9.8%	4 20.5%	5 16.7%	15 cases
j.	funds for travel	1 4.0%	2 2.6%	3 15.4%	4 28.2%	5 49.8%	22 cases
k.	appointments to administrative positions and committee appointments	1 13.5%	2 19.3%	3 22.2%	4 25.1%	5 19.9%	78 cases

11. [The Dean's] basic style in action is (Check One)
    22.1%   preference for one or a few departments
    17.4%   treatment of each department relative to status/productivity
    ____   among counterparts at comparable schools
    27.5%   equal treatment for all departments
    22.7%   I have insufficient basis for judgment
    9.7%   no clear tendency, in action, overall
    2 cases missing data

12. In my opinion, the overall record justifies a second five-year term for [the Dean]. (Circle One)

1	2	3	4	5	
Strongly Agree	Agree	Not Sure or Abstain	Disagree	Strongly Disagree	Missing Data
35.9%	18.8%	14.3%	9.8%	21.2%	4 cases

13. As a next-to-last step in completing this survey, do you have anything to add relevant to this survey?

    47% of survey respondents provide an average of about 1.9 add-ons per respondent.

    For summary themes, see attached pages Q13-1 through Q13-2.

14. After completing all the items, what is your opinion that the information from this survey will be responded to constructively?

1	2	3	4	5	
Strongly Disagree	Disagree	?	Agree	Strongly Agree	Missing Data
7.5%	11.2%	33.6%	32.4%	15.4%	8 cases

Appendix B   Survey Highlights Made Available to All Stakeholders

Survey Highlights

1. The responding population provides a probable replica only of the tenured population (Q1). The tenured response rate approximates 42 percent, if tenured N = 501 and if no discount is made for faculty targets not surveyed—due to leave, undelivered survey forms, or whatever.

2. Consistently, only 12.8 percent (Q2) of the responding population has been on the UGA faculty for less than 5 years.

3. The survey provides substantial context for what respondents see in A & S—to be continued (Q3), as well as to be started or stopped (especially Q4, and to a lesser degree Q13).

4. UGA can anticipate substantial turnover (Q5 and Q9).

5. Respondents see selves as substantially informed: on (Q6) re: "excellent opportunities to arrive at solid conclusions,": nearly two thirds report Strongly Agree (SA) or Agree (A).

6. Headship searches a target for action (Q7): over 37 percent Disagree (D) or Strongly Disagree (SD) that searches have been "very positive."

7. Q8 vs. Q11 deserve attention. "Professed style" is seen by nearly 50 percent as "equal treatment," while "style in action" is 27.5 percent "equal treatment."
   Also on Q8 and Q11, on average, 20% have "insufficient basis for judgment."

8. "Aspects of A & S administration" show substantial room for improvement:
   —only five aspects—c, d, e, h, & j—get 50 percent or more in two highest ratings
   —only one aspect gets 75 percent or more responses in two highest ratings, and that one is subject to quick decay—funds for travel
   —several aspects provide targets for early action because of "low" ratings:
      (a) resources;
      (b) sense of mission;
      (c) encourages input;
      (i) inspires confidence; and
      (k) appointments.

9. One reasonable interpretation of Q12 approximates 55 percent favoring reappointment of Dean.

10. Confidence that survey will be taken into account (Q14): 47.8 percent are SA and A; 18.7 percent are SD and D.

I.8

Family Life from an OD Perspective

The following is a case study, with a twist. It explores aspects of life in one ODer's family, and hence constitutes a study over an extended period of time about how we tried to live our lives together while powerful forces threatened to pull us apart. Other ODers may find meaning in it relevant to their own experience.

This writer learned many important things from Lee Bradford, whose centrality in OD and laboratory education is too little remarked, but one point stands out: It pays to do your OD work in rhythm with what you are going through in life, as well as in congruence with who you are. Consistently, during his "retirement," Lee began working with people in a similar situation (Bradford and Bradford, 1978). This writer has other ego ideals in this regard; for example, Joan Paris worked her last support group for the dying from her wheelchair, with her own death coming only a few days after the final session.

The basic strategy of Joan and Lee gives the ODer a kind of two-fer: one can better identify with the client, and one is in a better situation to learn things that can be applied quite directly to one's own life.

Thus, I sought to put Lee's advise to work in my role as an active consultant, while still according first priority to my growing family and second priority to my university responsibilities. I was a prodigiously frequent flyer for some 15 years and have remained active on-the-road in a slightly lower key for the two decades following. Altogether, my career has exceeded my expectations. I have been an active consultant in four or five major OD efforts, with one association lasting almost a decade and a second stretching over 22 years. In addition, and a great pleasure as well as an honor, the OD Institute in 1989 selected me as Organization Development Consultant of the year. Later I received the Institute's recognition as the 1997 winner for Excellence in OD Projects, Worldwide.

Part of the relative success in dealing with the demands of family and work, often at cross-purposes, can be attributed to insistent efforts to "do OD" within the Golembiewski clan. That theme will constitute the bulk of this essay.

My motivation—perhaps, my fear—was that I would be unavailable to my family at important or even crucial times. Certainly, the popular press contained much on the theme of the absent father or mother being associated with dire consequences for the family. Even within our limited circles, wife Peg and I know of several clients and friends who have had tragic experiences such as the suicide of a daughter or son, often drug-related.

To put the point in necessary perspective, I had plenty of help in being relatively successful. In part by native cunning, but more substantially by incredibly good luck, things went our way. Several elements promoted my family's well-being over the years:

- My wife, Peg, decided to be full-time commander of our homesite, or as I religiously entered on our joint income tax return, Peg was "domestic engineer, First Class."

  Her decision provided much more room for me, although Peg never finished her doctoral work and forfeited other possible personal and professional developments. Now, after 42 years of marriage, Peg still says she made the correct decision, for her and for us.
- We always had a fiesta involving the kids when I returned from a consulting trip of any length. Hence, when I had some slack time, it wasn't long before our kids got antsy about the next fiesta. "When are you going consulting?" I'd hear.
- The kids always had access to a telephone credit card, and still do. Dad was only a quick dial away, and still is, now that our kids have their own families.
- I cut back my consulting about 50 percent, and kept it there, when our oldest child moved into adolescence.
- At least once each month, two or more of us went on a "consulting-plus" trip together.

SOME OD PERSPECTIVES ON MAKING ONE FAMILY OUT OF SEVERAL SETS OF WANTS AND NEEDS

To reinforce native cunning and good fortune, OD activities and perspectives were applied to give our family a better-than-even chance of responding to full schedules and demanding priorities. At first, Mom and Dad were the principal actors. Increasingly, however, the three children got involved in various ways. Later, as the children evolved their several and often-separate lines of activities, they became the central actors.

The goal was to help in making a reality out of the concept of "one family" as the scaffolding that gave structure to several evolving sets of needs and wants. The underlying metaphor is taken seriously. "Scaffolding" implies supporting form and structure, but still leaves a lot of room for growth, experiment, or chance within that supporting network.

How did OD help with building this scaffolding and modifying what variously had been built or was under construction? Here, your writer has to simplify grievously. Initial attention goes to a kind of template for value-loaded interaction. Then, two separate sections turn first to the kids and then to their parents, to illustrate how OD perspectives and approaches were utilized to give form to the dynamics within that template.

THE GENERAL TEMPLATE: REGENERATIVE INTERACTION TREATED AS VITAL

As with most of this writer's work in OD, the character of our interaction dominated in building the scaffolding within which our individual personalities were given guided freedom for development. Throughout our life together, it has been essential to choose regenerative interaction over degenerative interaction, and by a very wide margin.

The basic distinctions between these interactive styles have been made in several places, both in this casebook ("A Grumble or a Meta-Grumble?") and elsewhere (e.g., Golembiewski, 1993a, especially pp. 30–72). So summary treatment is possible here. In various ways, our family strived to achieve a special combination of four variables:

- *openness*, or telling it as it appears to the teller;
- psychological *owning* of ideas or feelings;
- *risk*, or the threat of interacting in the system; and
- *trust*, or each person's confidence in the ability and intentions of all system actors to work things out.

Specifically, our goal was to approach a High-High-Low-High profile, a combination labeled regenerative interaction.

In sharp contrast, our interactions with people are often degenerative: Low openness, Low owning, High risk, and Low trust.

In either case, the four variables constitute a basically recursive model. By hypothesis, changes in any one of the core variables will cycle through the full interaction system, inducing appropriate changes in all the other variables. That is why those in degenerative interaction can't seem to win for losing: even benign intentions may be interpreted distrustfully, for example, and a degenerative system thus can reinforce itself as system members fail to give one another the benefit of a doubt.

The two interaction patterns can have prominent consequences— some better to approach, and some to avoid. Degenerative interaction, in effect, discourages raising real issues, which means that even determined effort will fail because it solves the wrong problems. Obviously, such consequences are better avoided.

ILLUSTRATIONS FOR SMALLER PEOPLE

There might seem to be limitations on regenerative interaction with children, certainly with regard to their experiencing the fuller senses of ownership. But the problems were not insurmountable, as three illustrations suggest.

Beat on Dad

Both Bob G and his wife, Peg, had concerns about his busy travel schedule: if nothing else, the schedule could raise the possibility of unfinished business, which travel could exacerbate. For example, consider the following worst-case scenario. Assume Dad disciplines one of the children just before leaving on an extended trip, during which absence, the target of this attitude readjustment grows seriously out-of-shape concerning that last experience with Dad. "I hope his plane crashes in flames," an angry child could say; and in the worst-case scenario, that event might happen, with a probability proportional to one's frequency of travel.

And then? The wishing child might come to believe in his or her personal complicity in such an event. And the offending Dad would have an eternity to be sorry about his irresponsibility in leaving one of the parental pair's responsibilities in such a vulnerable state.

How does one avoid such worst-case possibilities, even if remote? Our family, by happy consequences, established a ritual called "Beat on Dad."

Each trip was preceded by a debriefing experience. Dad would lie on the floor of the family room, and the kids were encouraged to respond as they wished—pushing, punching, hugging, or whatever. The mode and intensity of their responses offered an estimate of their unresolved issues with Dad. On occasion, the exuberance of one or more of the kids would provoke a "time out," when attention would shift to a discussion of the reasons for that exuberance. Peg typically served as facilitator.

"Beat on Dad" was ritual fun, and sometimes revealing. I recall one occasion, long after the ritual had not been practiced because the children were in their late teens. "It's time to 'Beat on Dad'," one teenager announced. And we got right to the time out.

Most of the time, the contact was desultory. "Oh, Dad, you just want a rub-down," I recall hearing during one of the less-intense experiences. "Why just not ask for it like an adult? No unfinished business this time."

Initially, I wrote that the situation to be avoided was rare, but since the first-draft of this essay our kids have come forward with cases in point. Our son, now a nephrologist, tells of his own invention to counteract thinking ill of his Dad, who was off somewhere. It was raining hard, but the youngster went out to the basketball hoop, bargaining with God that he would make one hundred jump shots in exchange for one boon: that Dad be allowed to return safely from a trip, despite the son's initial displeasure.

Contracting

By far the most useful OD technique was contracting, in the conventional sense. Any family member or combination of members could call for contracting, at any time, which in practice often took place during our "family conference."

You know how this one goes, following Harrison's (1972) useful design. Each participant generates three lists: a list of good things in the family, a gripe list, and a wish list.

Then contracting would start. If one person wanted A, the question became, what would that person stop, start, or continue that would get others to do what was required in return for their supplying A? As soon as they could do so, the children prepared a block-print or cursive document, and we all ceremonially signed it. (No big deal. Our children each signed their own tax returns at early ages, and Peg and I were often startled at the youngsters' understanding of even arcane provisions of the Uniform Act for Gifts to Minors.)

Various forms of contracting worked for a long time around our home. Kids could begin to play the game after age three or so, and we still had sessions when our young adults were in their twenties. The teenage years were the halcyon days for the approach.

Our heaviest reliance on contracting came when the kids were in 8th, 9th, and 10th grades, respectively. We parents were enthusiastic about a relocation to Vanderbilt University and sensed no great negative reactions from our offspring. So we all emplaned to Nashville, where we were planning to pick a house, attend the Grand Old Opry, and so on. The kids were exemplary: in a rational-technical mode, one child developed a list of criteria and associated points to guide the decision; all joined in rating the several residences we visited; and we all went to the Grand Old Opry, despite the view of two of us that country-and-western music was "yucky."

Eventually, it became clear that the kids had played it cool but could not continue the pretense. On our way back to Georgia, all three wanted a contracting session. The depth of feelings varied, but all were interested in talking about contracts keyed to our staying in Georgia. Our oldest child put it on the line most directly: if we were to withdraw her from her Georgia high school, she would run away from home!

So we contracted the flight away, and for some time afterwards. The kids got what they wanted, in different ways and degrees; and the parents drove a hard bargain that lasted for years.

Overarching Goals and Identifications

OD has always emphasized the relevance of overarching goals and identifications, on this general theme: A person who knows why, and accepts it, can usually handle almost any what and how (e.g., Golembiewski, 1993b, pp. 289–291).

We parents initially had a major advantage here, and we tried to emphasize the things that united us. A useful device was our philosophy of handling money. For example, when one kid or parent got a $5 bill for a present, the money went into three pots: $1 for the person's operating fund for discretionary spending; $2 into an education and development fund; and $2 into general family revenues.

This drew what we saw as useful lines around "ours" and "mine." The kids got the message in a hurry: for example, they often would frame a want in terms that justified using general family funds. We parents might well encourage them to choose either discretionary money, or the education and development fund. Many wants diminished in intensity, on two general principles: don't use discretionary money, if you can avoid it; and don't jeopardize the long-run development fund.

ILLUSTRATIONS FOR LARGER PEOPLE

This essay has been fun to write, but its length is already considerable, and greater self-discipline here gets reflected in two illustrative uses of OD approaches and perspectives. The first is a yes; and the second a clear no, except under limited circumstances.

A Definite Yes: 3-D Image Sharing

Several consulting teams of which I was a part had major roles in developing this intervention; indeed, we may even have innovated it in relative simultaneity with other ODers (e.g., Beckhard, 1967; Golembiewski and Blumberg, 1967).

The design is a simple one, and can be adapted to pairs or small groups. Each participating person—e.g., the two bonded adults in a family—responds to three basic questions:

- How do I see myself?
- How do I see the other?
- How does the other see me?

Conveniently put down on paper—independently, by each of the two adult partners in a relationship, for example—the two sets of responses can be put to multiple cross-checking purposes. For example, does A see his or herself in terms that are largely compatible with how B sees A? What differences exist between the two sets of perceptions? And so on.

Conventional contracting follows—e.g., what A can stop, start, or continue in exchange for what A wants B to stop, start, or continue.

For other details, see also the case under Perspective II titled "A Second Kind of Crisis."

This simple design permits useful and detailed analysis, in pairs as well as in complex managerial situations (e.g., Golembiewski and Kiepper, 1988, pp. 33–55). Especially when schedules are tight and absences are frequent, 3-D Image Sharing can be a powerful resource in moving toward regenerative interaction, as well as in preserving that condition, while inducing quality time together in the process. In effect, 3-D Image

Sharing emphasizes increased owning and openness, and promises more regenerative interaction by derivative improvements in risk and trust. The independent preparation of each 3-D Image permits individuals to calibrate the precise version of reality they are willing to share with their partner, a possibility leavened by the knowledge that the partner is independently making similar choices.

A Pretty Clear No, Under Most Conditions

Not just any old design will constitute a reasonable next step toward regenerative interaction. 3-D Image Sharing generally works, in some part because participants can variously varnish the truth if they judge an issue too touchy at a specific time.

Let me briefly describe a design that heard the music but got the words wrong. The setting was a "marriage encounter" at a church setting. One facilitator asked all attendees to write on a sheet of paper three true things about themselves that they couldn't even dream of telling their spouse.

Next, the facilitator solicited volunteers to share publicly items from their lists. More revealingly, the facilitator challenged such sharing by asking, "Who is brave enough to get the ball rolling?"

Well, you can guess what happened, given the high probability that in a group of even small size someone can be encouraged to do or say almost anything by a persistent authority figure. That high probability constitutes one reason for the responsibility that facilitators must bear for questions they ask, and for areas of exploration they suggest.

Let me cut to the chase. That first item was pretty powerful, and more items followed quickly. Then, some attendees spooked. In sum, trust-building had been insufficient to support the level of openness and owning demanded by the exercise.

The facilitator "asked for it," in effect, and got some products which some participants were not prepared to hear, let alone deal with. Perhaps later would have been better, but the exercise does not qualify as a next step in initial efforts toward openness; it constitutes a very large leap. More appropriately, a facilitator might ask for examples from one spouse of ideas or feelings *since the session began* of which they believe their partner is not aware. That stipulation sharply bounds the universe, of course, while encouraging more regenerative interaction.

In any case, the 3-D Design got ample usage in our evolving family, as well as in many assemblages of larger people.

INSTRUCTIONS AND QUESTIONS

Most ODers have families, of course; and we all have clusters of relevant others. What aspects, if any, of this case study with a twist seem applicable to your own relationships, familial and otherwise? Make a list of possibilities.

References

Beckhard, R. (1967). The confrontation meeting. *Harvard Business Review*, 45(2): 149–155.

Bradford, L. P., and Bradford, M. J. (1978). *Coping with emotional upheavals at retirement*. Chicago: Nelson-Hall.

Golembiewski, R. T. (1993a). *Approaches to planned change*. New Brunswick, NJ: Transaction Publishers.

Golembiewski, R. T. (1993b). *Handbook of organizational consultation*. New York: Marcel Dekker.

Golembiewski, R. T., and Blumberg, A. (1967). Confrontation as a training design in complex organizations. *Journal of Applied Behavioral Science*, 3(4): 525–547.

Golembiewski, R. T., and Kiepper, A. (1988). *High performance and human costs*. New York: Praeger.

Harrison, R. (1972). Role negotiation. In W. W. Burke and H. Hornstein (Eds.), *The social technology of organization development*, pp. 84–96. Washington, DC: NTL Learning Resources.

I.9

Go, or No-Go?

The day was a significant one—for an OD program in a multinational firm, for several internal ODers and their external consultant, as well as for an opposition in Human Resources that was getting bolder.

Two topics dominated the agenda. Gary Roberts and his OD team would provide an update on some just-concluded research on several Quality of Working Life (or QWL) initiatives. Then, the floor would be open to sketching the next action steps to be recommended to the firm's chief executive officer and chief operating officer.

Things had gone from bad to worse, as far as the two sides involved in the long-planned meeting were concerned. The OD team had gone to great lengths to involve Human Resources executives on several pilot projects, but to no great effect. As the word got around about the enthusiastic reception of the pilot projects, the HR clique faced a difficult choice: to get on board, however late; or to persist in raising difficulties that the pilots allegedly implied for "standard operating procedures," however positive the short-run effects.

And suddenly the stakes had been raised. Several days before the meeting, the firm's CEO and COO mentioned that they "would be sitting in." Like the proverbial 500-pound gorillas, not only would they sit in, but no doubt they would see that their agenda, if any, got worked.

The OD team had deliberately tried not to lobby their position with the executives, lest HR prominents later complain about having been sandbagged. Now it seemed likely that the HR cluster had been less restrained, and might even have convinced the two top executives that too many practical problems would overbalance any advantages of going operational with the pilot projects.

Facing the real possibility that they had been outflanked, the OD team nonetheless waited for events to unfold. Whatever else, the data attributed very positive effects to the pilot projects. Indeed, the major unexpected event in the testing was a very pleasant one. Members of a "control group" wanted an immediate extension to their worksite of the "experiment." They had seen enough to demand the "treatment," loudly and at several levels of management. Moreover, there was no point in risking further antagonism of HR, especially this late in the game.

So the meeting began with the bantering common to the organization. When the CEO and COO entered, together, it was clear to all that they wouldn't be just "sitting in." The executives were here to "call signals," if not to "carry the ball."

Gary's pulse started to race, and a quick scan of the conference room indicated he was not alone in his reaction. But the suspense did not build very long. The CEO asserted his primacy: "We would all profit if Gary Roberts put today's festivities into early perspective. He has served as guru to the OD staff and management of the pilot projects, as we all know. Gary?"

Gary started with a brief survey, in part to nail down the foci of discussion, but also to give himself a bit of time to consider alternatives.

INSTRUCTIONS AND QUESTIONS: PART 1

You are Gary Roberts. Did the CEO intend to help you, or to set you up as the target for today?

Decide on your major theme or themes. And quickly! You can think while you talk about some stage-setting details. But what's your theme?

PART 2

Some boilerplate having been reviewed in a few minutes, Gary tried to nail his theme. The words still ring in his ears:

> "Gentlemen, we are not here to reinvent the status quo. Basically, we will review the data that establish we can move ahead, with benefit to the employees and profit to the corporation."

"Great," said the CEO. "I see Gary has his usual stack of papers reporting results in detail. We'll have him talk 5 or 10 minutes to review the highlights for us. And then let's devote the rest of our two hours to detailing our course for the future."

Gary and his colleagues were delighted to be "hustled along" in this way. "It was nice to have the floor," Gary noted aloud, "but others might have something to say about the sudden new agenda."

There were no takers—at least not publicly.

INSTRUCTIONS AND QUESTIONS: PART 2

1. Evaluate Gary's tactics. Speculate about possible long-run and short-run effects.
2. Should the OD team take any special pains to inform the HR team about what occurred?
3. As one of the HR officials, what would you believe about the CEO and COO appearing at the meeting, with little notice?

PART 3

The OD team, in effect, whistled as they went back to their offices. Some commiseration was extended to the members of the critical HR staff, whose "doors had been slammed shut" by the two executives. Events continued to cascade around the OD team, and no special contacts were made with the HR staff. Implementations concerning "going operational" with the pilot projects began uneventfully.

INSTRUCTIONS AND QUESTIONS: PART 3

1. What are the major short-run effects?
2. Do you expect long-run effects for HR and OD activities?
3. If so, what kind of defensive plans should the OD team consider, based on the following premises?
   - Executives can have short attention spans.
   - "Staff" officials can have long memories.

I.10

Keep It Quiet, Guys!

PART 1

Jerry, Stokes, and Bob had shared a number of successful OD ventures in American R & D. The first two men had recently been promoted into new jobs (see Figure I.10.1), and Bob remained one of their main external consultants. The three men had big plans, they liked one another, and their confidence in each other was very high.

Their collaboration would be enhanced, they all hoped, by the recent movement of Ron into a staff job with Jerry (see Figure I.10.1). Ron's position typically had been held by a physical scientist, but Ron had come up through Human Resources and had strong OD interests. Stokes and Bob were major supports of Ron in the new job, and Jerry went out of his way to ease Ron's entry into a position for which, it is safe to say, there had been several attractive candidates with more conventional job histories. Moreover, not all research or corporate interests were equally strong supporters of Jerry's efforts to provide more OD resources for research.

Consistent with expectations, the now-augmented quartet soon embarked on major cultural and structural changes in research, which featured Jerry's commitment to a more open and confrontational style than had dominated in that arena for decades. Research directors had changed—indeed, too frequently—but *a* style tended to persist, and it emphasized larger degrees of autonomy for individual scientists as well as for research missions. Jerry saw a more collaborative research in his vision of the future.

There was plenty for all four men to do. Typically, Jerry, Stokes, and Bob spent much time together. Ron was busy coming to know and to get known, which included a large number of interviews from among sev-

Figure I.10.1 Simplified Chart for American R & D and Parent

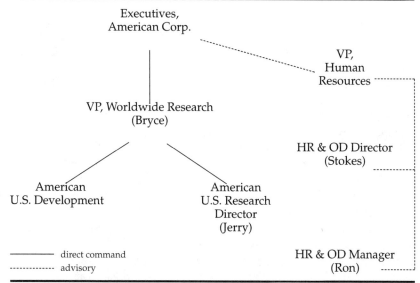

Executives,
American Corp.

VP,
Human
Resources

VP, Worldwide Research
(Bryce)

HR & OD Director
(Stokes)

American
U.S. Development

American
U.S. Research
Director
(Jerry)

———— direct command
------------ advisory

HR & OD Manager
(Ron)

eral hundred research scientists and other personnel. As much as possible, Ron was directly involved and he was always fully briefed when he was occupied elsewhere.

Details are available (Golembiewski, 1991), but a major issue developed suddenly. Jerry became a candidate for a high-level job elsewhere—for responsibility and for dollars that all had expected might come in perhaps eight to ten years, but not now. As surprised as anyone, Jerry told Stokes and Bob of the possibility, about which he required absolute confidentiality. Ron was not to know, Jerry said; and the same held for Bryce, the vice president for worldwide research. Why the secrecy? Perhaps basically the chances of Jerry's selection were seen as slight, if not nonexistent. But "being in the hunt" was too attractive to reject, even at early stages of the selection process.

INSTRUCTIONS AND QUESTIONS: PART 1

1. You are Bob. What do you do in the face of this demand?
2. What is Jerry's thinking?
3. How should you and Stokes respond? And why?

PART 2

Stokes and Bob agree to respect Jerry's demand—to "keep it quiet," but not without some reluctance. They lose no opportunity to revisit the situation as the weeks roll on. Jerry remains adamant, and that only makes things harder for Stokes and Bob. Once or twice, they come close to posing a direct choice for Jerry: either let at least Ron in on the possibility, or we put the brakes on several Research projects. Both men cool down, however. Basically, too many people are committed to too many projects to be so solicitous of their own feelings and reactions, especially when the odds of Jerry's selection are so low.

At best, Stokes and Bob emphasize that their relationship with Ron has been compromised. This is true regardless of whether Jerry stays or goes. Ron will know as soon as possible after the decision, but that will not preclude major consequences for Stokes and Bob.

Possibly even more consequential is the fact that Stokes and Bob are working closely with Bryce on several matters. He also is to be kept in the dark. While respecting confidentiality, however, Stokes and Bob are alert to situations in which Bryce could be hurt by lack of knowledge of the possibility of Jerry leaving. Moreover, substantial momentum has developed for several OD programs, and good faith has to be preserved even if everyone recognizes that not everyone can know, or should know, everything about all aspects of operations at the very earliest time.

Matters quickly become worse. Not only is Jerry offered the high-level position, but he accepts.

Stokes and Bob are the first to learn of the decision, from which Jerry deliberately kept them distant. But Jerry does want both men to help him plan the follow-on, both long-run and short-run—touching the bases with Jerry's old employer and associates, and planning for entrance to the new job.

INSTRUCTIONS AND QUESTIONS: PART 2

Bob and Stokes are now faced with a scenario that had seemed unlikely to occur. What should you do? Focus on several realms of consideration:

1. What should you say to Jerry?
2. What should you do in connection with your personal and working relationship with Ron?
3. What should the two of you say or recommend to Bryce—in connection with your own relationships; about the short-run and longer-run fate of the several OD projects in Research; as well as about Jerry's replacement?

Another source (Golembiewski, 1991, pp. 470–479) details what was actually done in this case. Readers may eventually want to consult that source to compare their approach to coping with that of Stokes and Bob.

However, we advise against consulting the other source until you have completed your own diagnosis and prognosis. To be sure, that other source contains detail beyond the present sketch. But enough has been revealed here to give you a realistic statement of the conditions associated with Jerry's departure.

Reference

Golembiewski, R. T. (1991). American research and development, A–D. In A. M. Glassman and T. G. Cummings (Eds.), *Cases in organization development*, pp. 455–479. Homewood, IL: Irwin.

I.11

Jack, Your Comments Are Neither Responsive Nor Helpful*

Jack Billingsley is an active and ambitious young OD consultant, and he has been revelling about being in the "big time, for the first time" during his present assignment. He has begun working with several division heads—first-reports to a CEO—whom he has barely met.

One day Jack receives a call from the office of the CEO, out of the blue. "Fletcher would like to see you," he learns from a semi-familiar voice Jack associates with one of the CEO's immediate aides, "and not only is sooner better than later, but immediately would be best of all."

Jack decides to provide the best, although that means rescheduling some family business that he had planned. He is in Fletcher's anteroom within 90 minutes. He enters the inner sanctum 15 minutes later.

Fletcher gets to the heart of the matter. "I have been pleased with your work with the division officers, and I'd like your help with one of them—specifically Bob."

To cut to the chase, Fletcher definitely sees Bob as moving into a staff role from his present line assignment, but Bob resists. Bottom-line, reassignment to staff would put him outside the "engine room" of the organization, Bob has concluded. So Bob has announced to Fletcher that he will not accept the move, period.

Fletcher has decided to persist, but to do so indirectly through Jack. "Please talk to Bob," he requests, "and get him to see the realities of how the shift will be good for both him and the organization, and especially for him."

A few exchanges follow, but they are brief and do not change the original message. So, Jack responds with a studied recap of what he had

*This situation arises for all ODers in many forms. One typical context can be found in Henning (1997), among numerous other sources.

read in many books and heard in consultant shoptalk. "It sounds like you and Bob have some important matters to discuss, one-on-one. Of course, I'll be pleased to sit in as a third person, a facilitator. But this appears to be one-on-one business."

Fletcher looks down at his desk and replies in a measured tone, "Jack, your comments are neither responsive nor helpful."

INSTRUCTIONS AND QUESTIONS

1. You need to respond to Fletcher quickly and confidently. What do you say?
2. What do you predict about the consequences of your possible response, both short-term and long-term? Distinguish at least two cases.
   - For example, you might say, "I'm sorry you react negatively, Fletcher. But I don't see my role that way."
   - Or you might say, "On quick second thought, I misspoke myself, I'll get to Bob as soon as he is available."

   In this second case, what will you say to Bob? And how?
3. Design a Dilbert cartoon depicting Jack's dilemma. See Adams (1996), or a broad range of popular media outlets that feature the Dilbert comic strip.

References

Adams, S. (1996). *The Dilbert principle*. New York: Harper Business.
Henning, J. P. (1997). *The future of staff groups*. San Francisco: Berrett-Koehler Publishers, Inc.

I.12

Volunteer Turnover in an ASO

PART 1

Judy Green has just taken over as director of volunteers in an AIDS Service Organization, or ASO. She faces a big job. For one thing, there have been three other occupants of her position in the last 18 months, and none of them was able to slow down the flood of volunteers leaving the agency, let alone stop it.

Judy vows to do better, a whole lot better.

But Judy is a new kid on this, or any, block. This is only her second job, and the first one was as an intern who rotated through several major areas of a distant ASO. She has a master's degree in community health from a good university, and she is usually a pretty confident person. But she does wonder a bit, now and again, whether she has really won this job, or whether she was the loser, if you know the feeling.

Judy goes proactive almost from the start. For example, she helps assemble a loose consortium of other ASOs in her region, writing the ASO heads and asking them to appoint representatives to a planning group. All heads quickly reply and name a representative, with several suggesting that Judy take the initiative and schedule a first meeting.

She does just that.

The planning group gets off to a curious start, from Judy's point of view. Quickly, she is elected chair by the four other ASO representatives who attend. They have all been around for several years, and one—Phil Abrams—acts as if he's been around for several years too long. He hardly talks, and seems generally uninterested. But he's always there.

As chair, Judy pushes the issue of losing volunteers, and one of the planning group's first tasks becomes a survey of why so many volunteers are leaving these ASO agencies. All five ASOs represented seem to have a retention problem, and they all worry about losing good people and useful data. Brief conversation follows, which suggests no one has developed a plan that has a reasonable chance to get a handle on retaining volunteers.

The planning group does not seem likely to set any speed records. For the first couple of meetings, indeed, members of the planning group do only a little business and then soon adjourn for pizza and beer. Judy waits, more or less patiently.

At a later meeting, the five-person planning group Judy heads—four males and herself—are sitting around the table after designing one section of the survey. Several members decide to guess the pattern of responses they will get on this section, whose purpose is to get a sense of why volunteers leave.

Table I.12.1 presents the options open to survey respondents, and the planning group has decided to permit no write-ins on the ground that this will make processing easier.

Judy does not agree, but it's clear to her that she will probably lose this one if she persists, so she goes along to get along. Even Phil seems against her on this point, and the three other members clearly do not share her views.

Somebody suggests a betting pool, with each member of the planning group putting in a dollar. The winner will have the highest rank-order correlation between his or her guesses about how the items will be ranked, as compared with the actual coverage rankings by all respondents. Everybody has fun with this one, Judy included.

Judy remembers something about "rank-order correlation" from her graduate work, and makes a note to consult her old statistics textbook. Judy doesn't want to appear ignorant in the planning group. Most members seem interested in projecting a sense of being with it, except Phil Abrams.

So, dutifully, Judy sits down and estimates the rank order of reasons survey respondents will give for leaving volunteer posts in the ASO.

INSTRUCTIONS AND QUESTIONS: PART 1

Take Judy's role. Use Table I.12.1 to estimate the average rank of each item when all surveys are scored.

Table I.12.1   Reasons for Volunteers Leaving Their ASO

Numbered Items on Survey	Your Guess About the Average Rank of Each Item
1. I seemed to feel tired all the time.	_____
2. I did not feel that my input was being given proper attention.	_____
3. I found myself being overwhelmed by the demands.	_____
4. I found relationships with other volunteers and staff were strained.	_____
5. It became costly to volunteer, given travel and associated costs.	_____
6. My friends gave me little, if any, support.	_____
7. Other demands in my life took on greater importance.	_____
8. Responsibilities and expectations were unclear.	_____
9. I felt the organization was losing focus on its mission.	_____
10. I just could not deal with witnessing any more pain.	_____
11. I had to spend more time at work.	_____
12. I began to feel numb; I just could not care anymore.	_____
13. I grew concerned I might get AIDS from exposure to the virus.	_____
14. I changed my mind about AIDS as a national health priority.	_____
15. I did not feel as though I was part of a team.	_____

PART 2

Time passes, as Judy gently reminds the group at a subsequent meeting. A subgroup of three takes on responsibility for preparing the survey forms, almost before Judy finishes reminding them of the group's commitment. The three men—not including Phil, as Judy notices without surprise—will distribute a copy of the survey to each member of the planning group. Each member, in turn, will make as many copies as needed.

The rest of the survey procedure seems simple:

- Each member of the planning group will send a survey form to each volunteer who left his or her ASO within the last six months or so, along with a personalized note encouraging a response.

- Completed forms will be returned for scoring to the three-person subgroup.

A job well begun, if a bit slowly, Judy concludes, as she moves on to other things.

Not long thereafter, things start to get a bit more complicated. Judy receives a call that is apparently from one of the ex-volunteers. The conversation goes something like this:

Caller: What a chicken outfit you represent, Judy.
Judy: I don't know you.
Caller: Well, I don't know you, either. But I do know that if anyone uses someone else's survey items, you should give them credit. The form you sent me was taken, almost word for word, from the *Journal of Health and Human Services Administration*, Vol. 19, No. 3, Winter 1997. And you omitted some of the most revealing items, Judy. Shame on you!

INSTRUCTIONS AND QUESTIONS: PART 2

Check the facts on this one. What's going on?

PART 3

Judy has a growing sense of having been sandbagged by a cluster from the planning group, although she has been too busy to check the accuracy of her phantom caller's message. She can't be sure, yet, but she has a growing suspicion that the three people processing the survey were the most active in bringing up items for inclusion on the survey. They also seemed to vote together.

Judy had tried to get a few items included, but she had been unsuccessful. A few suggestions were voted down, she recalls, but she can't remember any of them but her own items.

Then, one day, Judy gets a note from the survey subgroup. They are now ready to discuss the results of the survey. They suggest an early meeting to review the results, and they even specify a date, place, and time.

With their note, the subgroup encloses the survey results, part of which are summarized by Table I.12.2.

Table I.12.2   Survey Results, Rank-Order of Items, as Reported by Three-Person Task Force

Numbered Items on Survey	Average Rank Order on Survey Items, Rounded-off to Nearest Whole Number
1.	5
2.	7
3.	8
4.	9
5.	12
6.	14
7.	1
8.	4
9.	6
10.	10
11.	11
12.	13
13.	15
14.	2
15.	3

INSTRUCTIONS AND QUESTIONS: PART 3

1. What should Judy do next? She is a bit miffed, feeling that, as chairperson, she should have been accorded the discretion to call the meeting. But her concerns do not stop there, especially after she checks the local library. Almost all of the survey items do come from the source her caller identified, usually word for word.
2. What seems a reasonable action plan for Judy at the upcoming meeting?
3. Is there anything else Judy needs to check, in addition to doing this pre-planning?

PART 4

Judy gets nervous while doing the planning, and she seeks help from a "shadow consultant" who operates within an OD perspective. Judy cannot identify the source of her unease, but her doubts not only exist—they are growing. Judy reports that she doesn't "get it," but she is concerned that "it is getting to her."

INSTRUCTIONS AND QUESTIONS: PART 4

You are the ODer Judy contacts. In the context of the narrative above, you are left with three basic questions:

1. Is this a job for an ODer?
2. How can OD and the ODer help?
3. Who, if anyone, is trying to yank Judy's chain? And why?

1.15

Should You Help Build a Team?
If So, How?*

As a young OD consultant, you come upon two sets of materials that strike your fancy. One is a list of quotations from clients who have requested help in team building, and the other is a figure for classifying team-building efforts.

PART 1

Motives for Team Building

Clients have articulated several clusters of rationales or needs and aspirations associated with team building or development. In general, those rationales are variously accessible and comprehensible to client, consultant, or both. In brief terms, these rationales can be expressed as follows:

1. "I face tight time and dollar constraints, and I believe team building can help accelerate what needs doing. If we know one another's strengths and weaknesses, and can more efficiently increase the former and reduce the latter, the job is more likely to get done on time and within budget."
2. "We just need a limited check-up—a kind of socio-emotional audit, a fine-tuning, to help us realize we're OK enough."
3. "I am really concerned about my managerial potency, about my confidence and ability in making decisions. Team building seems like a

---

* Materials are drawn from R. T. Golembiewski, *Approaches to planned change: Macro interventions and change-agent strategies, part 2,* pp. 460–461. New York: Marcel Dekker, 1979.

good way to share the burdens, to lighten my load of responsibility, and perhaps to avoid total criticism or blame if things go wrong."

4. "Joe Wright did some team building, and he tells me it was great. I admire Joe more than my father."

5. "Many other managers in my organization are into team building, and a guy has to adapt to organization fads, however curious they may be."

6. "I am an unreconstructed autocrat, but a clever and devious one. My young guys want team development; I'll give it to them. I'd promise them anything to get them to produce more and better."

7. "I have a new team, and I want us to get to know one another quickly, so as to get some vital work done more expeditiously. My supervisory style is mildly autocratic, and I intend it to remain that way. But you can't work fluidly with people you barely know. So I'm for team development, up to a point."

8. "I'd like for the rest of my team to learn what an incompetent rat Joe Brown is. He's slippery enough to play one person off against another. I want to nail him in a group situation, where his incompetence and duplicity are there for everyone to see."

9. "We've got to do something different around here, even if it only buys some time, as long as it seems reasonable. I'm interested in team building in that sense."

INSTRUCTIONS AND QUESTIONS: PART 1

Rationales for team building require surfacing not only for their own sake, but especially because they influence the choice of a suitable learning design.

For some of these needs and aspirations, indeed, there is no design in which an ethical ODer can participate.

Make a rough sort of those rationales. Do any contraindicate team building? Which rationales suggest good bets for successful applications? Are you uncertain about judging some rationales, or perhaps all of them?

PART 2

A Schema for Classifying Rationales

Figure I.13.1 provides one way of judging the various rationales for team building, or at least sorting them. In addition, the figure may help

Figure I.13.1   A Typology of Client's Intent as to Impact and Orientation of a
Specific Consulting Episode

Orientation to Consulting Episode

	Needs and aspirations basically accessible to self and consultant	Needs and aspirations basically not accessible to self and consultant
Client's Intent to Deal with Possible Systemic Implications of Team Building	Relatively limited — III	I
	Relatively open-ended — IV	II

enrich an ODer's appreciation of the ethical and normative choices associated with team building.

INSTRUCTIONS AND QUESTIONS: PART 2

You may find Figure I.13.1 helpful in addressing the following questions.

1. Can you assign the several rationales to one of the four cells, without
    undue violence to either the cells or the rationales?
2. Can you see clear reasons for not facilitating team building in any of the
    four cells? Detail your concerns.
3. Can you conceive of changed circumstances that result in a movement
    from one cell to another that would justify terminating a team? Speculate
    on how you would go about doing that, consistent with the Statement
    reprinted under Perspective IV later in this book.

I.14

Who Is the Client?
A Case of "Systems Politics"

PART 1

The ODer and his client CEO were collaborating in a large urban public agency, and their conversations often turned to this question: Who is the client?

The client was preoccupied with the question, while the ODer was biased in a largely opposite direction.

For the ODer, when only individuals or small groups are involved, clarity about "who is the client" patently is useful and even invaluable. At the politics/administration interface, however, "the client" is typically Janus-like, with multiple and competing interests. That interface exists in all organizations, but often will appear more sharply in public organizations—i.e., at the "seam" at which political appointees and civil servants interface. A similar interface exists in all organizations, as at the level at which a person may lose a job for any and all reasons, including the whims of the superior.

The ODer's argument was direct: preoccupation with trying to define "client" may be paid for in terms of cultivating local loyalties and loss of systemic impact. The consultant should assist in seeking and solving problems, rather than defining sponsorship, while being as clear as possible about whatever multiple clients are being served by any single intervention.

The implications seemed clear to the ODer. An identification with the system versus the parts reinforces the intervenor's catalytic role, and also should signal that the intervenor intends to rise above "office politics." This does not suggest being "above it all," the ODer emphaɔizes. Rather, the ODer is thus able to play "systems politics" better and more credibly.

The issue became a hot one for the pair, who confronted it more than once. For example, the CEO had decided on a major appointment, he informed the ODer. The proposed appointee was saleable for various reasons, but the ODer soon concluded that the appointee's basic attraction was that he posed no threat to the CEO. The CEO agreed. He was bypassing an individual who possessed better credentials for the job but who also posed a greater threat to the CEO.

The appointment might be good "ward politics," the consultant agreed, but its systemic implications were serious. To illustrate, the CEO over time had importuned several subordinates to develop "strong backups," for all the usual public reasons but also to make it easier for the CEO to reassign and terminate employees. The CEO encouraged others to "put it on the line." But when he had his chance, he—like most of them—was motivated to take the easy way out. Few would be fooled, the OD consultant guessed. And the more threatening candidate had the greater competence and experience, hands down, both men agreed.

The CEO was not impressed after several iterations of the ODer's argument. The CEO held firm in his decision.

INSTRUCTIONS AND QUESTIONS: PART 1

What should the ODer do? What major consequences are likely to flow from the CEO's chosen course of action?

PART 2

The ODer came to believe this was "put up or shut up" time. The ODer would play systems politics, if in restrained ways. First, he told the CEO, "This appointment is such a big issue that, if we aren't on the same page, I don't see how we can maintain the mutual confidence that has made us such a good pair. I will resign at the end of the week if you go forward with the appointment."

The CEO reconsidered, and the pair's talk immediately turned to highlighting for all who would listen how the CEO had "bitten the bullet to set an example for one and all." This would be "good medicine for the system." Besides, the CEO concluded, the odds were better than even that the new appointee soon would "dig his own grave with his mouth."

"Good enough, if not charitable," the ODer noted.

Second, the ODer thought it wise to spend some time with the new appointee. The CEO balked but finally agreed, in terms steeped in realism: "If you can help him, that will help me, if I play it with any finesse. And if you mess him up, or can't help, that also will help me."

The CEO and ODer grew philosophical. "Here's another point at which we have differing viewpoints," the CEO noted. "A systemic orientation seems to increase the consultant's vulnerability, and it apparently clashes with the reasonable advice that the change agent needs a client, first and foremost." The CEO added, "Why not leave well enough alone? You pushed me pretty hard to change that appointment."

"Reasonable enough," the ODer responded. "But we're operating at the politics/administration interface. Tactics well designed to secure and safeguard *a* client, in short, often are counterproductive for maintaining a systemic role."

Indeed, the ODer admitted a fatalism in this regard. He assigned a very high probability to one of three outcomes in cases of interstitial consultancy, or operating between several levels of the organization or several clients:

- Either the consultant comes into a situation in which the "balance of power" initially recognizes the value of some external playing an interstitial role;
- or the consultant quite quickly can encourage such a balance of power;
- or the consultant is very unlikely to ever become effective in trading back and forth across the politics/administration interface.

The need to quickly legitimate the interstitial role at the politics/administration interface rests on numerous considerations, two of which hold a distinct prominence in the ODer's experience. Unless that legitimation occurs quickly, the consultant likely will either come to be, or to be viewed as, too closely identified with one of the subsystems to be a credible interstitial player. Moreover, appropriate balances of power at the interface typically are temporary. So, the premium definitely is on getting something done quickly, which implies a disciplined boldness.

The ODer advised that "getting out quick" when a supporting balance of power does not exist, or when it cannot be quickly induced, often will enhance a consultant's credibility, if nothing else. "This just is not a propitious moment," the OD intervenor announces, in effect. "There may be other, better times."

"I get it, now," the CEO observes. "Consultant freedom is just another form of nothing much to lose."

INSTRUCTIONS AND QUESTIONS: PART 2

1. Does the CEO really get it?
2. How do you react to the ODer's "fatalism"? How applicable is it when the ODer is dealing with only a single individual or a small team? Does it seem a reasonable strategy at entry, as well as at more advanced stages of consultation?

I.15

Transitioning Toward a Team-Based Organization

Based on Susan Albers Mohrman and Allan M. Mohrman, Jr.

Assume that you are an OD intervenor who has been tasked with developing an experiment with team-based organization at a worksite where the traditional bureaucratic model guides the structuring of work. Specifically, consult Model A in Figure I.5.2 in Case I.5, "A Grumble or a Meta-Grumble," which provides your starting point.

Basically, you are authorized to *develop an action plan, with a structural design as well as relevant recommendations concerning implementation and evaluation*. Directly, your plan will *add* a team-based S-unit to the three S-units in Model A, while retaining the latter three units. The flow of work remains A + B + C, which yields some product or service.

Model B in "A Grumble or a Meta-Grumble" can be used as a general guide for this add-on to Model A.

Table I.15.1 provides a summary of the challenges and issues you may expect to encounter in designing this team-based add-on.

Table I.15.1   Challenges and Tasks in Transitioning to a Team-Based
Organization

Area	Challenges	Key Tasks
Design	Designing the teams	Fitting teams to strategy Autonomous or integrated work processes Chartering teams
	Embedding the teams in the larger system	Forging connections between teams Connecting teams to the larger system
	Aligning contextual systems and power	Performance management systems Information systems Decision-making processes Communication practices
Capability Development	Team and management capabilities	Team development Team leadership development Experiential learning
	Design expertise for ongoing self-design	Team-based design framework Assessment and diagnostic practices
	Beliefs and assumptions	Surfacing deep-seated assumptions Learning from experience in a new mode of operation
Implementation	Achieving critical mass	Proceeding quickly enough to establish a new modus operandi Eliminating old practices and structures that interfere with teamwork
	Sequencing	Developing support systems and implementing new structures Just-in-time capability development

continued

Table I.15.1   Challenges and Tasks in Transitioning to a Team-Based
Organization *(continued)*

Area	Challenges	Key Tasks
	Managing concurrent change process and task functioning	Integrating change processes with new work processes Avoiding dichotomy between team activities and "getting work done"

Reprinted with permission of author and publisher from "Fundamental Organization Change As Organizational Learning: Creating Team-Based Organizations," by S. A. Mohrman and A. M. Mohrman, Jr. In W. A. Pasmore and R. W. Woodman (Eds.), *Research in organization change and development*, Vol. 10 (1997), p. 212. Greenwich, CT: JAI Press, Inc.

INSTRUCTIONS AND QUESTIONS

1. How does Table I.15.1 facilitate your analysis?
2. Some entries in Table I.15.1 may stump you, in summary form. Consult the full article (Mohrman and Mohrman, 1997) to get further guidance on any points that are obscure or puzzling.
3. You may want to include more detailed analysis than "A Grumble or a Meta-Grumble" can support. In this case, you may consult the following sources:

    Robert T. Golembiewski, *Practical Public Management* (New York: Marcel Dekker, 1995);

    Robert T. Golembiewski, *Approaches to Planned Change* (New York: Marcel Dekker, 1979), Vol. 2.
4. Don't be surprised if you cannot accommodate several—or even many—of the points in Table I.15.1 to the sparse details provided by the case "A Grumble or a Meta-Grumble?" Do your best.

Reference

Mohrman, S. A., and Mohrman, A. M., Jr. (1997). In W. A. Pasmore and R. W. Woodman (Eds.), *Research in organization change and development*, Vol. 10, pp. 197–228. Greenwich, CT: JAI Press, Inc.

I.16

Six Events in the Life of a New Voluntary Agency

Patricia D. Nobbie

BACKGROUND

In a United States protectorate composed of several islands, three parent support groups formed a coalition and received funding from the U.S. Department of Education to start a Parent Training and Information Center. These projects, which exist in every state, provide information, support, referrals, and training to families raising children with disabilities. The federal funding for the Parent Training and Information Centers comes under a specific section of PL94-142, the Individuals with Disabilities Education Act (IDEA).

Though their children were technically in a United States school system, island parents of children with disabilities constantly struggled for adequate services from the special education system. Their children often went without qualified classroom teachers, not to mention speech, physical, and occupational therapists, and regular transportation. Class action lawsuits filed on behalf of the children had been pending for years.

The parents were excited and energized at the chance to run their own operation and to deal with other parents the way they wished to be dealt with. Better services for all eligible children were sought.

The board of directors of the new agency—named the Disabilities Information Network, or DIN—hired the first four staff, with a clear preference going to the parents of eligible children. June, the executive director, has a teenage daughter who is mildly disabled. She is a white "continental" from California who plans to move to one of the islands at the end of the first grant year. She has extensive experience working for grant-funded nonprofit agencies. Her husband is a designer for a major computer company who will "telecommute" from the island, traveling to the U.S. as needed. June has received permission from the board to commute to work until she and her husband can move their children to the islands at the end of the school year.

Olivia is June's executive assistant and will also work 20 hours per week as an Information Specialist in June's office on the main island. Olivia is a unique individual. She has a visual impairment that prevents her from driving but does not limit her much in other arenas. She is a singer who performs regular gigs at bars on weekends. She has worked as an advocate in special projects for another federally funded advocacy agency, as well as for the local Division of Mental Health. She is African American, originally from Harlem, and lived in Florida before she moved to the islands. She knows everyone.

Carol is the Information Specialist on the smallest island. She is a white lawyer with a daughter who has autism. Her husband is deceased, and she works minimally to avoid jeopardizing her eligibility to receive death and SSI benefits for herself and child. She has been an aggressive advocate for her child, who is doing facilitated speech, a fairly controversial method. The child is in a regular class at the local elementary school, with a full-time personal assistant. Carol's knowledge of the special ed laws is seen as a real asset.

Diane, the fourth staff member, is also a white continental who has lived in the islands for more than 10 years. She has a daughter with Down syndrome. She has also aggressively advocated for her child, and participated in many of the planning efforts that got DIN to its present state. She has a personal relationship with several board members.

In addition to being an Information Specialist for DIN, Diane has her own business, which provides private tutoring for private school students as well as for children with learning disabilities. She is married to a West Indian, whom she met soon after her arrival on the islands. She is well known, especially by parents and professionals in the special education system.

The board of directors for DIN is composed of seven members: five women and two men. Five are parents who have children of varying ages with disabilities. One member is a lawyer with Legal Services. One is a professional employed by the local Department of Education, Division of Special Education. All but two are local islanders.

Note that white continentals compose only 10 percent of the islands' population. The majority are African American, "Down-islander," Hispanic, or Arab.

PART 1: ESTABLISHING THE OFFICES

June and Diane hit it off immediately. They have similar working styles, share progressive ideas about people with disabilities, and are both well-educated. June relies on Diane for information about the local system. Theirs becomes more of a cooperative working relationship than that of boss and employee.

As the work begins to settle down in the offices on three different islands, June realizes that Olivia's technical and organizational skills are severely lacking. She has difficulty following directions, is not facile with the computer, misplaces paperwork, neglects to give June messages, and so on. June, who is competent where Olivia falls short, tries several ways to help Olivia grasp her responsibilities. June sees Olivia's people skills as a real asset. However, June gets increasingly frustrated, because her time is precious; every few weeks she must go to California to check on her family. June relates some of this frustration to Diane, who knew Olivia from another project. In fact, Diane is glad she doesn't have to work in the same office.

It gets to the point where June feels she may have to fire Olivia, so she begins developing documentation. All the employees are on probation for 90 days. June states conditions for continued employment on interim evaluations, which Olivia signs.

A month later, a consultant arrives from New Hampshire to assist June in completing the design of administrative procedures for the three island offices and to design training for the special education laws with the first groups of parents. One training session will take place on each island.

On the morning of a crucial meeting that is being held on Diane's island, Olivia misses the plane. She has all the training materials, which do not arrive until noon. When June sees Olivia walking up the driveway to Diane's office, June takes Diane aside and informs her she's going to fire Olivia.

INSTRUCTIONS AND QUESTIONS: PART 1

Assume you are the New Hampshire consultant.

1. The labor laws in the territory have very specific parameters for firing an employee. Although Diane doesn't know them specifically, she has a bad feeling about this sudden move. What should she do?

2. Immediately, what should Diane do with June?
3. What should you, the New Hampshire consultant, do—if anything? You were sent to assist the new agency to deal with all issues, including personnel matters.

PART 2: DISMISSAL

June does it: she fires Olivia, even before she enters Diane's building. June gives Olivia cab fare so she can get to her friend's house where she will be staying.

Diane is put off-balance by this move. Once back in the office, Diane listens to June and the consultant describe Olivia's behavior from the night before, when they were training on June's island. Olivia was without cab fare home, or a ride, and got very agitated at the end of the meeting. She began asking people for money or transportation and loudly complaining. The consultant, a straight-laced professional manager, was very embarrassed. June was very angry at what she considered to be immature and unprofessional behavior. Olivia's missing the plane added fuel to the fire.

Diane files this information away, glad she is not in the director's shoes. June has not consulted the board, attempted mediation, or even consulted the lawyer on the staff. Diane knows there will be repercussions.

INSTRUCTIONS AND QUESTIONS: PART 2

In an OD course, your assignments deal with consultant empathy. In this setting, you are encouraged to play several roles-of-the-other:

1. As Olivia, what are your reactions and your options?
2. Is there anything Diane should do about the situation? What are her feelings?
3. What should June do at this point? Relate this action to her reactions about what seems to be going on.

PART 3: RESIGNATION

In early spring, June leaves for California to begin the move with her family. She appoints Diane acting director in her absence, but not without some resistance from the board, which neither June nor Diane understand.

A few weeks later, Carol, the staffer from the third island, calls to ask what Diane thinks about June's resignation. Diane has heard nothing. Carol says she got a fax, and sure enough, a newly arrived letter sits in Diane's front office. It states that because June's husband's company is reorganizing, her husband cannot telecommute and, moreover, must remain in California indefinitely.

Diane is devastated, even though June's letter asks the board to make Diane the acting director while they look for a new director.

The board quickly, almost embarassedly, accepts June's letter and her recommendation. However, they never send Diane a letter formally acknowledging her change in status. Diane learns only through DIN's accountant that her pay rate has changed. But the board will not pay her the same salary as the preceding director. In any case, Diane is now doing the work of at least two people. A great deal of responsibility has been put on Diane's shoulders. First, the new grant cycle will soon begin, and Diane will have to negotiate a five-year, half-million-dollar grant, as well as finish out the funding allocations from the first-year grant. Second, Olivia has filed a wrongful discharge complaint with the Department of Labor, and Diane will have to attend the hearing to represent DIN. The agency is also right in the middle of an extensive ADA technical assistance project, and had been planning to apply for money from the Developmental Disabilities Council for a year-long training program to teach policy-making and advocacy skills to a group of 20 parents.

At the same time, Diane is beginning to detect an undercurrent of backlash against June coming from several of the board members. Apparently, some of them didn't like her. They were not impressed with the way she fired Olivia. One member says he felt she was cold, not friendly.

This greatly surprises Diane, but she does remember that the board actively resisted June's request to appoint her as acting director, as well as refused to increase her pay temporarily while June was away. These inactions hurt Diane's feelings very much. Did the board not feel she deserved it? After all her years of volunteer work with this same group of parents? In fact, the chairperson of the board was a parent whom Diane trained and took to conferences to enable her to take over as a representative for the parents of younger children once Diane's child became ineligible for the Early Childhood Special Education Program (at age 5). Yet, this individual seemed to offer the least support.

In spite of everything, Diane decides she wants to apply for the director's position, and tells the chairperson of her intent.

INSTRUCTIONS AND QUESTIONS: PART 3

Consider this an extension of your OD coursework about "walking a mile in the shoes of others."

1. You are Diane. How would you proceed on the issue of a pay raise while you are acting director? Do you merit the same level of pay that the preceding director had received? Or perhaps more because you are doing June's job as well as your own?
2. How should you, as Diane, handle the wrongful discharge hearing?
3. How much initiative should you take with new projects, funding, and other business, knowing a search for a director could take three months or so?

PART 4A: WRONGFUL DISCHARGE HEARING

Diane is coached on the procedures for the hearing by the Legal Services lawyer who is on the board of directors. Diane finds, as she suspected, that there were no firm legal grounds for the firing, despite June's prior documentation of poor work habits. Olivia is suing for all back pay and damages.

Diane is reluctant to have Olivia back, since Diane would be her supervisor.

In the eyes of the chairperson, DIN has no choice. It only remains to settle the financial aspects. Diane attends the hearing with a great deal of anxiety.

INSTRUCTIONS AND QUESTIONS: PART 4A

Building on Parts 2 and 3, take the role of the OD consultant.

1. The federal grant prohibits paying damages in law suits. What kind of wrongful discharge settlement should Diane seek? What kind of conditions can she impose on Olivia?
2. How can Diane arrive at a settlement that will relieve the agency of its culpability, without financial compensation?
3. How active a role should you play in counseling Diane, as a recently assigned OD resource person and facilitator?

PART 4B: AMICABLE SETTLEMENT

After taking statements, the hearing officer reviews the labor law for all parties, and Diane must concede that firing Olivia for missing a plane is disallowable. She realizes that the whole issue comes down to what June wrote about the reason for the discharge. Despite the fact that just cause for firing had accumulated in her documentation, June only wrote about Olivia missing the plane as *the* reason for dismissal. This is an important lesson for Diane.

Olivia drops her demand for damages and most of the back pay. She really just wants her job back. She agrees to another 45 days of probation. The hearing is concluded.

In the hallway afterward, Olivia tells Diane that she really wants to work with her, that she had liked the job, but that she had found it hard to work for June. She says she'll have no problem working for Diane, and she will do her best. Diane appreciates this apparently sincere statement on Olivia's part, and stresses to Olivia that she will have to run the office alone until a director is hired.

To Diane's relief and delight, she has no problems with Olivia. Diane gives her concrete instructions, and things get done. Diane begins to gain confidence in her managerial skills. Olivia becomes her staunchest supporter during the director search, which gets very uncomfortable for Diane.

PART 5: GRANT NEGOTIATION

Diane contacts the grants officer in Washington, and they begin working on the grant negotiations. Diane and June wrote the grant, so both are familiar with every detail.

At this point in the fiscal year, with two months left, there is approximately $20,000 left over from what was budgeted for the first year and had not yet been allocated. Most of this comes from salaries that went unpaid. DIN was funded beginning July 1, but staff was not hired until November 1. In addition, the agency is saving money now because it is short one staff member. June, thinking ahead just before she left for California, had successfully requested an extension for the use of this money, so they have until August 31 to spend it.

With June gone, Diane has to find an acceptable use for the $20,000; otherwise the authority to spend it will lapse. June finds out what is allowable under the grant, and also contacts the consultant from New Hampshire. Then she writes a proposal for spending the money, which she faxes to New Hampshire, mails to Washington, and delivers to the chairperson of the board. She has very little time to encumber the money. The new, five-year, half-million-dollar grant cannot be negotiated until the issue of the leftover funding is resolved.

What is in the proposal? It had occurred to Diane that after the first year of operation, which had its rough spots, DIN could use a regrouping or renewing exercise. The purpose of forming a coalition originally was to bring three parent groups together to procure better services for their children with disabilities. Yet the groups had not interacted except through the executive director.

Diane talks to a few parents and finds they would also like to get together and have a planning exercise, as well as socialize. Diane finds out through another contact that she can get a speaker from ARC, the Association for Retarded Citizens, for free, if the agency will pay the airfare. Diane begins planning a one-day conference, with the ARC woman as keynote speaker, break-out planning sessions, and a luncheon. The federal grant will not pay for food, so Diane plans to use some money left over from the original planning grant, which was locally funded. She arranges for a restaurant, and details the expenses, including transportation from the other islands, child care, lunch, speakers, as well as miscellaneous expenses. The total comes to around $4,500.

Diane "has" nearly $20,000 at her disposal, and if she doesn't spend it, it will be returned to Washington. She knows agencies avoid returning money to Washington, because it will make it that much harder to justify the needs for the new grant budget. She plans to spend the rest of the money on a new computer and printer for the third office; new books, tapes, films, and subscriptions for the Resource Library; brochures; and posters; as well as bulk-rate plane tickets for the board and staff to fly to meetings. In mid-June, Diane submits a written proposal to the chairperson and hears nothing, so she continues with her plans.

A few days later, the chairperson calls, asking about the airfare costs, which Diane explains. The chairperson expresses some doubts about the idea, but doesn't tell her not to proceed. Diane, feeling that this exercise would be particularly helpful to her if she were to take over as director, goes on making the arrangements.

The next day, Olivia calls and reports she overheard one of the board members grousing about the "cockamamie" idea that the acting executive director came up with for the retreat. The board member added, "Only a continental would come up with an idea like that!" The influential complainant is an older man from down-island who has two older daughters with physical and mental disabilities, and who checks in regularly with the secretary of the advocacy office where the DIN is housed.

Diane is stung. After checking around discreetly, she finds she has very little board support for the mini-conference. But Diane has confirmed with the restaurant, reserved the bed and breakfast where the speaker will stay, made plane reservations, and agreed to the speaker's schedule.

INSTRUCTIONS AND QUESTIONS: PART 5

Continue in the role as OD consultant to Diane.

1. Diane has not yet informed the parents as a whole about the luncheon, nor has she sent out invitations. What should Diane do? What is the significance of the remark, "Only a continental would think of something like that"?
2. Help Diane gain insight about why the board didn't openly communicate their concerns about the mini-conference plan. Also, help Diane understand the board's lack of formal input on how the excess funds are spent.
3. Explore any risks Diane is assuming in making these spending decisions on her own. What are her options?

PART 6: THE DIRECTOR SEARCH

Diane ends up cancelling the retreat, which causes her some embarrassment because of the commitments she made. Nonetheless, she assumes the responsibility, and does not even mention the board's objections when talking to the people involved.

The whole situation puzzles Diane and tires her, and she wonders what is up between the board members, their feelings about June, and now maybe about her. Diane is sad that the whole spirit of the parent effort has taken a back seat to what she sees as a cultural conflict. Yet she is committed to the idea of DIN and feels she can make some positive advances as the executive director. Diane even tells the headmistress of the private school where she has been tutoring and consulting that she is seeking full-time employment as the director. Consequently, Diane will be unable to teach the following year.

The search process seems to take forever, and Diane can't understand why they don't simply hire her. She knows the workings of the agency and appreciates the grant parameters better than anyone.

Indeed, Diane had been approached about being the director before June's hiring, but Diane had not wanted to cancel her teaching commitments at mid-year, so she took the Information Specialist job, which was only part-time, at $10 per hour, one-third of what she made as a tutor and consultant. At the time, she was less interested in the remuneration than in the excitement of beginning a new project that could have far-reaching positive outcomes. Diane was also aware of what she would gain in knowledge in the areas of advocacy and policy-making.

The directorship pays $32,000 a year. To continue to work as an Information Specialist for $10,000 a year would be difficult for Diane.

Diane knows that according to the federal grant guidelines, the job has to be posted, and so on, but she also knows the board has come up with few qualified candidates. Diane is also a parent of a child with a disability, and it is the agency's written commitment to give parents priority for staff positions.

Diane begins to feel that the board wants to hire someone local, and not white. She understands this; the agency serves predominantly local parents. Yet Diane feels she is an exception because, although both white and a continental, she is married to someone from the region, and has fully participated in all aspects of the community during the 10 years she has been a resident. Moreover, despite Diane's level of education and sophistication, she has a reputation for being approachable and comfortable with everyone. She also realizes that if someone else were hired, she would be in the uncomfortable position of having to train that individual, and she mentally role-plays how she will deal with this. She contemplates quitting, but her family really needs her extra income and, more importantly, Diane feels very connected to the parents she is working with.

Finally, the board chairperson informs Diane when her interview will take place. Unfortunately, Diane alone has the keys to the agency, so she has to go over to the office early to open it. Another candidate is scheduled before her. It is a local attorney who often takes pro bono cases for disabled individuals and who has participated in Diane's ADA seminars.

The lawyer asks Diane if she will be interviewing him, and she says, "No—you are interviewing for my job." He is startled, and says, "Oh no, why, I think you are very good at it." Diane explains the acting director arrangement and emphasizes that she is also applying for the directorship. He expresses his support for her but then goes to his interview.

Diane is asked to go home and come back later for her own interview. Once home, she thinks the chairperson will call her when she is to come, since she doesn't know who else has been scheduled, and she doesn't want to run into any other candidates. No call comes. Finally, Diane just goes over to the office, and finds everybody ready to leave, insistent that they told her to come back in two hours.

Now, they can only reschedule her interview.

Diane protests. This uncertainty has gone on long enough.

The board members persist, however, and the interview is rescheduled a few days later. Diane gets no reaction from the other two members who have come to do the interviews with the chairperson. They both were friends from other times and places outside the agency. Diane is confused and hurt.

INSTRUCTIONS AND QUESTIONS: PART 6

Continue in your role as OD consultant to Diane. Among other possibilities, you as OD consultant could help direct attention to issues such as the following:

1. How do you help Diane understand what happened?
2. Speculate on Diane's feelings and how you can help her surface and deal with them.
3. Role-play various ways Diane could approach the training scenario she imagines if she isn't hired as executive director. She will have to train any new director; that alone is certain.
4. Should Diane just quit and let the board face the music without her help?

PART 7: RESOLUTION

A few days later, Diane has her interview via conference call with the chairperson and a board member from the other island. It is over in one hour.

The next week, Diane must open up the agency on a Saturday for the board meeting that will decide her fate. She must also first give the quarterly report, for which she has prepared carefully. She doesn't want any more surprises like the luncheon, so she has all the financial figures ready for the board. She has an itemized list of the supplies and equipment she has already purchased, and she wants their input on how the remaining money should be spent.

To her dismay, the board members merely glance at the figures, then ask her to leave while they debate the directorship. She goes to sit in the front of the office. A little while later, they call her into her office and inform her that they have hired another woman, who was previously a middle manager at AT&T. She had also run a work training program for rehabilitation clients. She was not the parent of a special needs child, nor disabled herself; nor was she local, but she was African American. Board members express hope that Diane will stay on and assist the new director. The meeting adjourns.

INSTRUCTIONS AND QUESTIONS: PART 7

As OD consultant, you are debriefing yourself at an early opportunity, so as to extract as much learning, personal and organizational, as possible. Among other possibilities, you may be called on to help the new director get off to a good start.

1. Examine this small history from a cultural perspective. Despite the common bond of parents dealing with disabilities, other motivations are driving the board members as well. There is a cultural dichotomy between those "born here," and outsiders ("continentals"). Is this attitude coming into play? Were Diane and June sufficiently sensitive to this? Is there anything they could have done differently?

2. At various times, June and Diane were puzzled at the reactions of the board members to events in DIN. Recall the board's resistance to appointing Diane as acting director, the undercurrent of bad feeling toward June after she resigned, and their lack of public input to Diane's plan to spend the remaining first-year grant money. How do you evaluate the communication between DIN's staff and the board?

3. Did the board handle the hiring process appropriately? Considerately? Is consideration important?

4. How do you think Diane will deal with the new director?

I.17

Organization Termination in the Nonprofit Setting*

Dorothy Norris-Tirrell

Nonprofit organizations (NPOs) grow increasingly common, with perhaps a million being legally constituted in today's America. Hence the relevance of this case, which charts why and how one NPO merged itself out of existence.

THE CASE: CHILDREN'S REHABILITATION SERVICES[1]

Children's Rehabilitation Services (CRS) was established in 1958 by the Charity Guild of Fort Lauderdale, Florida, with the mission of financially supporting therapeutic services for foster care children experiencing behavioral problems. CRS's mission quickly changed to direct service provision after the local community service council identified a special need: short-term residential-based facilities for emotionally disturbed children, boys in particular.

The new organization's board of directors thoroughly researched the concept of residential treatment and its utility for ultimately developing an innovative treatment program. The trend in residential programs in the late 1950s centered on long-term treatment programs that placed

---

* Reprinted with permission of author and publisher from *International journal of public administration*, 20(12), 1997, pp. 2181–2184. New York: Marcel Dekker, Inc. References have been variously changed.

[1]The information for this case was collected by the author over a period of one year. Interviews were conducted with board members, the executive director, the clinical director, the guardians of clients, and a range of external stakeholders including funders, regulators, referral agencies, and competing nonprofits. Additionally, a wide range of documents including annual reports, IRS Form 990s, and auditor reports were reviewed.

children in large institutions and separated them from their parents for the duration of treatment. The group home approach chosen by CRS was innovative in two ways. First, the program focused on the development of a homelike treatment setting, admitting only six boys at a time. Second, the program used a five-day plan: Children stayed at the CRS facility for five days (Monday through Friday) and then returned to their parental or guardian family each weekend. The treatment program's goals were to provide emotional care and support for the boys, to assist them in the development of better coping and peer skills, and finally, to reunite them with their parental or guardian families. Treatment centered on the role of the houseparent in creating a homelike environment.

By August 1960, the board had purchased a house, hired houseparents and opened the doors of its first group home for emotionally disturbed boys, aged six to fourteen. A second home opened in 1964 originally serving girls but after two years was altered to serve boys. The treatment approach and number of clients served (12 maximum at any time, with six at each group home facility) remained unchanged throughout the life of the organization.

The volunteer board of directors handled all day-to-day operations of CRS from purchasing supplies to client admissions until 1982. In 1982, CRS sought funding from the United Way of Broward County and licensure as a group home from the State of Florida, Department of Health and Rehabilitative Services. Both United Way funding and licensed group home status were received later that year under the condition that the agency would employ an administrator and a clinical director. Even though both positions were filled as part-time, the hiring of the professional staff created new expenditures that were greater than the revenues generated through the United Way and state contracts, leaving the organization with an annual operating budget deficit. Funds from restricted endowment accounts were used to cover the debt.

In 1985, at the suggestion of the United Way, several children's residential treatment programs in Broward County merged to form a new agency, thereby pooling resources and increasing efficiency, service scope, and capacity. CRS was approached but eventually elected not to be a part of the merger even though financial and legal opinion was favorable and strong support existed for the merger. The new "merged" organization was funded by the United Way, the state, and the county, and quickly became a respected agency in the community while CRS continued to experience an annual operating deficit.

By the late 1980s, demands for accountability and decreasing availability of funds resulted in increased scrutiny by current and potential funders and questions regarding the effectiveness of the CRS treatment program. CRS decision makers failed to answer these questions satisfactorily, leaving stakeholder relationships negative and unstable. By fall 1990, the organization's survival was threatened due to the continued use of endowment funds to cover the operating deficit and its inability to generate new revenues. After a six-month concentrated effort to raise funds and at the urging of their United Way allocations panel, a board committee was appointed to explore the options available to CRS, including merger. In September 1991, the CRS board of directors unanimously approved the organization's merger with the agency that was formed out of the 1985 merger noted above.

INSTRUCTIONS AND QUESTIONS

It seems a useful OD rule-of-thumb that organizational phases or stages have significant implications for OD: different skills/abilities for managers may be appropriate at entrepreneurial vs. bureaucratic stages, for example; and OD interventions are ideally targeted not only to an existing organizational stage or phase, but the one likely to follow.

What does the literature tell us about organizational phases or stages? You as an ODer may want to consult sources such as the following:

- an excellent reader (Cameron, Sutter, and Whetten, 1988);
- an early model by a recognized ODer (Greiner, 1972);
- the interpretive summary from which the CRS case is drawn (Norris-Tirrell, 1997, esp. pp. 2179–2189); and
- various models of program termination (e.g., de Leon, 1983).

1. How do the models, generalizations, and insights derived from the literature help you to understand the events detailed in the case of CRS?
2. If you had been called in as an OD consultant at the time of the merger, how would the literature have influenced your orientations or interventions?

References

Cameron, K. S., Sutton, R. I., and Whetten, D. A. (Eds). (1988). *Readings in organization decline: Frameworks, research, and prescriptions.* Cambridge, MA: Ballinger Publishing.

de Leon, P. (1978). A theory of termination. In J. V. May and A. B. Wildavsky (Eds.), *The policy cycle,* pp. 279–300. Beverly Hills, CA: Sage.

Golembiewski, R. T. (1979). *Approaches to planned change.* New York: Marcel Dekker.

Greiner, L. (1972). Evolution and resolution as organizations grow. *Harvard Business Review, 49*: 37–46.

Norris-Tirrell, D. (1997). Organization termination in the non-profit setting. *International Journal of Public Administration, 29*(12): 2177–2194.

I.18

So, How Do You See Yourself as an OD Consultant? And How Do Others See You?

**Joanne Preston and
Robert T. Golembiewski**

Table I.18.1 lists a number of skills and areas of knowledge seen as relevant to the success of OD practitioners. The elements in the table usually have a clear meaning. When that is not the case, the reader may not find it convenient to refer to the original source for details. So the best advice in case of ambiguity or unclarity: move on to the next item.

The point of the exercise, after all, is not to be exhaustive. Rather, the point is to begin a process, using both self and others, for the development of both. Even a very short and very deficient list of skills and knowledge could be useful in this exercise, and Table I.18.1 is neither short nor deficient.

Table I.18.1 Critical Skill and Knowledge Profile for Organization
Development Practitioners *

Consulting Skills [†]

Entry and Contracting
Identify clients' expectations.
Say "no" to projects.
Build and maintain collaborative
relationships.
Communicate appropriate
qualifications and capabilities.
Discover clients' receptiveness to
change.
Respond to clients' concerns non-
defensively.
Confront clients on dysfunctional
behavior.
Quickly assimilate the unique
characteristics of client systems.
Clarify role in initial meeting.
Clarify expectations.
Identify clients' underlying
concern(s).

Data Collection and Diagnosis
Use appropriate processes to collect
data:
—questionnaire;
—interview design and use;
—direct observation;
—secondary information; and
—document analysis.
Plan data collection jointly with
client.
Clarify boundaries of confidentiality.
Facilitate openness.
Research root causes.
Nonjudgmentally document what
exists.
Probe issues as they surface.
Use computer, if appropriate.
Synthesize data into themes and
condense.
Involve those interviewed in the
interpretation.
Discover missing data.
Probe and explore hidden causes.
Encourage and build ownership of
data.

Identify underlying problems.
Identify clients' personal role in
problem.
Identify role of others in causing
problem.
Break problem down into smaller
parts.
Interpret data in a way that is useful
for the client.
Invite participation.
Confine to valid, pertinent, and
appropriate information.
Convey information clearly.
Protect confidentiality.

Intervention Design
Communicate intervention design
process to client and group.
Design is time-efficient and cost-
effective.
Design fits client systems' parameters.
Involve client system and stake-
holder in design.
Create appropriate organizational
links.
Develop a written plan that is logical
and simple.
Build the plan so buy-in exists at all
levels.

Intervention Implementation
Identify barriers and degree of
change readiness.
Predetermine the impact of changing
one part of the system on the
whole system.
Link ongoing change process to
structure and operations.
Maintain change momentum.
Give management responsibility by
working with their ideas.
Bring management and employees
together to discuss the intervention
and consultation.
Interview and question key people to
bring them together and identify
goals.

Table I.18.1   Critical Skills and Knowledge Profile
(continued)

Intervention Implementation *(cont.)*
Model desired behaviors for the client.
Bring top-level management together to collaborate in the intervention.
Regularly give and get feedback.
Adjust the pace of the presentation to fit the audience.
Use simple models to make complex issues appear simple.
Present information in sequential steps.
Change the model and approach to help facilitate the intervention.
Change the structure of interventions on the spot to meet the needs of the client.

Feedback
Confront client with all relevant data.
Give descriptive feedback.
Give feedback to client on personal behavior.
Do not take criticism personally.
Structure and control the feedback meeting to elicit client reaction and choice of next step.

Intervention Evaluation
Recognize progress, reinforce positive change, and correct negative change.
Establish a feedback system to continuously monitor the change effort.
Initiate feedback on the client-consultant relationship.
Choose the appropriate evaluation method.
Secure close of current project before going on to the next cycle.

Project Termination
Recognize when separation is needed.
Provide feedback on process to date.
Transfer process to client.
Facilitate the separation process.
Give feedback to client on

management of project.
Ask for feedback from client.
Contract with client about future involvement.

Maintaining Client Relationships
Confront the organization to bring out major issues.
Contact the client regularly to discuss issues.
Maintain close contact with management throughout contract.

Interpersonal Skills ‡
Active listening
Giving and receiving feedback
Rapport building and maintenance
Behavior flexibility
Assertive communication
Supporting
Conflict management
Establishing trust
Interruption avoidance
Political influence skills

Organization Development Knowledge and Intervention Skills †
Marginality skills
Effective use of appropriate consultative style
Process consultation
Team building
Organization development
Job and work design
Group diagnosis

Organization Development Knowledge Theory †
Whole systems change theory
Change management theory
Diagnosis theory

Presentation Skills ‡
Training and education skills
Public speaking

(continued)

Table I.18.1 Critical Skills and Knowledge Profile
(*continued*)

Specific Skills [‡]	**Managing Information and**
Facilitation	**Records** [‡]
Problem solving	Gathering, analyzing, organizing,
Project management	and reporting data
Conflict resolution	Disseminating information
Meeting leadership	Keeping records
Coaching	

Communications—Written [‡]
Writing correspondence, memos,
reports, or proposals

[*]From L. M. Dyer (1995). *Developing internal organization development consultants.* Master's thesis, Pepperdine University, Culver City, CA. Note that this table omits five clusters of skills with relevance to a specific employer.

[†]Primary skills and knowledge group.

[‡]Secondary skill group. Five other secondary skill and knowledge groups are omitted from this table.

INSTRUCTIONS AND QUESTIONS

1. Complete the form according to how you see yourself. For convenience, use the following five-point scale to rate your skills on each item.
   (Notice that you can rate a skill/knowledge item as "NR," for "Not Ratable," if you cannot make a judgment.)

NR	1	2	3	4	5
	Definitely Need Much More Work in this Skill/ Knowledge		Adequate in this Skill/ Knowledge		Superior in this Skill/ Knowledge

2. Arrange for a full set of ratings by one or more others who know you well enough to have an opinion about most items.
3. Meet with the other rater(s) to compare the sets of responses.

Reference

Dyer, L. M. (1995). *Developing internal organization development consultants.* Master's thesis, Pepperdine University, Culver City, CA.

I.19

Western Transducer Corporation*

Walter L. Ross

PART 1: BACKGROUND

Western Transducer Corporation (WTC) is a moderate-sized electronics firm ($20 million annual sales) specializing in transducers. Until recently, it had a virtual monopoly in its field. Established in 1965, WTC quickly developed a reputation for innovation, quality, and the ability to deliver on schedule. This reputation and an aggressive sales force resulted in rapid growth and expansion. This growth, in turn, created many opportunities for advancement, and the company shared the wealth with the employees through wages and benefits that were at the top of the industry. In the early years of the company's existence, few problems existed because of high morale, collegial relationships, and a "family" atmosphere that prevailed throughout the company.

As the company grew, departments became more highly defined and interdepartmental conflicts increased. New employees did not have the benefit of knowing what the company had been like when it had a "family" atmosphere. Consequently, they were much more prone to be critical of other departments. Because of the rapid growth, most supervisors received "battlefield commissions" in which they were promoted without the benefit of supervisory training. Many lacked the experience to be a supervisor, but were promoted on the basis of their potential because of the urgent company need and a commitment to promote from within. Increasing sales, labor shortages, and difficulty procuring materials contributed to increasing stresses within

*From the files of the Master of Science in OD Program, Pepperdine University. Minor editorial changes have been made. Published with the permission of the author.

WTC. In spite of these increasing pressures, WTC remained highly profitable, was seen as a "star" in the field, and generally was considered by employees to be a good place to work.

Organization

WTC is a subsidiary of a large multinational firm headquartered in the eastern United States. The president of WTC reports to a corporate group executive who is responsible for all the electronics companies owned by the parent corporation. Organizationally, the general manager of WTC reports directly to the president and is the chief operating officer. Four directors—the director of finance and administration, director of marketing, director of engineering, and director of operations—report to the general manager.

Frank McGuire, the corporate group executive, previously served as president of WTC. Six months ago he was promoted to corporate vice president of the electronics group. Prior to becoming president of WTC, he was director of marketing for the firm.

John Stevens currently is serving as president and general manager of WTC. Prior to Frank McGuire's promotion, he served as general manager and director of marketing. John is an engineer by training but has spent most of his career in marketing. He has been with WTC for 10 years.

Bob Thompson is director of marketing. He has held that position since John Stevens was promoted six months ago. Previously he held the position of marketing manager of WTC. Bob has been with WTC for six years. As director of marketing, Bob is responsible for marketing, sales, order processing, shipping, customer service, and pricing and estimating.

George Anderson has been serving as director of operations for six months. The person he replaced had been in that position since the founding of the company. George is a CMA and has just completed his MBA degree. He has been with WTC for six years, previously serving as controller and then as director of finance. When the decision was made to terminate the previous director of operations, George asked for the opportunity to move into operations. As director of operations, George is responsible for manufacturing, quality control, manufacturing engineering, production and material control, facilities maintenance, purchasing, personnel, and accounting.

Norm Smith has served as director of engineering since the formation of the firm. He is responsible for design, research and development, documentation, testing, and product repair.

Mark Jones is relatively new at WTC. He was hired to replace George Anderson as director of finance and administration when George became director of operations. Mark is responsible for finance, facilities management, and cost accounting. George Anderson still has general accounting reporting to him and is responsible for facilities maintenance.

Current Situation

WTC employs 2,500 people in three divisions. Competition has increased dramatically. New, small, aggressive companies are able to produce superior products at lower prices. WTC quality has deteriorated severely, and they seldom deliver orders on time. In fact, it is common for orders to be delivered three to twelve months late. Profits are becoming marginal and finished goods inventory is growing at a rapid pace. Morale is at an all-time low. Turnover is becoming a serious problem because of the labor shortage in the electronics field.

WTC officials realize that the firm has outgrown its systems. It is virtually impossible to accomplish anything on a timely basis. There is a great deal of in-fighting between departments. Communications are strained and ineffective. Managers use power and coercion in place of reason and persuasion. Long hours, a lot of unnecessary overtime, and devastating stress have replaced the formerly relaxed, confident, collegial atmosphere at WTC. It no longer is considered a great place to work.

About 18 months ago, Frank McGuire hired a management consultant to address the problems the firm was having with product quality, missed delivery dates, turnover, and interdepartmental fighting. The consultant, who described himself as a "behavioral scientist," consulted with the company for about nine months. During that period he conducted a company-wide survey and prepared several instrumented interdepartmental team-building learning designs based on the FIRO-B and LIFO instruments. Frank McGuire and George Anderson feel that the sessions were useful and badly needed.

Norm Smith and Bob Thompson privately objected strongly to the interventions and participated reluctantly. John Stevens felt very uncomfortable with the process but supported Frank McGuire. When John became president, he discontinued the interventions.

At the urging of George Anderson, John has agreed to consider bringing in a different consultant. Bob and Norm have objected strongly to the suggestion. Frank McGuire is urging John to get some help.

INSTRUCTIONS AND QUESTIONS: PART 1

You have been invited to meet with the executive group to discuss the possibility of an OD intervention in WTC. One hour has been scheduled for the meeting. George Anderson has provided you with the information contained in Part 1. You are instructed by George Anderson to create the agenda for the meeting and cautioned that you should be well prepared, with a specific proposed plan of action.

Respond to Anderson's instructions.

PART 2

The meeting is attended by John Stevens, George Anderson, Bob Thompson, and Norm Smith. Mark Jones does not attend.

Per your plan, you introduce yourself and describe your work experience and consulting qualifications, and then you present the "OD Cycle" as the process you would use with WTC.

For present purposes, the "OD Cycle" can be taken to be the conventional "action research" model sketched in the introductory materials elaborated in Perspective III of this text.

Beyond this introduction, you intend to discuss in detail the types of interventions you have used with other companies, explaining that the particular intervention activities selected would depend on the outcome of the diagnostic phase.

As you are presenting your background, Thompson interrupts you to inquire about your managerial experience and to ask which firms similar to WTC have hired you in the past. John Stevens asks for the names of references from your other clients. You respond to these interruptions and begin to explain your general approach to consulting.

Before you are able to elaborate on the "OD Cycle" model, the tensions in the group reveal themselves. Thompson states that the company already knows what its problems are and that people are too busy to take the time to participate in another diagnostic study. He thinks it would be a waste of time and money. Smith, who has been very quiet up to this point, agrees. Stevens asks you how long it would take to do a diagnostic study, specifically who would be involved, how much of their time it would take, and how much it would cost. You attempt to field these questions as best you can and return to your presentation. Anderson's attempts to be supportive are met with comments from Thompson that he doesn't think that this is a very good time to be taking people away from their jobs for this kind of program. Smith, who has continued to be quiet and sullen-looking, supports Thompson.

At this point, the meeting is 30 minutes old. Stevens announces that he has another meeting that he and Thompson must attend. He asks you if you would be willing to do a project on a contingency basis where your fee would be based on the increased profitability of the firm. As you are attempting to respond, he turns the meeting over to Anderson, apologizes for having to leave, and exits with Bob Thompson. Norm Smith also excuses himself, leaving you and George Anderson alone in the conference room.

At this point, George Anderson comments that he thought you handled yourself well, that the meeting was successful, and that he thinks that John Stevens was impressed by you. Anderson further states that you shouldn't be too concerned about Thompson and Smith because Stevens needs to start an OD project to satisfy McGuire, and besides it should be clear to you now how badly WTC needs it. Anderson offers to take you on a tour of the facility and suggests that you prepare a written proposal directed at John Stevens to conduct a diagnostic study of WTC. He volunteers to help you write and present the proposal to Stevens.

INSTRUCTIONS AND QUESTIONS: PART 2

Develop your proposal, after you decide what to do about Anderson's offer.

PART 3

Your proposal to conduct a diagnostic survey is accepted by John Stevens, and it relies on data collected through interviews with all managers and supervisors. This includes 12 managers (including the executive group) and 26 supervisors. Your survey produces the following major conclusions:

1. There are significant relationship problems between marketing and engineering, marketing and manufacturing, marketing and production control, engineering and manufacturing, manufacturing and production control, manufacturing and quality control, manufacturing and purchasing, and manufacturing and shipping.

2. Most managers and supervisors have been promoted without the benefit of formal management or supervisory training. Most supervisors did not have previous supervisory experience. Most managers were promoted in spite of the fact that they were not particularly effective as supervisors. Promotions have been based on need, and qualified personnel have not been available.

3. WTC has adopted a new policy of hiring managers and supervisors from large firms with significant management experience. This has created several problems. People within WTC who have supervisory or management aspirations feel that they will no longer have an opportunity to be promoted. The newly appointed managers and supervisors seem to have an air of superiority and treat the long-tenured employees as if they are "hicks."

4. The existing data processing systems are inadequate. Since the various automated systems cannot be integrated, it is necessary to manually integrate data from different departments. Not only does this create errors, but information is not available when it is urgently needed to make decisions. "Patch jobs" to update the systems have made them difficult to use. Very few people know how to use them.

5. Finished goods inventory continues to increase. The number of custom-built products also continues to increase. The company has been forced to hold special sales at a loss to reduce inventory of standard products. Of the 2,000 products WTC produces, more than half are special orders.

6. Manufacturing documents produced by engineering are seriously out of date. Manufacturing specifications often are different from quality control specs. Thus, manufacturing and quality control personnel frequently fight over whether products should pass inspection.

7. Cost and delivery estimates initiated by marketing for potential orders typically take 90 days to serially circulate from marketing to engineering to material control to purchasing to production control to manufacturing engineering to manufacturing to inspection to shipping and back to marketing. The personnel in these departments who are responsible for providing cost and delivery information feel that they are too busy trying to meet their primary

objectives to give a timely response. If they did so regularly, they would spend all of their time on that. Since marketing has to be responsive to potential customers, they quote price and delivery dates on the basis of historical data. Most orders have a 90-day delivery requirement.

8. With the volume of custom orders, it is taking about 90 days for engineering to begin work on a new order. Purchasing cannot order materials until the engineering order is released. There is a 30- to 90-day delivery period for most materials used in WTC products. Thus, the order usually is at least 30 days late before it even reaches production.

9. Each new order is scheduled into the production and inspection plan based on data provided by marketing. When the materials and engineering orders are not available as called for in the plan, the schedule has to be revised. This requires coordination with the engineering, purchasing, and marketing departments to revise the delivery schedule. Pressure frequently is applied in an attempt to speed up the process. Marketing pressures production control, and production control in turn pressures engineering or purchasing.

10. The quality and deliverability of material purchased from vendors has deteriorated significantly. With the pressures to meet production schedules, this has become a major problem. If materials from vendors do not pass receiving inspection, there is an additional delay of up to 30 days until replacement parts can be delivered. Purchasing has been criticized for not being aggressive enough in requiring vendors to meet their demands and in finding new vendors. Purchasing maintains that it is better to stick with vendors you know than to take a risk on new ones. Most of the vendors used by WTC have serviced the company for years. Most are small and are not equipped to handle the volume now required by WTC. Purchasing also points out that most of the problems are with special-order components.

11. The major material problem for WTC has been with crystals. Since they were unable to find a satisfactory crystal vendor they decided to produce their own. They still are having serious problems with crystal quality.

12. Marketing regularly applies pressure on operations to try to satisfy customer needs. WTC is developing a reputation of "baiting" customers by quoting unrealistic delivery days and delivering products anywhere from six to twelve months late. Marketing tries to persuade operations to change the production schedule to produce some orders ahead of others and to use material specified for certain

orders on different orders that they think are more critical. Operations resists doing so because it would significantly impact productivity and increase the likelihood of quality problems. When persuasion fails, Bob Thompson attempts to coerce George Anderson. When that fails, Bob brings in John Stevens to "explain the facts of life" to George Anderson. Because of this, personnel in the operations division perceive WTC to be "marketing driven." There is a great deal of animosity between operations and marketing and lack of respect for John Stevens within the operations division.

13. John Stevens currently is acting as general manager as well as serving as president, even though his schedule does not permit him to take an active role as a general manager. As a consequence, the individual divisions operate autonomously. John has indicated that he will select one of his division managers to become general manager within the next six to twelve months based on his perception of who has performed best. The definition of "best" that appears to have been perceived is who has best achieved his division objectives. This has resulted in functional parochialism, which has been very detrimental to interdepartment cooperation and collaboration. Strong competitiveness and resentment have developed between Thompson, Anderson, and Smith. Finger-pointing is commonly used to blame failures on the other divisions, and accusations have been made that other divisions have sabotaged operations to make them look bad. Anderson keeps a lot of pressure on his staff to meet their objectives. There is an escalating problem of in-fighting and finger-pointing within operations.

14. One aspect of departmental parochialism is that departments view each other with suspicion and describe the managers and supervisors in other departments as unqualified.

15. It is unclear why personnel, general accounting, and facilities maintenance report to John Anderson, as Mark Jones is the director of finance and administration. Some people think that quality control should not report to the director of operations.

16. Turnover in skilled positions is high, and there is a tight labor market.

17. Wages and benefits are above the median for the area.

18. WTC uses an MBO system that is based on monthly, quarterly, and annual objectives. The two primary measurements are dollars of products shipped and cost of sales. Other factors are sales bookings, finished goods and material inventory, and labor efficiency. John Anderson is evaluated on dollars transferred to finished goods inventory, percent of orders delivered on schedule, and labor efficiency. Bob Thompson is evaluated on sales bookings. It is

unclear how Norm Smith is evaluated. Mark Jones is evaluated on profitability, and John Stevens is evaluated on sales and profitability. Yearly bonuses based on personal objectives can be as large as 50 percent of an executive's annual salary. The engineering, marketing, manufacturing, quality control, production and material control, and manufacturing engineering managers also are included in the bonus program with a potential to receive as much as 25 percent of their annual salary in bonuses.

19. The monthly reporting system creates a cyclical phenomenon in which the pressure for production increases as the month progresses. Operations tries to finish as many orders as possible to pad its numbers. Consequently, the first two weeks of each month are spent building sub-assemblies. Operations does not receive credit for dollars produced until products are shipped, and marketing is evaluated on finished goods inventory. Thus, both divisions have an incentive to ship products by the midnight deadline each month. This usually means a lot of overtime in the last two weeks of each month with manufacturing, inspection, and shipping working around the clock for the last two days of each month to ship products by the month-end deadline. The cycle is repeated each month.

20. Since operations is measured by dollars shipped, there is an incentive to build "big-ticket" items as well as standard products that are easy to build and can be inventoried. There also is a disincentive to cooperate with marketing when they want to alter the schedule. Marketing has an incentive to keep the inventory of finished goods low and thus tries to control the volume of standard products produced. Operations argues that producing standard products is an efficient way to fill in the production schedule when there are engineering or material delays on special orders. Marketing tends to push special products because they are easier to sell.

21. George Anderson recently hired three very strong managers to clean up his operation and "do battle" with marketing and engineering. All three have significant experience with large electronics manufacturing firms. The quality control manager has taken a very firm but objective approach to managing his department. He has earned the respect of his own staff and of people in other departments and has made some significant improvements. He has found it necessary to replace several of his supervisors. The material control department was merged with the production control department to create the position of manager of material and production. The person hired to fill this position came to WTC with the reputation of being bright, outstanding in the areas of systems develop-

ment and management, extremely demanding, blunt, and nearly impossible to work with. He has fired several people. Others have quit. Those who remain, as well as people in other departments, are extremely intimidated by him. He has declared war on anyone who stands in his way. The marketing supervisor who is required to interface with him on production scheduling is so intimidated that she is barely able to function and is developing psychosomatic symptoms of stress. The new manufacturing manager is very nearly as strong as the new material and production control manager, but he uses his power in a much more political way. Performance has improved considerably under these new managers, but tension, open hostility, and turnover also have increased significantly.

22. Product quality is at an all-time low. Scrap and re-work is becoming costly. WTC management is becoming increasingly concerned about rising production costs caused by quality problems and overtime costs. Marketing is becoming concerned about WTC's declining image with regard to quality and deliverability.

23. Most WTC managers complain of a lack of leadership at the top and feel that a general manager should be appointed as soon as possible.

INSTRUCTIONS AND QUESTIONS: PART 3

Assume you are John Stevens.

1. What do you do about these findings?
2. What's your first step?

PART 4

After reviewing the findings, John Stevens decides to go ahead with an OD project. A series of meetings of the executive group facilitated by you produces the following objectives:

1. Improve the percent of the manufacturing schedule built and shipped on time each month.
2. Improve product quality.
3. Increase production volume.
4. Improve the labor efficiency ratio (labor cost/dollars transferred).

5. Reduce finished goods inventory (dollars).
6. Reduce overtime—especially unscheduled overtime.
7. Reduce turnover.
8. Reduce the number of changes in the production schedule.
9. Improve vendor quality and deliverability.
10. Improve supervisory and management skills.
11. Improve departmental and interdepartmental working relationships.
12. Improve morale.

INSTRUCTIONS AND QUESTIONS: PART 4

You are the OD consultant. Recommend a plan of action to achieve the listed objectives.

Among other considerations, be sure to take into account the stages of organizational growth reflected in this case. Perhaps the most well-known set of phases or stages can be found in these sources:

*   Chandler's (1962) effort to categorize the evolution of several specific American businesses.
*   Greiner's (1972) simple but useful generic model.

References

Chandler, A. D., Jr. (1962). *Strategy and structure*. Cambridge, MA: MIT Press.
Greiner, L. (1972). Evolution and revolution as organizations grow. *Harvard Business Review*, 4(4): 37–46.

PERSPECTIVE II

ODers in Unusual and Even Exotic Settings

II.1

When the Client Dies: Reflecting on the Personal and Professional Ramifications of a Sudden Tragedy

Anthony F. Buono

INTRODUCTION

As a management consultant for the past 19 years, I have prided myself on being prepared for virtually any contingency. While I like to think that I have enjoyed many successful experiences and interventions as a consultant, I also realize that I have been involved—and have learned from—a number of less than successful projects. In some of these latter instances, I comforted myself with the rationalization that contributing events were simply beyond my control; in others, however, I am certain that a more experienced consultant (and, with the advantage of hindsight, I) might have approached the situation in decidedly different ways.

Developing the ability to deal with problems and unanticipated events may be thought of as part of the seasoning process in becoming a well-rounded consultant. As I reflect on my experiences, it is clear that one of the true challenges of consultation is preparing oneself to deal with the unknown: moving from not knowing what we don't know, to the realization that there is so much that we do not—*cannot* initially—know about a client or a situation that we must constantly re-envision our role and react to the inevitable discrepancies between our envisioned role and what is actually happening around us. Indeed, I must admit that one of the things I enjoy about management consulting is that, in literally every project, I learn something new—a new way to frame or conceptualize a situation, a different technique or a novel way to use an old one, a different way to handle a particular set of dynamics, and/or, perhaps most importantly, something about myself.

A recent event created such a unique learning experience, literally placing me in a personal and professional quandary. As I was completing the first phase of a merger integration consulting project, the client I was working with, a senior vice president of one of the merger partners, died suddenly at a corporate board meeting. From a contractual vantage-point, I had essentially completed our agreed-upon agenda. The only "unfinished" business was a joint discussion of my observations of a staff meeting and their reactions to the latest dynamics surrounding the merger. While I had submitted a written copy of my observation to the client, we postponed our usual debriefing meeting due to time constraints and the travel associated with the board meeting.

Professionally, I felt that it was important to share this information with the organization and not simply let it "die" with the client. Yet, since some of this information was sensitive and, especially if taken out of context, could be construed to be highly critical of some of the individuals on the staff, I was very concerned about whom to share it with. Personally, I was experiencing considerable discomfort in dealing with the death of my client. In addition to my own feelings of grief and loss, I struggled thinking about how I might proceed. It would have been far easier to assume an avoidance posture—waiting for them to contact me, when and *if* they did—rather than take a more proactive role. Yet, if I wanted to assert myself, what would be a reasonable "waiting period"? Since my relationship was stronger with the client than it was with that person's staff, peers, or the chief executive officer (to complicate matters, an *interim* CEO), with whom should I deal? Should I focus on all three groups (staff, peers, interim CEO)? Should I leave it to the organization? Once I began to assess the situation, such questions seemed to multiply exponentially.

This paper is written from a very personal perspective. The process of writing it has also had a profoundly introspective as well as cathartic effect. I started and stopped working on the manuscript several times, going from the feeling that the whole idea was too private, probably idiosyncratic and potentially self-serving, through some gallows humor (e.g., "too bad last year's conference theme 'Learning from Unusual Events' wasn't *this* year's focus"), to a commitment to getting my thoughts on paper.

THE SCENARIO

During spring 1996, I was contacted by Sara Cooke,[1] the senior vice president for administrative services for Interactive Computing Institute (ICI), a computer-based, open-platform-oriented research organization. ICI was involved in a friendly merger with Open Forum (OF), a European-based organization with a similar mission. According to Sara, the merger between ICI and OF, which had formally taken place three months earlier, was proceeding much more slowly than planned: internal resistance to the combination was high at both companies, no clear direction was coming from the top, and, as a result, no one was taking charge of the post-merger integration process. Although the combined entity assumed the new name Open Computers (OC), members of both merger partners still strongly identified with and referred to their prior affiliations.

For the next several months, I worked closely with Sara, her immediate staff, and ICI and OF's combined executive team to enhance their understanding of merger-related dynamics and post-merger integration processes. Following some early merger dynamics workshops, my function at OC was to "listen deeply," comparing members' perceptions with other perceptions, organizational realities, and "official" positions, helping these individuals to listen to each other with greater attentiveness, compassion, and understanding, and facilitating the problem-solving and decision-making activities that were within their sphere of influence.[2]

THE SHOCK

While I was sitting at my desk one afternoon grading papers that I had promised my class I would return the next day, the phone rang. It was Debbie Morgan, Sara's administrative assistant. I was pleased to hear from her. My immediate reaction was that Sara had returned from the board meeting and Debbie was calling to set up a meeting time. As I reached for my appointment book, Debbie literally broke into tears over the phone, saying, "Sara's dead. She was delivering an update on the merger at the board meeting when she slumped over the podium. They tried to revive her, but it was a massive coronary. Within a few minutes

---

[1]All names and organizational identities used in this case are pseudonyms.

[2]The process of "listening deeply" to one's clients, helping them focus on those aspects of organizational life in which they can exert some influence, was shaped by Buono and Nurick (1992) and Stein (1994).

she was dead. Everyone was stunned." As was I. As I sat at my desk, a state of disbelief quickly enveloped me as Debbie continued, "I wanted you to know as soon as possible. I didn't want you to call the office and find out that way."

I was silent. After a lengthy pause, I recall (with the advantage of considerable reflection and hindsight) stammering a disjointed series of questions something along the lines that Kübler-Ross (1969) would have predicted. "I just spoke with her two weeks ago. I don't believe it. We were going to meet next week when she returned from the meeting." (*Denial*) "How the hell can someone like Sara die like that? Things were beginning to really come together [in the merger]. It's not fair. She has a son my son's age." (*Anger*) "Did she have health problems before? I never saw any difficulties. Did she have any preexisting condition [beginning to think of my own family history of high cholesterol and my last physical examination]?" (A type of *bargaining*) "What is the reaction at OC? How are [staff members] handling it? Something like this really puts things in perspective. So much of what seemed important to fight for [in the merger] seems rather trivial right now." (*Depression*) "What are the funeral arrangements? Is OC planning on doing anything?" (*Acceptance*)

After I thanked Debbie for relaying the news, and, after exchanging a few pleasantries, we hung up. I stared into space for several minutes and slowly began to collect my thoughts. Thinking about the merger sensitization workshops I had conducted for OC, I found it ironic that the human toll I warned was associated with mergers—the anxiety, stress and strain, and related psychosomatic problems and health risks— would hit so close to home.

CONSULTING ROLES AND UNDERLYING DYNAMICS

This incident prompted considerable reflection about my role as a change-oriented management consultant. In reflecting on the various consulting roles I have played, I see myself as a temporary (short-term) rather than day-to-day "regular" member of the group.[3] As such, I am an outsider, a "stranger" (Stonequist, 1937) who might be thought of as a regular guest in an organization for a given period of time. During this period, I attempt to learn about the organization's cultural system,

---

[3]This conceptualization of the consultant's role was stimulated by a thoughtful discussion in Stein (1994:6–7).

emotionally encompassing as much as possible in order to help describe and interpret it to its members to facilitate their own understanding and knowledge about the breadth and depth of their own culture and its ramifications for the changes they are envisioning. While the "outsider" status lends itself to a level of objectivity often not available to full-time members (Park, 1928), in retrospect I typically try to obtain sufficient "insider" status to gain credibility without compromising my external position.

In this type of role, consultants are ascribed little, if any, formal authority. Rather, we tend to acquire status more informally, through our ability to network, mediate, and, in general, interact with people in the organization. The role of consultant as change agent may be understood as that of a temporary "attachment figure," helping organizational members to develop a sufficient sense of security that they are able to explore new ways of relating and working (Kahn, 1995). The behaviors that enable one to do this—communicating empathy, respect, warmth, and regard, and helping others to cope with uncertainty by giving encouragement and comfort as well as practical assistance and appropriate information (Buono and Nurick, 1992; Heard, 1982)—are precisely the type of interactions that develop personal relationships and commitments.

Working with Sara and OC over a six-month period, I had developed a personal commitment to the merger as well as to Sara and her direct reports. While there were obvious differences between us (white male and African American female), we were both in our late 40s and married, with 13-year-old sons. I recall one afternoon when Sara took a break from a discussion we were having—a debriefing of an extensive planning meeting held earlier that day with her group—to call home to check on her son. I found it difficult to suppress a smile as I heard her trying to convince her son of the importance of finishing his homework and household chores before departing for a friend's house. "Sara," I said laughingly after she had finished her phone call, "I just had the same conversation with my son yesterday." We joked for a while about the trials of raising teenagers in the 1990s and then resumed our debriefing.

While this sort of little break from work may seem rather trivial, I have found over the years that this type of sharing supports a bond between a consultant and his or her client. By establishing a sense of the client (and, in turn, the consultant) as a person, this type of informal repartee not only creates a greater level of consultant-client understanding and comfort, but it also begins to develop a foundation for trust and influence. And, as I discovered in this situation, when such personal relationships do develop it is just as difficult to deal with the death of a client as it is with the death of a friend.

Mirvis (1996) differentiates between the "onstage" (i.e., open, public) and "backstage" (i.e., confidential, private) roles involved in working with clients during change efforts. As I reflected on these roles, I realized that much of my dilemma was captured by this distinction. As part of my "onstage" role, for example, I tried to place the stresses and tensions that people were experiencing in the broader context of merger-related dynamics, making interpretive comments as needed and pushing for an action agenda when necessary. This discourse was carried out in a public forum, whether in a staff meeting with Sara's direct reports or in an executive committee meeting with her peers.

My "backstage" role, however, was quite different. In fact, while there appeared to be some progress through my onstage efforts, the real change (and success) was gleaned through more private moments and conversations, where I played the role of Sara's "sounding board." In these situations, I engaged in the type of attachment-oriented behaviors noted above, urging and helping her to pay attention to verbal and behavioral cues from her staff and peers, to "listen" for the true reasons and rationale underlying resistance to merger-related changes, and, in general, to bring to life the plan of action she was formulating. The dilemma was squarely placed on my "backstage" role and efforts. The need to continue in my public, onstage role was minimal. Even if Sara had not died, we both felt that the early training and merger-sensitization work that we had done had run its course. It was my backstage role that Sara saw as being useful in the merger's latter stages—my working with her as she processed the type of sensitive information that I was now faced with possibly sharing with others at OC.

FORMULATING A COURSE OF ACTION

Not surprisingly, in light of my academic orientation, my first step was to search the literature. I could not find any discussion on this topic in past issues of *Consultation* or the *Journal of Management Consulting*. A wider search encompassing a host of consulting-related handbooks also failed to provide any guidance. Much of the advice that is available in this area is decidedly legalistic in nature. Using contractual terminology, for example, Hardwicke and Emerson (1992, p. 142) suggest that if performance becomes "impossible," a contract is "discharged by operation of law." Thus, in a personal services contract, they point out that the death or incapacitating illness of the *performer* would discharge the contract. Although "acts of God" (i.e., natural occurrences that render performance impossible, such as a flood) are also noted as reasons to discharge a contract, no guidance was provided for situations in which the client, rather than the "performer" (i.e., consultant), dies.

The literature on "organizational death" raised some interesting implications. As research has underscored, the same basic feelings (e.g., shock, disbelief, anger, bargaining, acceptance) and parting ceremonies (e.g., wakes, related rituals) that are found in individual death-related situations also accompany plant closings and acquisition-related terminations (Ginter, et al, 1991). Sutton (1987) has suggested a series of dilemmas that organizational members must work through if they are to effectively manage the demise of their organization: (1) *disbanding* versus *sustaining*; (2) *shielding* versus *informing*; (3) *blaming* versus *coping*; and (4) *delegating* versus *inventing*. While the human costs are obviously high in such situations, regardless of how well these dilemmas are managed, the key is to facilitate such basic functions as member motivation, information dissemination, impression management, and guilt assuagement. Within this context, the members of ICI (and, to a lesser extent, OF) could be said to be experiencing a "double-death" situation—the loss of an important organizational figure *and* the loss of the organization itself.

Overall, the literature provided little guidance as to how one might proceed in fulfilling personal commitments, even those that are not professionally necessary, when one's client dies. As noted earlier, while I had shared sensitive information with Sara just before her departure for the board meeting, we had not had an opportunity to discuss or act on it. Since this information raised some potential difficulties for an important set of upcoming merger integration decisions, I felt it was necessary to ensure that it was appropriately disseminated. Yet, while I knew which way Sara was leaning in her decision, since I did not know what her ultimate decision would be and did not want to be placed in a situation where I was potentially advocating a position that Sara would not have taken, I wanted to proceed with caution. Moreover, while I worked well with Sara's direct reports, my relations with some of her peers on the executive committee were far more tenuous. As Schein (1996) has noted, what you think you know about a client is, at best, a hypothesis that needs to be tested. This tenet especially applies to the client's colleagues, your view of whom is often influenced by discussions with your client. When that person is suddenly removed from the situation, your view of and relationship with these organizational others, as well as their view of you, are problematic at best.

My next step was to seek advice from friends and colleagues who engage in consulting activities. Once again, I was surprised that no one I spoke with had experienced or even known someone who had gone through a similar situation. Yet, since most of these individuals engage in the same type of process-oriented consulting as I do, they were clearly empathic, reflective listeners. The counsel I received from these individuals, as well as the sheer opportunity to simply discuss the situation with informed individuals, greatly facilitated my thinking. Drawing on a series of iterative discussions with an unsystematic, random sampling (i.e., whoever I happened to be talking to over a two-week period) of 12 of these individuals, I decided on a multi-phased course of action.

After a reasonable waiting period (approximately three weeks), I contacted one of Sara's direct reports, Curt Reynolds, OC's director of human resources (previously a member of ICI). At that time, I had not heard from anyone from OC since our early communication about her death. Curt and I had worked well together during my earlier onstage activities and he seemed like the best place to start. My initial goal was three-fold: (1) to see how Curt was *coping* with the situation; (2) to gauge his perception of the impact of Sara's loss on the rest of the group and organization; and (3) to test his feelings about getting Sara's group together for a final debriefing session. Based on an extension of Sutton's (1987) work, the focus of the meeting would be on *sustaining* the group as much as possible, keeping its members focused on the merger-related assignments that Sara had *delegated* at the last group meeting and encouraging them to *invent* novel approaches for dealing with the new realities of the merged organization. It was clear that Sara's sudden death was still having a profound impact on Curt and, through his expressed sentiments and descriptions, the rest of OC, and especially members of ICI. Our discussion about the group meeting and its agenda went well and, as we concluded our conversation, he noted that as soon as "things calmed down a bit" he would set up the meeting.

The second phase involved a similar meeting with Sara's peers, OC's combined executive group. I was especially curious as to how the group was proceeding without Sara, who her new replacement might be, and what role that individual would play. Other issues emerged from merger discussions, such as the extent to which certain individuals from OF might use her demise to serve their own agendas, prompting for a reorganization that would have been difficult, at best, if Sara were alive. While Curt agreed that a similar session with the OC executive group was a good idea, he felt that he did not have the authority to request such a session. Although he had been assigned to "sit in" with the group in Sara's place, it was clear that he felt the role was temporary. My approach, therefore, was to contact the interim CEO, discuss the situation with him, talk on a general level about the debriefing session with

Sara's group (being careful not to share any information that could be construed as being damaging to any of these individuals), and proceed from there.

The third phase was to meet with the new CEO. Since he was coming on board within the next couple of months, this would be a good opportunity to provide him with a context for the merger-related work I had been involved in as well as a greater sense of the changes that had been taking place in the organization. Throughout these interactions, one of my goals was to make it clear that I wasn't using this process to seek out additional consulting work and that there would not be a charge for any of the debriefing sessions noted above. If other opportunities did emerge from these interactions, I would, of course, be happy to stay on, but my intent was to finalize what I had done thus far and not to set the stage for future endeavors.

EPILOGUE

As difficult it was for me to deal with this tragedy, the situation was far more difficult for Sara's colleagues at OC, particularly those from ICI. She had been a highly respected and valued colleague, and, based on comments from the interim CEO, her peers, and subordinates, a source of reason and equilibrium during a time of merger-related chaos and instability and the "death" of ICI per se. To complicate matters, the sense of grief and loss associated with Sara's death was exacerbated by the voluntary termination of ICI's chief financial officer (CFO), who had left the organization just weeks before Sara's passing. His departure, in essence experienced by many of his colleagues as a symbolic death, further underscored the need for an organizational mourning period and accompanying interventions. As Zaleznick (1989) argues, however, organizations by their basic nature have a tendency to encourage rapid adaptation of their members, encouraging them to quickly abandon roles without disruption. As a result, a fear of loss and a built-in intolerance for mourning pervades organizational life (LaFarge and Nurick, 1993). A lot of *shielding* (Sutton, 1987) appeared to be taking place throughout OC.

As the consultant who was working with (perceived as "related to") the deceased executive, however, I began to realize that my presence served as an unpleasant reminder of the tragedy. In essence, there was an automatic recognition of Sara through me, a recognition that some people clearly preferred not to deal with. Thus, it may not be uncommon for those who were very supportive during the consultant's earlier efforts to suddenly attempt to avoid him or her. Curt, for example, delayed setting up the meeting as promised and took several days to return my phone calls. Within this context, it is important to understand the nature of projection, transference, and countertransference, as emotional legacies from the past spill over into the present, readily influencing the ways in which people respond to each other (Hoffer, 1955). Such emotional realities of group life are not extraneous to structure and action but rather take us to the heart of the human experience in groups (Stein, 1994).

To some extent, I think that I continued to process this experience until, as Stein (1994) has eloquently phrased it, my reasons and rationale caught up with my heart. In retrospect, I feel that, perhaps, I always knew what I wanted to do—felt I should do—yet had to struggle to articulate it sufficiently to bring it to the surface. As Diamond (1993) suggests, especially in interventions focused on change, process, and development, the ideal of reflective participation often manifests itself in highly emotional and personal experiences as we, as consultants, attempt to more fully understand the complexities, realities, and intersubjective meaning of organizational life. Coming to grips with Sara's death and my activities as her consultant has led me to reexamine my own values, goals, and the roles that I attempt to play.

INSTRUCTIONS AND QUESTIONS

This is a complex case, and it focuses on issues that get little attention. But as author Anthony F. Buono notes in the opening of this case, all ODers should take pride in being ready for whatever comes along.

In this sense, you may find it useful to address the following questions:

1. Have you had any experiences relevant to this case? How did Buono's past experience apply?
2. What did Buono see in the literature that provided help and guidance? Can you add to his inventory?
3. What in the change agent role is relevant to cases such as this one?

References

Buono, A. F., and Nurick, A. J. (1992). Intervening in the middle: Coping strategies in mergers and acquisitions. *Human Resource Planning,* 15(2): 19–33.
Diamond, M. A. (1993). *The unconscious life of organizations.* Greenwich, CT:

Greenwood Press.

Ginter, P. M., Duncan, W. J., Swayne, L. E., and Shelfer, Jr., A. G. (1991). When merger means death: Organizational euthanasia and strategic choice. *Organizational Dynamics, 20*(3): 21–33.

Hardwicke, J., and Emerson, R. (1992). *Business law*. New York: Barron's Educational Service.

Heard, D. (1982). Family systems and the attachment dynamic. *Journal of Family Therapy, 4*: 99–116.

Hoffer, E. (1955). *The passionate state of mind and other aphorisms*. New York: Harper.

Kahn, W. A. (1995). Organizational change and the provision of a secure base: Lessons from the field. *Human Relations, 48*(5): 489–514.

Kübler-Ross, E. (1969). *On death and dying*. New York: Macmillan.

LaFarge, V., and Nurick, A. J. (1993). Issues of separation and loss in the organizational exit. *Journal of Management Inquiry, 2*(4): 356–365.

Mirvis, P. H. (1996). Midlife as a consultant. In P. J. Frost and M. S. Taylor (Eds.), *Rhythms of academic life*, pp. 361–369. Thousand Oaks, CA: Sage.

Park, R. E. (1928). Human migration and the marginal man. *American Journal of Sociology, 33*: 881–893.

Schein, E. (1996). Managerial consulting: Who is our client? Who should be our client? Distinguished Speaker Presentation, Academy of Management, Cincinnati, Ohio, August.

Stein, H. F. (1994). *Listening deeply*. Boulder, CO: Westview Press.

Stonequist, E. V. (1937). *The marginal man*. New York: Russell and Russell.

Sutton, R. I. (1987). The process of organizational death: Disbanding and reconnecting. *Administrative Science Quarterly, 32*: 542–569.

Zaleznick, A. (1989). *The managerial mystique*. New York: Harper and Row.

II.2

Consulting at a Distance

Craig C. Lundberg

SOME ORIENTING ISSUES AND CONCERNS

Several years ago I had a consulting experience like none before or since. I have thought about it often, turning it over and over in my mind. My captivation with that experience, on the one hand, is easy for me to understand—it was unique in so many ways, and so different from my other consultancy experiences. My continued fascination, however, stems from the many questions it raises, from Was it OD? to How might I have behaved more effectively?

I confess to several beliefs that prompt this sharing. One is that we can learn more from unusual or extreme cases than from typical ones. A second belief is simply that we must describe and share our experiences carefully to learn from them. Lastly, if we share what's puzzling, bothering, or intriguing us, our OD colleagues will usually help us make sense of it.

While OD as more or less intentional change continues to evolve, both in theory and practice, most conventional thinking continues to elaborate or modify it as a multi-stage process reflecting Lewin's original model—unfreezing, change, refreezing. Kolb and Frohman's seven steps of planned change are typical: scouting, entry, diagnosis, planning, action, stabilization and evaluation, and termination.[1] Such simple, linear sequences are seldom followed, however, in actual practice. Experienced ODers know that such a sequence is occasionally, or even frequently, truncated, interrupted, delayed, or aborted. And they know that the sequence is subject to many distortions such as lack of goal and

[1]Perhaps the first overall planned change strategy was developed by Lippitt, Watson, and Westley in *The Dynamics of Planned Change* (New York: Harcourt, Brace, 1958). The best known sequence of stages, however, is probably that described by Kolb and Frohman (1970), in "An organization development approach to consulting," *Sloan Management Review,* 12(1): 51–65.

problem consensus and clarity, favorite or even pre-packaged intervention tech-
nologies, restricted diagnosis, client dependency, hidden agendas, and the like.
Whatever your current understanding of the OD process, the following case will
probably not fit it very well.

THE SIT CASE

It all began, as do so many engagements, with a telephone call. The
caller, Ed, identified himself as the full-time OD person with the South-
western Indian Tribe (SIT)[2] located two states away. Ed said he'd surveyed the OD literature and had come to believe that Dr. W, one of my
colleagues, had the values and experience that the SIT needed. Ed had
tried unsuccessfully to reach Dr. W and had called me in hopes that I
might set up a meeting.

Ed noted that he had been working with the executive branch of the
tribal government for nearly four years, that he was "probably in over
his head," and that he believed some external assistance was needed
for the tribe to go forward.

Ed also made it clear that the SIT was seeking free consulting. He
suggested that he and several others could come to my city to meet with
Dr. W and any others who might be interested in working with the SIT,
pro bono. We picked out a date a month away. I said I would try to get
Dr. W and several others from our academic organization together so we
could mutually explore the possibilities of helping SIT.

On the appointed day at 10:00 AM, Ed, who turned out to be an Anglo,
and three Indians in their thirties came to our conference room. There sat
Dr. W, Dr. M, and Dr. C—experts in OD and leadership, strategy, and
socio-technical systems, respectively—two advanced students (one
familiar with the SIT, the other an experienced management consultant),
and I. After introductions, the next two hours were devoted to questions by my colleagues and responses from our Indian guests. We
learned much of a general background nature: that SIT was little studied
by anthropologists and others; that SIT was quite poor as a tribe and
heavily dependent on the revenue of one mining firm beyond the usual
government support; that while the Indians present all held college
degrees from major universities, most of the tribal members had little
schooling; that the SIT culture and language were unique; that the tribe
had no experience with consultants; that SIT was really a set of about a
dozen villages on its own mesa distributed over a vast, high desert

[2]All names of persons and organizations have been disguised.

region; and that one neighboring tribe was perceived as increasingly encroaching on their lands.

During this questioning, Ed was largely silent except in response to questions about SIT culture, which were almost always referred to him.

As we reconvened after lunch, Dr. W pressed for what our guests wanted from us. The response focused on a general belief that the executive branch of the SIT was antiquated, highly bureaucratized, and badly needed redesigning to become more effective. No specifics were offered. The only stipulation was that since this visit was unauthorized, and since the tribal council would probably not approve of outsiders becoming involved, any future consultations would have to be free and take place at a distance from SIT.

As time was running out, everyone murmured agreement to meet again to pursue some sort of joint work. It was decided that Ed would call me again to set up another meeting, whenever the Indians could next visit.

Ed did call, nearly two months later. He and his colleagues would be visiting in two weeks' time. An afternoon meeting was agreed upon. I notified my colleagues. I then read two ethnographies about SIT.

When the SIT members appeared for the second meeting, I was joined only by the two doctoral students—my other colleagues gave one or another excuse for not attending. The meeting began with one of the students who had kept extensive notes recapping what we had learned about the SIT, its executive branch, and the consulting constraints. I chimed in with some points I had read about SIT in the ethnographies. To our surprise, the Indians—Sam, David, and Tom, SIT executive director, assistant director, and fiscal officer, respectively—gently "corrected" almost everything! They made it clear that no published materials accurately described the tribe—secrecy was a strong tribal value. They noted that, as Anglo-trained members, even they weren't privy to some inner tribal matters.

During the next several hours, we basically retraced the ground that had previously been explored, but two aspects of this meeting were different from the first one: we wrote almost everything on newsprint, and the Indians often disagreed among themselves. Ed, as before, was mostly silent.

By afternoon's end we had agreed on a couple of things to work on, voiced by Sam: to examine the functions and structure of the executive branch, with the idea of suggesting improvements. Moreover, we'd try to meet again in two months' time.

With that the Indians and Ed left, with the former going off to spend the coming weekend in the city. The students and I went to a local pub to debrief and, over a couple of beers, agreed that we were getting a much better feel for the Indians' situation, that the afternoon's conversation reflected a real openness to our assistance, and that none of us felt very sure of what might happen next.

Six weeks later, Ed called to suggest a half-day meeting in two weeks, again on a Friday. I agreed to his proposal. On the scheduled day, however, I alone greeted Ed and four Indians, two of whom I'd not met before. Sam and David were back, joined by Joe, the head of the police force, and by John, head of personnel.

In this, our third meeting, the pattern of future meetings—just with me—was established. Each meeting was attended by Sam and Ed and two to four of their associates—at least one always a new face—and we worked for about five hours. Typically, also, the meeting flow fell into sequence: we began with small talk; they informed me of current events on the reservation during which I probed modestly; they told me what parts of the actions we had talked about they had initiated, again with clarifying questions from me; and we focused on some issue or topic and jointly talked it through to some concrete suggested action, always recording the discussion on newsprint. Then, the Indians left to enjoy some event in the city, and Ed visited his mother in the suburbs.

The third and subsequent seven meetings were always held in a conference room near my office. They occurred irregularly, separated by from one to three months but always on a Friday. During the third meeting, two things happened that stand out in my memory. One was my compliment to Joe about his cowboy boots. I noted that they were obviously handmade and had stirrup marks. This prompted a conversation about horses and riding in which Joe and the others learned I was an ex-rodeo-hand as well as an experienced horseman. The other incident was when I noted to Joe and John that their departments paralleled two of the tribal clans in the old days, and this led to an examination of other parallels between the old Indian social structure and the modern form of their government. Both incidents, I now see, accorded me a degree of trust not present before.

In the third through tenth meetings, spanning nearly a year, we dealt with a series of topics. My notes show that we twice redesigned the formal structure of the executive branch; redefined the job descriptions of department heads; outlined a renegotiation with the mining firm in which the tribe increased its revenue; revamped the recruitment and selection process for executive branch managers; redesigned Sam's biweekly meetings with his department heads; practiced task analysis, role analysis, and team processing with whoever was present; and designed a joint meeting with the tribal council. By the sixth meeting onward, I found myself more and more cautioning them against adopting theoretical organizational and managerial solutions without careful adaptation to the SIT culture. To illustrate, I urged them to seek opportunities to learn about SIT ways: visiting kivas and village elders, dressing less "Anglo" during tribal ceremonies, and so on.

By the seventh meeting, Sam, David, Ed, and I agreed that a crucial relationship that needed work was the one between them as key members of the executive branch and the members of the tribal council. The council members were all elders, elected from the villages; and the council was the arena where major political and fiscal decisions were made. We strategized on how to get the council better informed on executive branch affairs and how to build better relationships with council members. Some of this was simply a matter of trading on old family ties, some on Sam and his associates playing down their Anglo education and experiences, and some emphasizing reappreciation of Indian traditional views regarding nature, family, community, and individual dignity.

Our ninth meeting was attended by Charlie, head of the tribal council, and by his assistant Bill. While Bill sat silently throughout this session, Charlie and I hit it off quickly and easily, the meeting concluding with a plan for a series of presentations by Sam and his departmental associates to the council. That memorable meeting ended with Charlie inviting me to visit the reservation "next time I was in the area." Ed also was invited to help redraft the tribal constitution.

As the months and meetings went by, I learned to be less and less surprised when my Indian friends reported that they had not fully implemented the plans of our last meeting. More and more I took their report on current events and whatever they had done as simply the starting point for that meeting's work. I had grown to like Sam and David and the others. Ed continued to call me to set up meetings, but basically only served as a resource person on the technical aspects of tribal government and on current political affairs. I saw my role as having become a meeting facilitator, a technical resource on management and organization, and a gentle brake on expectations. I frankly loved my ongoing education about the SIT.

The tenth meeting was devoted in its entirety to designing a long weekend in which Sam, the department heads, and the tribal council were going to go off on a large houseboat together to "get better acquainted and do some joint planning." We touched on everything, from how the cooking was to be shared, to an agenda-setting exercise, to how the piloting of the houseboat should reflect tribal status, to how to handle potential conflicts, to bait for fishing.

Sam led the discussion, and everyone contributed vigorously. As far as I could tell, consensus ruled the resulting designs. Ed was quiet, as usual, but his smiles gave away his positive feelings. The weekend we were planning so effectively had great potential for encouraging much other needed work. I recall telling my wife how great it had been, how helpful I had felt, how warm I felt toward my Indian "brothers."

Two weeks later, Sam called me to report that the weekend had indeed been a great success. His hopes for it had been more than satisfied. I would learn the details on their next visit.

The weeks passed. About two months after talking with Sam, I initiated a call to Ed, but got passed along until I had Sam on the line. Sam, clearly subdued, told me that Ed was no longer employed by SIT. According to Sam, Ed had an affair with the wife of a council member, it had been discovered, and Ed was dismissed. Sam was uncertain about what this meant for our work but said he'd get back to me before long.

That call never came.

CONCLUDING COMMENTS

This case of "consulting-at-a-distance" seems to break with much of what has become the conventional wisdom of OD consultancy. For example:

- *None of the consultants ever had any in situ knowledge of the client system.*
- *Clarification of who the client was never occurred.*
- *The generation of what Argyris terms "valid information" (i.e., explicit and verifiable) didn't seem to happen.*
- *Contracting between the client system and consultant(s) was vague at best.*
- *It is difficult to see that any planned change or action research sequence of steps was followed.*
- *Consultant and client roles changed and blurred, as did their relationships.*
- *No clear change strategy was apparent.*
- *Client motivation seemed to be highly variable as to type and strength.*
- *Diagnosis was both intermittent and partial.*
- *Consultant interventions often seemed to be entwined with other behaviors.*
- *Action that was planned was only partially enacted, and explicit assessment was nonexistent.*

Any reasonably experienced OD practitioner will no doubt be able to extend this listing. Most consultants will probably believe they would have behaved differently than I did at several points in the case; in fact, I would do some things differently now. Unusual and unorthodox as this consultancy was, I nevertheless believe that some real good did occur. OD consulting across both geographical and cultural distances is different and difficult, yet may be more and more needed.[3] Of course, what is mostly needed are appropriate models. Perhaps by pondering the SIT case we can all be better prepared.

INSTRUCTIONS AND QUESTIONS

1. How would you label the author's facilitation? Was it "shadow consultation" or something else?
2. What do you like most about what the author did?
3. What would you do differently from the author?
4. Did the author miss a valuable opportunity to develop systemwide credibility when he did not act on Charlie's invitation to visit the tribe? Should the author have raised the issue of payment for expenses?
5. Do you see any way to move beyond the last-reported condition—i.e., to reopen a dialogue with SIT?

---

[3] Cross-cultural consulting has acquired a long history and considerable literature. Interested readers should turn to the field of applied anthropology, especially the journal *Human Organization*.

II.3

A Cast-Iron Sponge of a Client*

An ODer was contemplating doing some work with a CEO, but worried that the man might prove to be a "cast-iron sponge." That is, the CEO reputedly heard almost all feedback and even encouraged it, but no real change seemed to result from the effort. Instead, the cast-iron sponge remained pretty much as it had been.

Interviews with the CEO's subordinates confirmed this view. Indeed, a picture emerged with almost total agreement about the CEO. His basic style suggested a preference for laissez-faire, but often featured a quick reliance on potent authoritarianism when things did not go well in his eyes.

In his own way, however, the potential client was very responsive to others. That is, the CEO periodically built up concern and even hostility in his subordinates, but his timing in scheduling "ventilation" sessions was pretty good. Subordinates saw these sessions as "kiss and make up." Then another iteration soon followed. The CEO would again drive the resulting "era of good feelings" into the ground just as if no "kissing and making up" had occurred.

The ODer shared these concerns with the CEO. "Now, that's the kind of openness I want," the CEO said. "If you can only get my colleagues to do half as well."

The ODer agreed to serve as the intervenor, but with a faint heart. A conventional design seemed appropriate, for openers. It would have two components: a confrontation phase between the CEO and the group of his subordinates; and a contracting period, when the CEO and subordinates would bargain about what one party wanted the other to *stop*, *start*, or *continue*. The ODer advertised his major and continuing interest in seeing that any contracts would be met.

* Adapted from Golembiewski, R. T. (1979), *Approaches to Planned Change, Part 2: Macro Interventions and Change-Agent Strategies*, pp. 382–383, New York: Marcel Dekker.

The CEO smiled benevolently. "Just what we need," he said, "agreements arrived at in public and in which we can all share—both in formulating and enforcing." He joined in enthusiastically, agreeing later to "start" a major policy in return for an agreement by his subordinates to "stop" something they were doing that displeased the CEO.

There were promises of greater things to come, and the CEO even contracted for 20 more days of the ODer's time over the next several months.

The experience and its follow-on proved a smashing success. So much so, in fact, that the CEO gave a dinner party for the OD intervenor, as well as for participants in the design. All spouses were invited. At the party, the ODer learned at the table that the CEO had changed his mind about the major policy he had agreed to "start." The change would be communicated to other participants at "some later date," the CEO announced when confronted.

Before it was possible to check out the news, the CEO asked the ODer to say a few words at the dinner about the further progress that the CEO and his team would be making with the ODer's help.

INSTRUCTIONS AND QUESTIONS

As the ODer, what would you say, briefly? Why?

For those interested in what the ODer actually did say, and why, as well as the CEO's response, see p. 383 of the source in the footnote on the first page of this case. (A hint: The ODer used only two words: the first was "I" and the second was "resign.")

II.4

A Second Kind of Crisis

You are an eager but relatively inexperienced ODer; and you have just read about a class of OD design that "floats your boat." It is labeled 3-D Image Sharing, and you can hardly wait to give it a try.

You found the description of the design during one of your infrequent trips to the library stacks, when *Approaches to Planned Change* seemed to stare out at you from the stacks. As fate would have it, the book popped open to page 140, and smack in the middle of the page were the standard questions for a 3-D design, which are adaptable either to individuals or groups. The author uses the generic term "Relevant Other" in formatting the questions:

- How do you see yourself in relation to the Relevant Other?
- How does the Relevant Other see you?
- How do you see the Relevant Other?

Quickly, you perceive that 3-D Image is a multi-purpose design, broadly applicable at various levels, in many settings, and relevant to a broad range of conditions. The book's author (Golembiewski, 1979, pp. 139–141) develops the following features of 3-D Image designs:

- They involve as participants either individuals in relationships or work teams in a common flow of work.
- They are intended to guide confrontations between individuals or groups who have real and unresolved issues with one another.
- They use the three questions above to engage processes of feedback and disclosure to help resolve such issues—e.g., to isolate how each party sees the other, to check on "consensual validation" as to whether both parties share perceptions and evaluations, and so on.
- 3-D Images are developed by each individual or group in a separate space, for later sharing of the full products to each participant, instantaneously, as it were.

- Typically, 3-D designs present opportunities for action-taking in a short time-frame.
- 3-D Images can be adapted to various decision-making and action formats, as in decisions about what to *stop, start,* or *continue.* Each participant can bargain with the other about items appearing on their two sets of 3-D Images. Thus, A may wish B to "stop" something on A's list, in return for "starting" some attitude or action that appears as a need on B's set.

Your attraction to the design is strong and remains so as you consult a research report on an application of the 3-D design. True to form, you skim that report—pretty tough going, but you get a general sense of it from Golembiewski's *Approaches to Planned Change,* Part 1, pp. 145–156.

In any case, you soon get your chance to try out the 3-D Image model—specifically, with two teams. One group is the Operating Committee, or Op Com, of a product line; and the second group comprises the subordinates of Op Com members.

The participants quickly get into the spirit of the design, but you are stunned by the results. Overall, both groups agree in their Images, but in ways that seem fruitless. For example, the subordinates see Op Com as a group of "sad sacks"; and the members of Op Com describe themselves in similar terms. Table II.4.1 reflects this dour agreement on one critical comparison of two 3-D questions. Other comparisons present much the same awkward picture, if with many variations.

INSTRUCTIONS AND QUESTIONS

Complete all cross-comparisons of the two partial 3-D Images in Table II.4.1.
    You are prepared for some blend of agreement and disagreement, and planned on using some of the latter to help reduce the former. The agreement is not only virtually total, but both sets of image-makers describe Op Com almost exclusively in negative terms.

1. Short run: the two groups of image-makers are sitting there, waiting for you to say something. What do you do, right then?
2. Longer-run: you chastise yourself for another example of skim-reading. Go back to the library, and check pp. 152–156 of *Approaches to Planned Change,* Part 1, to see if there was anything you missed on your earlier reading. Does your reading suggest any changes in your approach to OD?

Table II.4.1*

How Operating Committee Believes Subordinates See Operating Committee	How Subordinates See Operating Committee
Not communicative enough	Divergent and disunified
Floundering, indecisive	Lacking evidence of authority and decisiveness
Defensive, unreceptive	Spends too much time on non-key issues
Too involved in day-to-day operations and decisions	Poor catalyst
Overcautious	Does not communicate a sense of direction or purpose
Under tight corporate control, disadvantaged in competing for corporate resources	"Nice guys" (i.e., not very competent)
	Too much resistance rather than encouragement

* From Golembiewski, R. T. (1979). *Approaches to Planned Change, Part 2: Macro Interventions and Change-Agent Strategies*, p. 157. New York: Marcel Dekker. Reprinted with permission from the publisher.

Reference

Golembiewski, R. T. (1979). *Approaches to planned change*. Parts 1 and 2. New York: Marcel Dekker.

II.5

Is the Issue Confidentiality?
Or What?*

The atmosphere at the headquarters of Corporation Z was bullish, if hectic, and perhaps the dominant theme was that success had its mixed blessings. For example, the president bittersweetly discussed with an ODer and several others, with a boisterous joviality, the familial problems associated with his children (now nearing their majority) being owners of large blocks of shares he had earlier left in trust for them. Those shares were once worth pennies apiece, now each cost the better part of a $100 bill.

As part of his work, the ODer visited a firm, newly acquired by Corporation Z, whose members included the founding entrepreneur and many employees proud of their historic autonomy and substantial achievements.

In a private meeting with the head of the acquired firm, a major theme was the mixed fruits of success. The ODer briefly recounted the Corporation Z president's illustration of the familial paradoxes of corporate prosperity, among many other examples and much other talk.

A three-day meeting followed, one focus of which was a planned OD program for creating more open and trusting relations within the corporation. The ODer outlined an action plan and led what he took to be an almost unanimously enthusiastic discussion. The exception? The acquired firm's head was present but not enthusiastic.

Shortly after the meeting, the president of Corporation Z placed a conference call to the ODer, with his executive vice president on the

* An earlier version appeared in Golembiewski, R. T. (1979), *Approaches to Planned Change, Part 2: Macro Interventions and Change-Agent Strategies*, p. 459, New York: Marcel Dekker. Reprinted with permission of publisher.

line. The president recounted a conversation with the acquired firm's head in which the ODer's recounting of the discussion about familial problems was central. Expressing his strong opinion about a breach of confidence, the CEO of Corporation Z worried, "If that is what is meant by openness," to paraphrase the thrust of the comments by the head of the firm, "we don't need any more. Lord knows what other confidences the consultant would break."

The ODer admitted the illustration, stressed its very minor role in the discussion, and emphasized that he had not considered the illustration's content as confidential in the least. Supportively, the executive vice president reminded the corporate president that the latter had on several occasions himself used the illustration in public settings, in addition to the time the ODer heard the president's story.

More centrally, the ODer was puzzled by what the head of the newly acquired firm was after. Was his target the ODer? That seemed unlikely, even if possible. Was this a way of seeking some leverage in the post-acquisition fluidity? The ODer hoped not, because the potential leverage seemed slight, even if the basic issue had been credible.

The ODer preferred that he confront the firm's head about what he saw as a complex issue, preferably in the presence of the corporate president. The president did not consider the cost, effort, or risk worthwhile, given the delicacy of the early postacquisition days.

What was the next-best alternative? "Wall me off from the man," the ODer advised. He did not want to burden his consulting inputs with speculations as to the acquired firm's head's intent in raising the issue.

The ODer got his second-best choice, and expressed irony at this perhaps small matter in the context of developing an open and trusting system in Corporation Z. The essential meaning of the conversation was clear to the ODer: there would be no easy modeling of confronting behaviors in Corporation Z. The risks were very high.

INSTRUCTIONS AND QUESTIONS

1. Has the ODer missed something in this case?
2. What do you take to be the strategy of the head of the newly acquired firm?
3. Should the ODer have attempted to do something different from what is reported above?

II.6

It'll Only Be for a Short Time...

PART 1

OD consultants live and die with each client—sometimes a little, and sometimes a lot. Jan had suddenly become aware that the stakes in one consultancy had been both raised and changed.

"I'm nearly tapped out," she was told by Bill, an internal OD consultant of a multinational firm. "I need at least $5,000, or better still, $10,000, to get me over the hump. Can you loan it to me? It'll only be for a short time. Probably at bonus time, in about five or six months, I'll be able to pay it back, and maybe with a nice rate of interest!"

INSTRUCTIONS AND QUESTIONS: PART 1

Jan's mind is racing. What should she say to Bill?
   Some points seem clear enough:

1. Jan and Bill have been through a lot together over the past couple of years. So Bill's relying on her makes sense in that context.
2. Jan is a saver, and both have joked that she always puts away 10 to 15 percent of her pay, whatever her salary. As for Bill, he tends to be 5 to 10 percent overspent, whatever he makes.
3. Bill's recent expenses have sharply increased. He got custody of his two kids a year or so ago, and his travel schedule requires much costly child care. Moreover, one of the kids is in an expensive private school, and Bill's ailing mother took a big financial hit on her investments. So Bill faces mounting expenses there. This is not to mention the high alimony payments he agreed to pay not so long ago so as "to keep the divorce a civilized one."

4. Jan is mindful that $10,000 is only a small fraction of the consulting fees she has earned annually through Bill over the past few years.

   So there is always one way to get the money back, Jan muses sardonically, no matter how bad things get for Bill.

   But she runs away from this thought. No conflicts of interest for her, if she can help it. Even thinking about conflicts of interest was to be avoided. So what does Jan tell Bill?

PART 2

These thoughts flash through Jan's mind quickly, and she responds almost as soon as Bill has added a few more details:

> "OK, Bill; I guarantee I'll be your lender-of-last-resort. But please try other ways to get the cash—try real hard.
> "I will have to think through the details, but depending on how matters develop, we might have to revisit the ways we have done business in the past.
> "Take a bit of time, Bill, to review matters. If you decide to use me as lender-of-last-resort, give me two to three days to get the money.
> "Do you want cash, or is a check OK?"

INSTRUCTIONS AND QUESTIONS: PART 2

1. How do you expect that Bill will respond to Jan's offer?
2. And why? Specifically, what do you read into Jan's offer?
3. Will a check be OK with Bill?
4. Do you read anything into Jan's statement about "use me"?

II.7

Measuring Your OD Consultant

PART 1

I seldom get "cold contacts" over the phone, but this was one of them. The caller was the head commissioner of an urban county in Georgia, and I had seen his name in the newspapers. But I had never met the man. Nor did I even generally know what he had in mind, after three or four tries at getting some clues.

But I am especially solicitous of calls from government in Georgia, and especially from local government. They do little OD work, with a few exceptions. And I don't want to do anything to discourage them, at least prematurely. So I tried not to be agitated by several failures to get the commissioner to describe the nature of his possible business.

Hence, I noted, in my best summing-up tone of voice, "I hear that you want to see me, but also that you now prefer not to talk about what I might be doing with and for you. Right so far?"

"Your hearing is fine," rejoined my caller. "And our meeting won't take long. You might even enjoy the trip."

"Well, I can't give you a good price," I noted, "no matter how short the time we spend together. There's at least 70 minutes of travel each way, by car, and that could take much longer, depending on the traffic. I might have to charge you for a full day, plus expenses. But I'll try to get something else to keep me occupied in town." Success in that effort could reduce the charge to a half-day.

"Great, for either a full day or a half," said my caller, "I'll see you at 9:30 AM sharp, Wednesday next, at my office."

Well, he didn't appear at 9:30. It was more like 10:10 and, even before we shook hands, I could see he was displeased. We spent a minute or two in inconsequential talk. Then politely but firmly, he announced, "I have to be going. Busy morning, you know. Send your bill, and we'll turn it around as a special case. Here's an envelope you should use. Thanks for dropping by."

So that was it! I drove home; prepared a bill for a full day, since I had failed to get another assignment in the caller's town; and I soon put the commissioner out of my mind.

INSTRUCTIONS AND QUESTIONS: PART 1

1. Can you help the ODer understand what happened?
2. Would you have treated your "cold" caller differently from the way the ODer did?

PART 2

Several months later, I was scanning metro papers, and there was the commissioner—up front, and stage center. "I'll be a son-of-a-gun," I thought. "So that's what he wanted!"

Some facts: the meetings of elected officials presided over by the commissioner had been rough for a period of time, according to the news story, and things were getting worse. Tirades and name-calling were common and fisticuffs were not always avoided. One fellow commissioner had even taken to carrying an automatic pistol, which he would prominently display on his desk during executive sessions when the public was excluded. In public session, he would on occasion reassuringly pat the bulge that suggested he was "packing an equalizer."

Suppositions: the commissioner perhaps wanted a facilitator or conflict resolver, but only one large enough to deal with any uprisings as a kind of highly paid bouncer. So he was "measuring" his possible consultant in a very direct way. Somebody may have told him that I was a "big guy," but the commissioner needed to test that assertion directly. My poundage may have sufficed; but at 5 feet 10 inches, I may not have been sufficiently imposing for the commissioner's taste! *He wanted a meeting-facilitator-plus.*

INSTRUCTIONS AND QUESTIONS: PART 2

1. Does this possible explanation seem plausible to you?

2. Check on local governments as to whether they are experiencing the kind of incivility suggested above.
3. Assume that you are approached for a similar case of facilitating a meeting.
    - Would you accept the job, all other things being equal?
    - How would you approach your facilitation?

II.8

Oh, He's So Strong!

PART 1

Fred was feeling sorry for himself. He and his wife, Flo, had squirrelled away a couple of weeks at a favorite spot for fishing and reflection, but just before they arrived, the rains fell. Indeed, floods and wash-outs occurred. The skies promised even more trouble, in fact. Two days after their arrival, it was still raining hard.

Where to go now?

This negative reverie was interrupted by a phone call.

Did Fred have some time available in the next couple of weeks? That was the key question. The caller, Liz, had never met Fred, but had in mind a get-together at some convenient airport, and if there seemed some real compatibility with the OD teams already assembled, Fred would be asked to attend a three-day get-together scheduled within the next week.

Fred's mind was in motion. "So where in the next day or so could we meet? And where will the get-together be held?"

Liz's answers delighted him. "Well, we'll be at the Trout River Lodge for the three-day-er. And tomorrow I'll be in Denver, with a light afternoon," the caller noted.

"I'll be dipped," Fred replied, quickly upgrading his previously dour mood. "I can meet several objectives. Denver gets us within rental car distance of the Lodge, where we could fish, and reconnect until the three-day-er, if things work out." He added, "I'll assume you'll handle my expenses from where I am to wherever we'll be going...probably home...whenever our business is done."

"Sold!" Liz agreed. "And if things work out, your in-between stay at the Lodge also will be on us!"

"Well, thank you, beaucoup. See you in Denver. Is 4:00 PM good for you?"

INSTRUCTIONS AND QUESTIONS: PART 1

Fred's motives are easy enough to read, and the lateness of the contact encourages easy interpretations.

1. However, is this any way to do early contracting?
2. How could Fred have done better?

PART 2

Things seemed to go well enough in Denver—great, in fact. The contact, Liz, was the head of a headquarters OD staff and, although several rungs below decision-making levels, seemed comfortably in the saddle. In sum:

- Yes, the client was in a bit of a jam. Several senior people "hadn't worked out."
- The client firm was looking forward to a right-sizing experience and wanted the best data possible about what divisions to spin off or close within the next year to 18 months. Not that there were financial pressures. Rather, the client had decided to sharpen its strategic foci. This followed a period of great growth, usually by buy-outs for cash but on occasion via mergers for stock.
- The firm had "the best OD group that money could buy," but they were "not seasoned enough" to handle what was coming.
- Specifically, a "senior" external would be assigned to each of the several task forces, each targeted to one of the firm's multiple divisions, and would work with internal OD resources and division leadership to prepare for the right-sizing.
- There was no "master plan": Each task force would operate on the dictum "different strokes for different folks."
- Various activities could easily consume 30–50 consulting days for each task force member over the next year or 18 months.
- Fred's "senior status and publications" were seen as very useful.

There were several surprises, or even soft spots, however. The full corps of ODers had already met, and all but one task force had already been formed by an extended and tough process of mutual choices. That could not be undone, and then redone, Liz and Fred agreed.

So Fred's task force assignment, "if things worked out," would be to that single cluster that had not earlier settled on a "senior ODer." Not all the dynamics were known to Liz, she admitted, but "mutual agreement" seemed to underlay the failure to make a match. The two internal ODers assigned to this task force, both women in their late twenties, did prefer a female "senior" but seemed mostly troubled with the status of the original "senior." He was a "loser," both concluded, and in very little demand by the other task forces.

In addition, Fred was surprised by the assembled external "senior" consultants. Some of them had written about "organization change," but not one of them was known to him as an ODer. Liz counseled testing-out his surprise and potential reservations. "These folks are known to the CEO, and he wants them all."

Finally, Fred was "senior" even among the "seniors." He was 10 to 15 years older than the other external consultants, and perhaps a quarter-century older, on average, than the internals.

"If it's OK with you, Liz," Fred concluded, "I'll be pleased to sign on for the three-day-er; and we'll see what happens after that. My fit with the team will be critical, and we'd want a max-fit there, especially since we have to play catch-up ball."

"Not to worry," Liz assured him. "Things will go just great! I know it." She added, "And they tell us the fishing has been really great. That alone should justify the trip for you!"

INSTRUCTIONS AND QUESTIONS: PART 2

Despite his down-time and itch to fish, Fred's consulting antennae were twitching. Specifically, he was on the alert about:

- the dynamics of the large assemblage of internal/external resources;
- Liz's immediate interests; and
- Fred's fit with the two internal employees who had not "got on" with his "senior" predecessor.

Is Fred's list a reasonable one? Do you have any major items to add? Or subtract?

PART 3

Liz could not have been much less correct. For openers, the Trout River Lodge was one of those places you can get to only with great determination. And when you get there, bedraggled, you wonder why anyone would want to go there. If the river had ever been fishable, that had ended a long time ago. In addition, it rained, hard, for the first three days after Fred and his wife, Flo, arrived. And to top it all, Fred was the only one of the 20-odd attendees who had brought along a spouse or significant other.

Things went from bad to worse as the get-acquainted workshop got underway. In sum:

- For most of the time, reasonably enough, the task forces met separately to "build relationships." Not too subtly, several task forces demanded a public moratorium on the issue of "senior" assignments. That was agreed to, with only gentle expression of the usefulness of "revisiting" past decisions.
- Fred was not doing very well in "his" task force, for several reasons.
  1. The choice of the Lodge was the responsibility of "his" two internal consultants, which eliminated from conversation one of Fred's favorite topics.
  2. Early on, one internal acknowledged she had "not liked Fred from the start, even on paper."
  3. The two internals seemed to agree only on the usefulness of "icebreaker designs." That is, the immediate stimulus for the response above was to the question: "What kind of car do you prefer to own: Jaguar, Lamborghini, Porsche, or Audi?"
     Fred was not helpful: "I'd be delighted to talk about any matter of orientation, skill, design, or experience. But this leaves me cold. I prefer a Honda Prelude. And I would never buy a car, in any case."
  4. The two internals were not of a single mind; for example, Fred heard one say to the other, "You'll get both of us fired if you don't stop being so overt."

Cross-task-force talk was minimal, but on occasion arresting and possibly revealing. "Things go OK with your task force?" one senior attendee asked.

"You want the long or short form?" Fred responded.

"How about the latter?" the attendee chose.

"Not good," Fred revealed.

"So what else is new? One of your internals wanted to be paired with her current romantic interest, but that got derailed."

"Ah, so," Fred hissed at a possible clarifier of ongoing experience.

Back in "his" task force, Fred raised the topic of past choice-making, and some of what he had heard—albeit gently. "Just like I expected," one of his reluctant task force mates replied. "Confidence will be a real problem for us, with you carrying things outside of the group."

A long and spirited discussion of "absolute confidentiality" followed, with Fred getting most of the attention. One topic of conversation: "You wrote a piece about believing in something you called 'bounded confidentiality'—a really dangerous idea," one of the internal ODers observed.

"How else can we function, in general—both in our small task force, and especially in the larger assemblage?" Fred queried, with obvious irritation.

Matters in the large collectivity were not more satisfactory for Fred. The project leader was introduced—Maurice. He had worked with the CEO for years, and had been overseas on assignment during the first get-together of the task-forces-to-be. Liz had stood in. This surprised Fred, who was not aware that he might have to re-run several points he had already discussed with Liz. But nobody else seemed concerned.

Maurice reviewed his relationships with the firm, and especially with the CEO, emphasizing the essentiality of the task forces, whose efforts would be critical in the anticipated future "right-sizing." But Maurice would not go into details. In broad outline, task force members learned that each task force would be working with an individual division to "get operations in the best possible shape before the right-sizing." This process would take a year, more or less. Then the CEO and Maurice would meet with each task force as a prelude to developing a right-sizing plan.

"Now, here's some real substance to focus on," Fred thought.

After about 20 minutes of Maurice's stage-setting, no one raised the obvious issues. So Fred went ahead, building on the reality that "each task force will be working closely for a year with a division's leadership; and so an early key issue is what boundaries will exist for what gets communicated, to whom, and when?"

Fred continued, "The easiest way to approach this situation is to isolate several stages. Thus, six to nine months could be devoted to each task force working with its division, quite independently, under general guidelines decided upon while the task forces are together." Fred added, "Then, Phase II could shift into a descriptive mode for the CEO's purposes.

"To avoid conflicts of interest or roles, task forces might usefully rotate in this second phase, passing the ball from one task force to another, from attempting to improve division A, to later evaluating division B for sale, or whatever."

Fred noted, "I'm intrigued by how many people here seem to accept playing both roles in a single division. Myself, I see real problems with doing that."

A classic "plop!" followed. Or virtually so.

"Those are terrific thoughts, Fred," Maurice responded. "But [the CEO] wants something much more intimate and dynamic from each task force. We'll play it by ear for a while. But you won't have to wonder about what [the CEO] wants when he wants it. Oh, he's so very strong and determined, and this right-sizing has to go exactly right."

No other attendees at the general session seemed to have any concern about this preliminary scoping of these future relationships. Immediately, each task force would meet with division people—sometimes only the head, sometimes a leadership cadre. Assuming no veto at the division level, the task forces would set their own schedules for the next three months or so.

And then the three-day get-together turned back to break-out meetings for the several task forces. The topic for discussion: What is your favorite rock group?

Fred was deflated by the general session, and he had nothing much to add, in any case. He noted to the two internals, "I'm not much concerned with rock, especially now that our kids are no longer at home."

Fred added, "What does concern me is that just before the general session, we were doing a number on confidentiality. When, in the general session, I raised that issue as well as of conflict of interests and roles, I didn't hear a word from either of you two."

"Anything to add, now?" Fred asked, with an edge.

"That was Maurice's meeting, and he did not want any more talk," was the consensus of the two internals. "But we still need to know more about you to determine the synergistic fit of this task force. Now, Fred, what were you saying about rock groups? We can't always be responsive to your agendas."

INSTRUCTIONS AND QUESTIONS: PART 3

More or less, this is how things went for the evening session that began Day 1, and lasted through dinner on Day 2.

What should Fred do?

Liz has left; only three meeting slots remain; and Flo, Fred's wife, counsels: "Who needs this kiddie corps stuff?"

"Maybe the pressure will encourage some workable resolution," Fred wishes out loud to Flo. "It's clear what they're trying to do, charitably viewed. Call it bridging the generations. They need to be comfortable in what will be a high-pressure situation. And they're looking for commonalities in their own terms. So am I, perhaps too optimistically."

PART 4

Fred decided to see how things develop, but no major change occurred in the final three scheduled time slots.

Several days later, he got a call from Liz. "We need a get-together soon," she observed. "Things didn't go well for your task force, as you no doubt know. Things don't look good."

"I agree," Fred responded, "but probably for different reasons than the two internals. Why not just call it quits?"

"No," Liz replied, "let's try one more time. We're all going to be at the OD Network festivity next week, and a couple of hours should do it."

"I'm an optimistic guy," Fred replied, "and I trust that human dynamics tend toward benign effects, if given sufficient time. And you've done your share, and more. So, I'll be there, ready to see if we can build some base for working together."

"But that will be an expensive meeting for you," Fred continued. "I'm tightly scheduled, and 8:00 to 12:00 PM, Wednesday, is the only major slot I have open. And that needs to be double time, not to mention the premium for hazardous duty!"

"Will a full day's fee do it for you?" she asked.

"So be it," Fred agreed. "See you then."

INSTRUCTIONS AND QUESTIONS: PART 4

1. How do you assess the respective positions of Fred and Liz?
2. What do you guess Liz is trying to do?
3. And what do you think of Fred's approach?

PART 5

Liz and Fred met briefly, before the two internals arrived. "It's no-go," she announced. "And let's not go back into the details, please. My troops are restless, and I've got to go with them."

"How about a great dinner with us?" Liz offered, with what Fred took as a reference to the two internal OD staffers who were part of the projected task force.

"I believe it's a mistake to close it off this way," Fred responded. "But you have to make the call, and I respect that.

"As for dinner, Liz, I always enjoy your company. And let's we two do it some other time. But it's been a very long day. So let me beg off this time," Fred concluded.

INSTRUCTIONS AND QUESTIONS: PART 5

How do you respond to this conclusion?

1. Why did Liz close off any review of the details?
2. Will Fred send Liz a statement for a full day's fee? Should he?

II.9

Smelling a Consultant Ratbert

Debate often has raged concerning whether a consultant should empha-size what clients need or what they want, and Scott Adams decided to go one long step beyond that. He gave the client *something Adams wanted* that, in addition, was deliberately contrived to befuddle clients, if not to mock them.

If you need reminding, Adams is the cartoonist-author of the "Dil-bert" strip that takes a hard and often sardonic view of managers and the managed, including their consultants and gurus (e.g., Adams, 1996).

Adams decided to see how far he could go, up-front and personal. Play-acting as a consultant, he would deliberately attempt to confuse and confound a management group in connection with their mission statement (Associated Press, 1997). After seeking and receiving permis-sion from the CEO of a Silicon Valley firm, Adams targeted the exist-ing mission statement, which contained such commonplace prose as: "...to provide [the firm] with profitable growth and related new busi-ness areas" (Associated Press, 1997).

Adams was careful to disguise himself, but in curious ways. He was introduced in a memo by the firm's co-founder and vice chairman as "Ray Mebert." If that broad hint were not enough, consultant Mebert's credentials included his role on a "Taste Bright Project," allegedly to boost soap sales by a super-secret effort to improve its taste. Mebert also donned some facial disguise, but he had much to camouflage. "Dilbert" appears in more than 50 countries, in more than 1,700 newspapers, as well as in best-selling book form. And Adams' cartoons are posted on bulletin boards in business and public organizations everywhere.

Nonetheless, Mebert got away with it. As for the "Taste Bright Pro-ject," Mebert explained that many people in focus groups admitted that they had tasted soap, and his project team expected a substantial uptick in soap sales if they succeeded in improving its taste.

The clients seemed impressed.

Then Mebert went at their mission statement, hammer and tongs. He pushed his clients toward a new statement, which read in part:

> Our [mission] is to scout predictable growth opportunities in relationships, both internally and externally, in emerging, mission-inclusive markets, and explore new paradigms and then filter and communicate and evangelize the findings.

"You've all been had," Mebert concluded; and we are told the team-building participants took that revelation good-naturedly.

How would you identify consultants who are Mebert, if not Ratbert?

INSTRUCTIONS AND QUESTIONS

1. How do you react to Adams's "consulting" effort?
2. What does the "Statement" in Part III of this text have to say about this situation?
3. If you were involved in an OD venture with the firm's co-founder and vice chairman, what issues would you wish to check out with that person before involving others?
4. How would you identify consultants like Mebert, if not Ratbert?

References

Adams, S. (1996). *The Dilbert principle.* New York: Harper Business.

Associated Press. (1997). Smelling a ratbert. *Milwaukee Journal Sentinel,* November 16, p. 16A.

II.10

The Yellow Envelope on the Floor: Does Paying the Piper Imply Calling the Tune?*

It was a dramatic scene, in an apparently unobtrusive way. The casual observer might sense only a bit of untidiness, but those in the know were at once wary and alert to what was involved.

The scene? Visualize the sitting room in a comfortable hotel suite, and focus on the green-carpeted floor. More or less smack-dab in the middle of the central open space is an envelope, bright yellow. If you were to focus on that envelope, and if your eyesight is more or less normal, you would not have to get very close to see a bold legend, in capital letters:

Dr. Robert Golembiewski
Consultant

Now imagine time-lapse photography of that sitting room covering a period of five or so hours. People enter the suite and react in a similar way. They pause, and then move toward that envelope—as toward some known object. And then they veer away, as if repelled. Many people enter the suite in that half-day, but the envelope remains—not only in place, but unremarked although observed by all.

I write "observed by all," but that may overstate the case. Certainly, I knew about it, and so did my host-client—let's call him Tom, although that is not his real name. Indeed, he had tossed the envelope there...but I get ahead of my story.

So two of us definitely knew about that envelope, and tolerated that knowledge—each knowing the other knew, but both allowing the

* Adapted from Golembiewski, R. T. (1989). *Organization Development: Ideas and Issues*, pp. 52–56. New Brunswick: Transaction Publishers. Reprinted with permission of the publisher.

envelope to lay undisturbed throughout a long day of closely scheduled appointments.

If "observed by all" does overstate the case, however, it is not by
much. The common flight path of our visitors permits no other conclusion. The people coming through the suite that day recognized the envelope at a distant glance: it was the kind their organization uses for
nonpayroll checks such as those for expenses, consultants, and the like.
And hence they were attracted to it. Perhaps this came from mere curios-
ity, but I suspect most initially approached with an interest in helping.
But as they got close enough to see the addressee they knew that something was at stake other than carelessness or inadvertence. Hence, to a
person, our visitors veered away swiftly.

Our visitors were correct in their general wariness, and that is no surprise. For rising to positions of influence in the organization whose envelope lay on the floor—as all our visitors had so risen—requires great
sensitivity and far more than average caution and hunkering down
under uncertainty. Indeed, several of our visitors reconstructed the
essential dynamics between my host and myself, dynamics that led to
the yellow envelope getting on the carpet in the middle of the open
space and remaining there for hours.

What were the high points of those dynamics? My host had spon-
sored a set of team-building experiences for those reporting to him as
well as those in his broader organization, and it had been a rough experience for him. He had been forewarned that the processes might sting,
for he was in trouble with his staff, and for reasons that he substantially
created and perpetuated. But his need was great, and he was (in his
own words) a "bigger boy than most." So we went ahead, with my usual
team-building format:[1] individual interviews to diagnose the local conditions; a feedback session for all to sketch a possible design and to discuss the probability of success, given the diagnosis; and then a go/no-go
decision, subject to a veto by either the supervising executive or by a
number of subordinates, operationally defined as "more than 15 to 20
percent" having strong concerns about going ahead.

The decision to go ahead was unanimous, with the executive urging,
"It's now or never. Let's see if they have the stomach to take me on."

His subordinates took him at his word and even recommended more
than once over several days of energetic discussion that he consider res-

---

[1]Details of the entry design appear elsewhere. Basically, that design seeks to diagnose "conflict of
agreement" or "conflict of disagreement," and to predict the probable effects of the design appropriate
to each. See Golembiewski, R. T. (1979). *Approaches to Planned Change*, Parts 1 and 2. New York:
Marcel Dekker.

ignation as the only remedy. The executive was shocked and hurt. He alternated between seeing his subordinates as "ingrates," in the main, or as "gutless" for having held back so much and so long.

Nonetheless, quite specific contracts were hammered out, and usefully so, I concluded.

And now we were back to hold updating sessions with all participants. Individual contracts would be reviewed on our first day. Then a combined meeting would be held over the following two days—basically for looking forward, but with some early attention to reviewing the immediate past.

The executive and I met an hour or so before the first session with one of his first reports, and we both agreed that things had gone well after the team sessions. "Tough, and not uniformly upbeat, but necessary," we both agreed.

"And how about you?" I inquired in several cycles. "You took your lumps. Any unfinished business?"

"I'm great," he responded. "You know I'm a bigger boy than most."

But there seemed to be at least one snake in the grass. A minute or two before the first scheduled arrival—who would be on time; you could set your watch by it—the executive walked over to his briefcase. "Oh, by the way, I stopped by our controller's office to get your check." I prepared to say something bright, but had no chance.

"Here's your blood money," the executive announced. And he tossed the envelope in my direction. It had no chance to reach me, and fluttered to the floor—face up, as fate would have it—perhaps 10 to 15 feet from me.

We looked at one another—without speaking, as I recall—for a few seconds, and then came the knock on the door. Our first appointment had arrived. "Come on in, the door's open," we both said, more or less in unison. Our first appointment zigged toward the envelope, about equidistant between the executive and myself. And then he zagged. "Good to see you again, Bob," he said while extending his hand. "Let's go to work on our contract."

More or less, the same scene was repeated throughout the day, as individual first reports came by for one-on-one sessions with their boss to check on progress. I was the facilitator.

Our last one-on-one session finished, we had time to devote to our unfinished business. The first reports would soon be back as a group, for drinks and dinner, but we did have a break of an hour or so.

"We should talk about the envelope," the executive noted. "If we don't, my fantasy is that my guys will hug the walls when they come in. They know the business is between us, and I guess they're waiting for a signal from us that we've either got things square or we need their help.

"I also suspect," he added, "that since you didn't pick up the envelope during the whole day, you're not predisposed to ever pick it up. So, I suppose, if I don't pick it up, it'll stay there."

"Not so," I replied. "I'll be pleased to pick it up, and also to deposit it to my account. With three kids in private colleges, I know what to do with the money!

"But," I added by way of qualification, "let's both be clear on why that envelope lays where it does."

So we talked.

We covered some important topics together in the next 90 minutes or so. Let me abstract that discussion, which was sufficiently "finished" that evening for me to pick up the check, and for the check-thrower and I to embrace after I did.

The territory we covered in our talk was related to the limits on a folk saying: Who pays the piper calls the tune.

The sense of our talk was direct. In OD, that folk saying has very sharp limits. Who pays implies something, of course, but ideally, reliability and validity are not determined by that fact.

Several areas of agreement emerged from the discussion. They will be reviewed in outline form, which conveys the substance even as it underplays the emotionality. But so be it.

1. We agreed that his anger precipitated the throwing of the check. The team building had jarred the executive, and initially he suppressed his emotions. Much to his surprise, they later propelled him into an impulsive act. He had thought his defenses were stouter and his self-control greater. He did not remember using the term "blood money."
2. Throwing the check was not a premeditated act, but the symbolism had quickly become clear to both of us. The act was both an attack on me, and a test. If I simply picked up the check, I would be damned for what I did as a facilitator, and stamped as one whose future actions the executive could control, provided he bid higher than the others.
3. Picking up the check at the controller's office was an unusual act for the executive, but his conscious thought had been to express his thanks for my help in team building.
4. The first reports probably had a good sense of what the yellow envelope on the carpet signified. The executive was known as having a strong need to "get even."

5. I could not have picked up the check, even if I wanted, after the initial first report entered the suite. If I had done so, the word no doubt would have spread that I valued mammon more than process.
6. The executive could not pick up the check during the day, in part due to his own turbulent feelings and in part because he felt the ball was in the consultant's court, for good or ill.
7. Both of us were worried: he because of an act he saw as impetuous, even demeaning; and I because of what I may have communicated that encouraged such an act or, worse still, that gave the executive the sense that I might grovel for my fee.
8. We thought the one-to-one sessions had gone very well. The check *was* on the floor, but we both had sufficient trust that we would get to it when time permitted. And it would take some time, so we let the envelope lay.

So it went, and we were still in deep discussion when the first reports began to arrive. Quickly, expectantly, all were assembled.

"You guys want to talk about a yellow envelope?" the executive began.

"You bet," came the general reply. One attendee added, "We have learned to trust enough to wait, but we also need to process this one before my trust account is empty."

Discussion took a direct tack. One attendee explained, "Two months ago, that envelope would have stopped us cold. But I just knew we would learn from it, when we had process time. The envelope got my attention but, hell, you guys seemed to carry right on. After a while, I forgot about the damned envelope, and the check I knew was in it. But I remembered as I left the room, and took an arabesque around it!"

INSTRUCTIONS AND QUESTIONS

This case draws attention to two ways of responding to clients' feelings toward ODers.

Why two? To simplify, the case narrative focuses on Bob G. In reality, two consultants were involved, and both experienced the same episode with their checks. One consultant quickly and quietly picked up his envelope and put it in his inside coat pocket. You have read what Bob G did.

1. Of those two, which approach suits your style? Or would you choose a different response?

2. Do you foresee any issues developing between the two consultants as a result of this episode?

3. Imagine you are the consultant who picked up the envelope quietly. What are your reactions?

II.11

Welcome to Town, Big Guy!

PART 1

It had been a long and bumpy plane ride, traversing several time zones, and with a delayed arrival on top of it all. Moreover, it was the last stop of such a long trip that our vagabond ODer thought he might be able to find his own luggage without resorting to sight.

So, although the local clocks indicated 10:40 PM, it was much later than that, home time. There also were express-mail materials that had to be read to get some sense of the client. Lord knows what they contained.

Our ODer had met several principals from a computer software firm at an NTL laboratory for key executives, and the T-Group experience had "blown them away." The attendees invited the ODer to stop in for a day to discuss possibilities for follow-on with members of the firm's Executive Committee.

Several points were clear. Insistently, it seemed, one or more of the attendees had warned the ODer that they "started early," on the elemental grounds that this "left more time for partying." True to their word, breakfast had been scheduled for 6:30 AM the next day, with the casual explanation that they were this late only because "some loose ends" had to be dealt with prior to their getting together with the visiting consultant.

Moreover, from the start, the invitees noted that the "folks back home" could be in for a culture shock. The ODer would be the oldest attendee, invitees advised, suggesting with only partial tongue-in-cheek that the "age gap" might be too much to overcome. The ODer was in his late fifties; a "mod squad" awaited him.

So, the ODer was focused on a quick transition—getting into his hotel room, doing a bit of delayed reading, and hitting the sack at the earliest time, which was quite late. This was to be all the more prepared to deal with the self-professed "mod squad."

But habit took over as the ODer deplaned. One way that this ODer amused himself was to guess how he would be met, and that is what he was doing again this time. As he scanned the crowd awaiting the arriving passengers, he saw the usual collection of signs: Hi! Grandma and Grandpa; X Tools Greets John Jones; and so on. Then he spotted a greeting—in spangled lettering—he associated with his clients for tomorrow:

Welcome to Town, Big Guy!

That had to be his clients: informal, breezy, quick-paced, studiously irreverent, and not at all concerned about hiding their lifestyle preferences: Work hard, and play harder.

It also did not escape the ODer's notice that the greeting sign was held by a statuesque woman, high over her head, switching from tiptoes on one foot to the other.

It was a sight to behold, but almost exactly the opposite of what your ODer needed at that time.

"The guys at the office told me you were a swinger," my greeter added at full voice as soon as we were close enough to hear one another. "There are a lot of glorious things going down around here, and we've already lost a couple of hours. Let's get going. You can never tell what the evening will bring, let alone the morning!"

INSTRUCTIONS AND QUESTIONS: PART 1

1. How would you respond if you were the ODer?
2. Do you get a sense that the greeter has been set up? And by whom, as well as why?

PART 2

The ODer had no need to create any problems, but the greeter and he had already drawn substantial attention. "I'm beat," he announced to her, knowing only that she represented the firm. "I believe in giving my best to my clients, and I don't believe that would happen if I went out partying."

The female greeter did not hide her disdain: "A bummer," she announced to no one in particular.

INSTRUCTIONS AND QUESTIONS: PART 2

Should you somehow follow up on your greeter and her greeting? Or should you just let it go at that, unless she somehow raises the issue tomorrow?

II.12

Leaving "The Source"

Beth Levine and Barbara Reilly

CASE FOCUS

The focus of this case study is the exit process from what is being termed an "exotic consulting engagement." Why this case qualifies as an exotic experience, background about the client, and goals of the consultation are discussed to provide a context for understanding consultant exit from the system.

INTRODUCTION OF THE CLIENT

The Source is a nonprofit mental health delivery group located in the south-eastern United States. As a low-cost mental health provider, The Source serves a tri-county area northeast of a large city. The organization has been in existence for approximately 25 years and employs 10 full-time clinicians, three full-time clinician/administrators, and two full-time support staff. The Source also provides training to doctoral students and other interns.

Recently, The Source has had severe financial setbacks as managed care entered into the market. Higher-paying clients who in the past served to subsidize the cost of lower-paying clients have moved on to managed care providers. For example, a client with the ability to pay $60 per session might have helped to offset the expense of providing therapy to a client who could pay only $10 per session. With reduced mental health care costs, higher-paying clients can now go to any number of sources and pay $60 for a one-hour therapy session, thus eliminating the foundation of The Source's financial structure. We found The Source in a great deal of pain and ready for organization development as a potential remedy.

INTRODUCTION OF THE CONSULTANTS

Beth Levine is an internal consultant at Foster Wheeler Environmental Corporation, an environmental cleanup organization. She also provides consulting to other organizations. Barbara Reilly is a professor in the College of Business at Georgia State University in Atlanta, where she teaches organization development and provides services as an independent consultant.

The authors formed the primary consultant team, although other consultants participated in the role of new practitioners engaged in learning. As the lead consultants, we brought distinctly different backgrounds to the engagement. Reilly's practice has focused on corporate, high-tech, and manufacturing environments, while Levine's has targeted nonprofit and governmental agencies. Levine easily identified with members of the client system. In retrospect, she acknowledged that the consultation engagement felt like "going home." As a result, Levine had a natural affinity for the client that fostered a quick and easy rapport but also presented the risk of blurring the boundary with the client. While the client boundary remained crisp for Reilly, she found herself at times frustrated to the point of confronting her own value judgments in working with the client. From Reilly's point of view, the client system's nonprofit values (in contrast to traditional corporate values) created tension that slowed her development of client rapport.

PART 1

Overview of the Consulting Engagement

The executive director of The Source functioned as the client champion, although the client system was the entire staff. As articulated by the executive director, the consultants were brought in to "help us look at our organization, what worked, what didn't, and what changes needed to be made." The "looking" was the diagnostic phase of what grew into a one-year engagement. It consisted of a written survey, individual interviews, feedback to the management team, and feedback to the entire staff, which culminated in agreements about specific tasks to be accomplished. Diagnosis and contracting occurred over a span of two months.

The entire project included two separate contracts. There were at least three reasons for this approach. First, with two contracts, the client could feel a sense of completion sooner rather than later. Second, it was apparent that the type and amount of work could continuously expand as we proceeded.

The initial contract created a manageable boundary for the consultants. Third, we wanted to establish a productive rapport before even considering a lengthier engagement. The first contract addressed vision statement, mission statement, and establishment of measurable goals. It also referenced the option for a second contract that might involve organizational structure, role clarification, and conflict management strategies.

We completed the first contract in three months using traditional OD techniques such as brainstorming, nominal group techniques, fishbowl, modeling, activity-based team building, and targeted reading assignments. Upon completion of the first contract, momentum for the change process was uninterrupted and we moved easily and with much fanfare and celebration into the second contract. In contrast to the possibilities specified in the first contract, this agreement focused on the role of the consultants as process guides in accomplishing the goals the staff had established for themselves as a result of the first contract. The specified end date of the second contract was seven months from its start, or a full 12 months from the original entry into the system. Unlike the first contract, the second contract included no mention of additional work or phases that might be handled in a third contract.

During the second contract, more attention was devoted to individual coaching for the executive director, focused on leadership and on transferring facilitation skills to all members of the system. During the first contract, The Source had created several task forces to work on specific goals independently and report back to the larger group. Each task force had an identified leader, and we assisted that individual by providing facilitation of those meetings as well as individual coaching before and after the meetings. We also designed and facilitated sessions for the entire staff at six-week intervals to ensure organizational integration of the independent committee work.

The Exotic Nature of the Client

Three characteristics contribute to the exotic nature of this engagement. First, a majority of the members at The Source were Ph.D. clinical psychologists providing psychotherapeutic services. Second, the consultation was provided on a pro bono basis. Last, The Source lacked a traditional business culture. We will detail each of these three characteristics below.

The Therapy Environment

Having a group of clinical therapists compose the majority of the client system created a number of interesting qualities in our interaction with the client. They were a system long on "process" and short on "task." In contrast to corporate cultures in general, the client system at The Source embraced process work and valued emotions. Furthermore, members of the system saw themselves as sophisticated in these realms and were quite articulate in describing their experiences.

Many of the clinicians at The Source worked with couples and/or families, i.e., systems beyond the individual. It is not uncommon for a client system in OD work to consider itself "one big happy family." However, The Source considered itself a dysfunctional family. While they recognized the need for help, there was confusion about what that help would look like. With varying degrees of trepidation, most individuals expected the help to look like family therapy. Whereas most clients need to spend time understanding the OD process and how the consultant will work with them, in this case we spent a significant portion of the first session helping the clients understand the differences between OD and family therapy.

The Pro Bono Factor

The pro bono status of the consultation added a flavor of the exotic because we were not constrained by the constant filter of "will the client think this is worth the dollars they are paying?" This allowed us greater freedom in supporting an action learning stance as consultants. When the system was unanimous in choosing a direction that diverged from our "professional" opinion, it was easier for us to recognize the potential learning for both systems, regardless of the outcome. If their direction became a dead end, they would realize why we had a different suggestion and then be able to embrace our proposed task with enthusiasm, rather than out of respect for the consultant or from an inability to express their needs as they saw them. And, should they hit a dead end, we did not anticipate a boomerang effect involving their blaming us for wasted time and money. On the other hand, if their approach turned out to be successful, we would have an enlarged understanding of potential pathways for organizational change.

As we are with all clients, we remained constantly focused on not wasting client time. In other engagements in which the client is paying substantially for our time, similar situations have created an additional tension about the client's potential perception of the consultant's "time on the clock." As it happened, these clients did hit something of a dead end when they tried to work on their mission before reworking their vision. This was an instance in which we set aside our professional opinion in the hopes of achieving greater learning and understanding in the

Figure II.12.1   Differences Between OD and Therapeutic Systems

Characteristics	OD Systems	Family Therapy Systems
1. Size of system	Varies from individual to large system	Varies from individual to family unit
2. Choice in participation	Limited	Established through mutual agreement
3. Ease of entering and exiting	Permeable boundaries	Easy entry; rigid exit
4. Rituals and rules	Defined by organizational culture	Defined by individual family
5. Focus of goals	Organizational growth	Intrapersonal and interpersonal growth
6. Bringing work home	Greater ability to separate from the system (psychologically or otherwise)	Sharply limited ability to separate from the system
7. Structure	Formal	Informal
8. Catalyst for growth	Organizational	Personal
9. Role flexibility	Ability and expectation to shift roles	Roles prescribed and difficult to alter

long run. Interestingly, when we retraced our steps to pick up the vision piece, they did the work both efficiently and effectively.

The Absence of Traditional Business Skills

Many of the features that made this case unique can be traced to the client environment of mental health care providers, none of whom had strong business skills. The client was long on process and short on task (rather unusual from an OD perspective). In the task area, The Source lacked many of the taken-for-granted business concepts that we encounter with our for-profit clients. For example, in staff meetings a lack of structure often impeded performance. The group described their pre-intervention meetings as mired and bogged down. Meetings lacked leadership, a clear and focused agenda, firm boundaries on time, and a clear decision-making process. The employees were not "cared for" in a traditional human resource sense. There was no system for employee relations and human resource activities. Systems for tracking time and productivity and for providing recognition as well as rewards were absent.

What the client lacked in task skills, however, it compensated for (to a fault at times) by process skills. Early on in the intervention, it became apparent that this was a place where feeling statements were honored and valued. When a person began a sentence with "I am feeling," the rest of the group focused more intently. Contrast that response with a typical corporate environment, where "I feel" statements often are dismissed, derided, or never articulated in the first place.

INSTRUCTIONS AND QUESTIONS: INTRODUCTION AND PART 1

1. Based on Figure II.12.1, what are the major values underlying OD interventions?
2. What are the major values underlying family therapy interventions?
3. What do you see as the distinctions between OD interventions and therapeutic interventions? As you respond, consider the following aspects: size of the system, presence of structure, membership requirements, ease of entry and exit.

PART 2

Exiting the System

Although entry and exit are discussed as parts of the OD process, the majority of theoretical discussion centers on the entry process. In preparing this case, we failed to find any major research devoted to exiting the system per se. We saw the theme of exiting played out at two different levels during the consulting engagement. One level was a client system and individual exits from that system through staff turnover. This was a source of extreme pain that eventually became an area of growth. The second level was the dynamic between the client and consultant systems. As the engagement neared completion, the circumstances of our own exit became prominent for us and the executive director, in particular.

Employee Exit from the System

When we arrived at The Source, we were surprised by the difficulty and pain experienced by individuals exiting the system and the resulting pain felt by the system. Turnover was high, primarily because many therapists were unable to tolerate The Source's limited compensation. Issues related to exiting the client system were of concern for all members of the system. After a decade of limited turnover, professional staff had been turning over at a rate of two out of ten per year in the last three years. Additionally, the majority of professional staff had arranged partial exits by shifting to part-time status.

Both the partial and complete exits were fraught with guilt on the part of the individuals who were exiting, feelings of abandonment among those remaining, and pain for all parties. Individual decisions about departures tended to be shrouded in secrecy initially and, when made public, the system response was to try to convince the person to stay. The ensuing negotiation would generate a drawn-out process and heighten the guilt for one or more parties. The individual who was preparing to leave became painfully aware of abandoning not just friends and colleagues, but clients as well. Uniformly, the need to earn more money was the catalyst for leaving, which resulted in a sense of "copping out" for some exiters, while others resented the inability of the agency to increase their compensation. Those who stayed felt guilty for trying to cling to those who were leaving and increasingly felt put upon and burned out as they inherited their former colleagues' case loads and administrative duties. As a person's exit neared, the system norm called for a two- to three-hour group exit process.

Exiting, as a distinct issue, did not surface explicitly in either of the consulting contracts, but it was embedded in the work around organization structure, role clarification, and conflict resolution. By working on these issues, the system began the metamorphosis from identification as family to identification as organization, and the new identity allowed more freedom in exiting. Not only could individual members navigate the boundary more effectively to meet their personal needs, but the system could recognize and embrace the need for permeability. In evaluating the consulting engagement, personnel at The Source indicated tremendous satisfaction and pride in the growth they experienced in this specific arena. Several departures of staff occurred near the end of the project. Those who remained reported that they had felt genuinely happy for the person leaving and had been able to offer understanding and support.

Consultant Exit from the System

In contrast to their growth and satisfaction regarding their own exits from the system, the members of the client system were less than satisfied with the consultants' exit process. The last session, our semi-official exit from the system, consisted of a three-hour meeting with four specified objectives:

1. Approve plan to move forward on organization structure.
2. Initiate involvement of staff in budgeting process.
3. Put closure on consultant contract.
4. Maintain momentum for change/metamorphosis.

As was our tradition, preparation of the agenda was done in conjunction with the executive director. She stated her need for our assistance in helping the group achieve the first two objectives. Our main goal was to reinforce the embryonic sense of optimism we had seen unfolding, as represented in the last two objectives. We knew at the time that this was a very packed agenda.

The first objective, approval of a new organization structure, was handled through presentation of a proposal, group discussion, individual evaluations, and group decision-making. Given all the work that had preceded the proposal, with involvement from all members, it was no surprise to us that approval was unanimous. We were pleased to observe the strength of leadership exhibited by the executive director and the ability of the group to make a decision. The Source felt very different to us from the way it had been almost 12 months earlier when we had begun the process.

To accomplish the second objective, involvement of staff in budgeting, we developed an interactive exercise that was intended to be fun and also to help the clients feel safe in being creative about an area (finances) most of them approached with fear and lack of knowledge. When the activity was introduced, several members questioned the value of the activity and offered small suggestions to modify it. We incorporated their suggestions and the activity proceeded, but we observed mixed energy levels among the small groups. During the whole-group report and action planning, we again observed varying levels of energy. Nevertheless, the large group did come to agreement on certain actions that were generated through the activity, and individuals did accept responsibility for specific action steps.

The executive director's two primary objectives had been met, and now it was time to move on to closure. At this point, less than 20 minutes of our meeting remained. As we moved into closure on the contract, we began with our own observations of their growth as an organization and emphasized the reasons we believed they had cause for optimism. These reasons included their improved ability to make group decisions effectively, the approved organization structure, the subcommittees they had formed for specific initiatives, and the improved leadership. We presented them with a metaphorical gift: a child's toy that appeared to be a stuffed caterpillar but included a hidden pocket containing a butterfly that emerged when the caterpillar was turned inside out. We stated that we wanted the toy to remind them of their own metamorphosis, and how proud they should be about what they had accomplished. We then invited comments about what the project had meant for them. Each person offered a comment, and they were consistently appreciative of the work we had done with them as well as the many hours we had volunteered in order to do the work. Several individuals mentioned an expectation of missing us, and one person said she realized she had just assumed there would be a third contract, that she had not realized we were actually ending the project. There were many hugs and requests to stay in touch.

Subsequent feedback indicated the client system was very pleased with the engagement as a whole, that they recognized the value of the tasks accomplished and the dissipation of much of the pain that had been present initially. However, those at The Source remained less than satisfied with the exit process.

INSTRUCTIONS AND QUESTIONS: PART 2

1. What unique exit needs would you anticipate with this environment?
2. What needs and feelings about the consultant exit might individuals in the client system have had?
3. What needs and feelings about exiting might the consultants have had?
4. What do you think was the source of the dissatisfaction with the exit?

PART 3

Exit Perspectives, Again

We were provided with data from a work session held two weeks after our official exit. At this time, the executive director collected individual comments, both positive and negative, and forwarded those to us. This was the first indication we had of the extent of their need for a better exit process. While the positive feedback addressed our entire year of activity, the negative data focused primarily on the exit process. From the written evaluation we received came this excerpt: "After last meeting everyone seemed to admit they had lied at the last meeting—only gave positive feedback." As consultants, this motivated us to do some reanalysis. This section represents a deep, albeit delayed, analysis of the entire exit process.

Executive Director

Our last session and opportunity for exit was shaped jointly by the executive director, Reilly, and Levine. The executive director, as client champion, had requested a focus on two specific tasks because she felt inadequate alone to manage resolution of them. However, we observed her providing strong and effective leadership in bringing closure to the tasks. She knew the cultural norm of a lengthy and rich exit process, but she did not share that with us prior to the final meeting. In fact, we learned about that particular norm only after we had completed our engagement.

Three possible explanations occurred to us regarding why this information about the importance of an intense exit process had not been shared. First, the executive director may have felt confident about her own abilities to manage an exit process after we were gone and made a decision to forego consultant contact for this work in favor of our presence for tasks about which she lacked confidence. While it is clear she did manage to facilitate the system's need for authentic closure by leading a session devoted to evaluating the engagement after we were gone, it is equally clear to us that she could have facilitated the task goals without us as well. A second factor contributing to her non-disclosure of exiting norms may have been her own feelings of ambivalence about the consultants' exit, with the omission operating as a form of personal denial. A third and more harmless possibility is that the executive director just plain forgot to mention the norm for an intense exit ritual.

System Perspectives

We have several interpretations of what was happening within the system as our exit approached. Within the system as a whole, there may have existed an expectation of a third contract. While all participants knew we were technically working under a second contract, we do not recall if we spoke to this point as explicitly with the whole group as we did with the executive director. In this system of therapists, their reference point was always that of therapy, from which we had differentiated OD. Looking back on the distinctions we developed with them on the first day, the reference to time frames is conspicuously absent. Therapy generally continues until it is determined by the client *and* the therapist that the work is complete. In the practice of OD, the time frame is generally bounded by a contract that also specifies activities, tasks, or outcomes.

Working from their own frame of reference, system members may not have truly recognized that the last session signified a final contact with the consultants. If they were "caught off guard," they simply may not have had the capacity to access an honest internal assessment of the process. If the reality caught up with them subsequently, the session led by the executive director may have captured their reactions to the realization of the exit—e.g., ambivalence, abandonment, hurt, and anger—rather than their assessment of the exit process.

Consultant Perspectives

Our explicit intentions around the closing were to provide The Source with a sense of accomplishment about the completion of significant work and to support them in feeling optimistic about their ability to move forward in a productive manner. Another goal was to leave with a sense that everyone in the room recognized we had honored our commitment to them as consultants. The two consultants had some needs in common and some that were distinct, as reflected in Figure II.12.2.

In retrospect, we can see the impact of our affinities for the client, and how these affected our interaction with the client. While we had many common feelings at exit, there were a few notable differences. From Reilly's perspective, the most interesting difference was her own lack of sadness or feelings of loss or guilt regarding separating from the client. In fact, this was the first time Reilly could remember not feeling a sense of loss at the completion of a contract. As we discussed this in retrospect, it became clear that Levine was consulting from inside the system (where exits were tougher) and Reilly was consulting from outside the system (sometimes too far). We were both trying to move our personal boundary, Reilly getting closer and Levine trying to escape from within the system. Levine made sure there were mechanisms such as contracts and formal work products to allow for her exit. Levine reported comfort in the balance provided by Reilly. The ultimate goal of the consultant is to get as close to the system as possible without cross-

Figure II.12.2   Consultants' Objectives and Reactions to Exiting

---

Exit Objectives Common to Both Consultants

- Closure of contract
- Reflect The Source's growth as an organization
- Personal closure

Exit Objectives Unique to Reilly or Levine

Reilly	*Levine*
Have a win for them	Presentation of optimistic metaphor
Have a win for me	Recognition of self
Leave the client hopeful	

Consultant Affective Reactions to Exit

Reilly	*Levine*
Ebullient at idea of completion	Aware of guilt about leaving when more needed to be done
Aware of absence of guilt	Relief

---

ing over and becoming part of it. While neither one of us was "there" individually, as a consultant system we were balanced.

An additional concern was our need for optimism. We now realize that our desire to infuse the clients with optimism was so powerful for us that we may have stifled any expressions of doubt or insecurity. This was one place where Reilly and Levine did not balance each other. Because both consultants had such strong feelings supporting optimism and the need for optimism, the clients may have been overwhelmed at times. Additionally, in managing our own internal tensions between the sense of relief about bringing closure to a pro bono project that had consumed much more time than either of us had anticipated, we may have conveyed an attitude of not wanting to hear anything but the "good stuff."

Our intention to confirm the completion of the contract to everyone's satisfaction may also have contributed to the clients' dissatisfaction with the exit. We may have been too quick to honor the executive director's request to focus on tasks in the last session, because we wanted to leave her feeling satisfied with the services we provided. From our current vantage point, it is more obvious that the final session was only one of a long series of interventions. The reality was that our contractual obligation for specific tasks had been met long before the last session. Perhaps by focusing on wanting to leave her feeling good about the work we did in the last session, we did not give her or the group credit for being able to recognize the work we had done all year.

Ultimately, our primary source of dissatisfaction was the lack of balance in the process. In affirming the client system's success and growth so energetically, no space was left in which to express sadness concerning the separation and regrets about what was not accomplished. This was as true for the consultants as it was for the clients. A secondary source of dissatisfaction was the limited amount of time devoted to the closure process. It generally takes more time to get in touch with difficult or ambivalent feelings and, with the clock loudly ticking, it was certainly expedient to touch only on the positive realm.

INSTRUCTIONS AND QUESTIONS: PART 3

1. As a consultant, what major learning do you extract from these dynamics?
2. Why is it a good idea for consultants to reflect on all needs related to the exit process?

PART 4

Exit Perspectives

We have gleaned several valuable lessons from our experience in bringing this engagement to closure. Most of these apply across the board to consulting situations, but two lessons relate specifically to our "exotic" client. First, we now know that this type of client system, i.e., clinical psychologists or therapists, is likely to pay more attention to and expect a lengthier exiting process than is the norm in most business environments. With this type of client, then, we will push for a longer period of time devoted to closure. For all clients, we will attend more carefully to surfacing expectations about closure. Second, we have experienced what we think is a reluctance of pro bono clients to critique free services—an attitude of gratitude, if you will. This makes the process of payment, no matter how small, vital. With payment comes the freedom to critique.

Taking a lesson from the Gestalt Consulting Approach, that model identifies closure and withdrawal as two linked but distinct pieces. Closure requires an anchoring of the learning, or an opportunity to make meaning of the experience. Withdrawal is the final step and includes affirmations of what was accomplished and acknowledgment of what was not, as well as appreciation for the effort put forth, regardless of the accomplishment. What transpired during our last 20 minutes with the client was the withdrawal step, albeit without acknowledgment of what was not accomplished. The closure that comes from actually making meaning of an experience did not precede the withdrawal, and therefore the client experienced "unfinished business" and the discomfort associated with that state. It is hard to say whether our intentions would have been better served by using the limited time to work on closure activities rather than withdrawal. We still believe employees of The Source needed a dose of balanced optimism. However, recognizing two distinct components of the exit process provides the opportunity to make choices about how to balance the time devoted to each component in future engagements and provides a heightened awareness to the importance of the exit process.

Even the most sophisticated process-oriented client systems cannot escape the fact that organizational themes around specific issues envelop the system. They cannot be "fixed" and filed away, because they will always require the organization's attention. For The Source, this reality was played out in the resurfacing of secrecy and withholding in the last session. For the consultants, it was a reminder that the goal is not always to help clients "feel better" but rather to help them be better able to recognize their own unique themes and thereby become better at assessing and modifying their behavior relative to those themes.

INSTRUCTIONS AND QUESTIONS: PART 4

As an ODer, please evaluate these "exit perspectives."

1. How do you react to the perspectives?
2. How do those perspectives fit with your experiences as well as the theoretical perspectives you value?

II.13

Shadow Consulting to an OD Consultant*

William B. Wolf

PART 1

Many of the best executives with whom I have worked seem to have almost psychic powers of awareness as to what is going on in their organizations. Again and again I have witnessed actions where an executive asks a penetrating question revealing a significant problem. Frequently I have heard their subordinates ask, "How in the hell did he spot that?" My explanation is that through deep involvement and intensive experiences, one learns to react to minimum clues, to interrelate data and notice what is incongruent, and to recognize what is experienced, felt, and thought. The following case gives a sense of what I am describing.

A friend of mine called me and asked if I would help him in a consulting assignment. He was doing organization development consulting for a company. Most of his work had involved training workers in group problem-solving and conducting team-building sessions with the supervisors. He had been working with the firm for about six months and had more or less exhausted his bag of tricks. He wanted to keep the client. They were paying him $1,000 a day plus expenses. My assignment was to advise him as to what to do next.

What I did was visit the firm. It was a single-unit, corrugated carton company. My tour of the facilities revealed what I would say was a normal or unexceptional plant. The equipment was standard. There was no

* Reprinted with the author's permission from William B. Wolf, *Stories from Managers, Consultants, and Other Mortals.* Clinton, WA: 1996.

evidence of new or innovative manufacturing techniques. I interviewed two workers. Then I interviewed the vice president of sales and the comptroller. After that, I had lunch with the executive vice president.

My friend, the consultant, was eager to learn what I recommended. We met for dinner, and he immediately asked, "If this was your consulting job, what would you do?" I answered that I would buy expensive presents for the main executives and tell them I was too busy to take the job. My friend was furious. He wanted to know how in the hell I came to that conclusion. I explained, "You are being used as a placebo in a criminal money laundering scam."

INSTRUCTIONS AND QUESTIONS: PART 1

You are Wolf's OD friend. In addition to being angry, how do you deal with Wolf's summary conclusion? Why do it that way?

PART 2

My friend's immediate reaction was to demand, "How in the hell did you arrive at that conclusion? You were only around the plant for about four hours." I explained that when I had lunch with the executive vice president I told him that it seemed like the president of the company was on the edge of criminal activities. The executive vice president said, "On the edge, hell! He's in the middle of it."

I was then interrogated as to how I had arrived at my conclusion. It took me a while to figure that one out. What seems to have happened is that, from habit, the train of thought had run through my mind without my being conscious of it. However, there was a logic to it and it illustrates the nature of the thought processes involved. As I reflected, I put together the intermediate steps that led to my conclusion. The train of reasoning developed from the following information: Both of the workers I interviewed told me that the company was bought out about two years ago, that a gangster-polluted union represented the workers, that soon after the new owners took over there was a strike, and the strike was settled after the union president's house was bombed. Since then, relations between the union and management had been cordial. The story was so unusual that I checked it out in my subsequent interviews.

The vice president of sales told me that sales had been increasing at a phenomenal rate. I asked if there were any new products. He said, "No." I asked if he had hired any additional personnel. He said, "No." I asked if there were any major advertising campaigns. He said, "No." Then I asked how he accounted for the increase in sales. His answer was that he had started giving pep talks every morning and they were very effective.

The comptroller was a man in his middle forties. We got into a friendly and relaxed discussion. When I asked how he had come to be in his job, he told me that he had been shattered by the breakup of his marriage. He had taken to drinking heavily. He had drifted to the Bahamas, and while he was there he had met the president of the company. The president was in the Bahamas on business. They liked each other. The comptroller went on to tell me that the president helped him give up drinking and gave him his present job.

The executive vice president was a flamboyant Irishman in his middle fifties. When he spoke of the president, it was as if he was referring to a deity. Moreover, he told me that this was the twelfth turnaround that he and the president had engaged in. They had done well in each.

What could explain these facts? The only explanation I could think of was that it was a criminal operation where they were salting the sales revenues and thus laundering their money. My prediction was that the company would be sold and that within six months the old management would have disappeared and the new owner would be in deep trouble. A follow-up validated this prognosis.

INSTRUCTIONS AND QUESTIONS: PART 2

1. How do you evaluate Wolf's review of the thought processes and inquiries that led to his basic conclusion?
2. How do you guess Wolf's OD friend responded to the explanation?
3. Can you think of any other hypotheses that would explain what Wolf has learned by interpreting the results of interviews?
4. Can you generalize about Wolf's method?
5. Does Wolf's recommendation for the consultant's exit satisfy the statement of guidance for human-system intervenors abstracted in Perspective IV?

PART 3

To me, this vignette illustrates the processes and outlook one needs in most administrative work. That is, one should have a broad perspective of the phenomena being dealt with, the ability to recognize what is experienced, and the capacity to understand the interrelationship of the parts to each other and to the whole. One needs to recognize that almost everything is related to everything else. Most important, everything can be explained provided one has adequate information, a good framework for analysis, and the power of synthesis.

The above is a general philosophy. It has general applicability. In essence it holds that everyone should, at heart, be like a good scientist. We need to gather data, form hypotheses, check them for congruence with the various aspects of the phenomenon, and recognize interdependencies.

INSTRUCTIONS AND QUESTIONS: PART 3

1. As you reflect on your own practice or the experiences of others, can you think of other possibilities for OD being used as a placebo, a pacifier, or a deflector of attention from significant targets?
2. Does your experience suggest a criminal connection for one or more of your clients?
3. Does the OD literature touch on this issue?

PERSPECTIVE III

Leading Organization Change via Action Research: An Integrative Experience with a Single Case

III.1

Jake White

Glenn H. Varney and James M. McFillen

PART 1

Pat Spritely returns a call from Jake White on Wednesday the 3rd, setting up an appointment to discuss what Jake describes as "an out-of-control problem." During the call to Pat, Jake mentions that he is about to send a letter to all key account representatives regarding new customer calls and wants to discuss the letter with him.

Pat meets with Jake and, through a series of questions, learns that "several high-potential customers" have called Jake complaining that their key account representatives have not contacted them as Jake had promised. The potential customers have waited for three days and still have not been contacted.

Pat also learns that Jake has an assistant, Nancy Jacobs. Jake is so anxious to get going that Pat almost misses his quick reference to Nancy.

Jake gets to his bottom line quickly: Does Pat believe he "can get to the heart of this problem"?

INSTRUCTIONS AND QUESTIONS: PART 1

1. As Pat, what is your first impression of Jake?
2. What knowledge and skills do you, Pat, clearly have as a new holder of a master's degree in OD that qualify you to work on this initial view of the issues Jake raises?
3. Identify any knowledge or skills that may become useful or necessary but which you have only superficially or not at all.

4. Is there anything you, as Pat, need to guard against as you start working with Jake?
5. What additional information do you need? With whom do you need to talk?
6. Given your provisional reactions, will you accept Jake as a client? And with what degree of initial enthusiasm?

Be sure to check and re-check the Introductory Orienting Cues for Perspective III on pp. xv to determine whether they can help you respond to these instructions.

After a re-check, return to the introductory materials, beginning with page xxi. They will later help you, the reader, deal with Part 2 of this case.

PART 2

Pat realizes that if he is going to help, he will need to arrange another meeting with Jake and perhaps with other members of Jake's department who can provide more information and additional perspectives on the situation.

At this point, it is tempting for Pat to express confidence in himself and to answer quickly that he believes he can help Jake. However, he will need to test his own competency and availability before saying that he'll help.

Pat answers "yes" to Jake's request for help. Jake agrees to meet with him next Monday the 8th, from 10:00 until 11:00 AM. Pat asks if he also may speak with Jake's assistant, and Jake agrees. Pat makes arrangements for the meetings with Jake and his assistant, Nancy. Now Pat must think about the questions he needs to ask.

On Monday, Pat meets with Jake, and the meeting is essentially a dialogue. To illustrate:

Pat: This situation started because new customers reported that key account representatives had not called on them as you had promised. How many customers are involved?

Jake: First, they are potential customers, not new customers, and we expect our key account reps to make these calls. There are eight potential customers and two key account reps involved.

Pat: Why do you think the calls have not been made?

Jake: These two guys are "old-timers" who think they are in charge. My guess is they were out playing golf or something like that.

Pat: How many potential customers called you?

Jake: Three.

Pat: I assume you set up this arrangement directly with the potential accounts. What did you tell them?

Jake: Yes, I did. I told them they would receive a call in a day or so.
Pat: After talking to the eight potential customers, what did you do?
Jake: I told Nancy to get the word out to all key account representatives.
Pat: Anything else I should know at this point?
Jake: Yes, I need this problem fixed now! The only reason you are here is because my staff recommended you.

Pat's next meeting is with Nancy, Jake's assistant. Pat walks to another building to meet with her. She is working in an open office with the inside sales order-entry staff. The quality of this dialogue can be suggested with a few brief excerpts:

Pat: How did this situation with the potential customers get started?
Nancy: Because Jake makes promises that can't be met.
Pat: What do you mean?
Nancy: He is like a gunslinger, always shooting from the hip without talking to others.
Pat: What happened in this case?
Nancy: Jake called me a few days ago and told me he wanted all key account representatives alerted to be prepared to call on some new accounts within a few days.
Pat: What did you do?
Nancy: I sent out a letter to all 10 key account reps.
Pat: May I have a copy of the letter?
Nancy: Sure, I'll get it for you.

Nancy is interrupted by several telephone calls in quick succession. Between calls, the dialogue continues:

Nancy: Some things have come up that I must take care of right now. Can we continue this discussion in a few minutes?
Pat: Well, I need to get back to Jake before I leave and give him a preliminary report, so I don't think I'll be able to get back until later.
Nancy: OK! Thanks, and good luck!

INSTRUCTIONS AND QUESTIONS: PART 2

1. Develop two or three hypotheses to explain what is happening in this case.

2. Study what is already known about this type of problem. Pick one or two theories, concepts, and/or research findings that can support your hypotheses.
3. Consider how Nancy feels after you tell her that you "need to get back to Jake before I leave and give him a preliminary report...."

    In responding to these possibilities, you will find it useful to refer to the introductory materials, pp. xxv–xxx. They provide some orienting cues as you move from scanning and assessment through diagnosing and the analysis and alignment.

PART 3

After meeting with Nancy, Pat is soon ready to get back to Jake. Pat meets briefly with him and explains that he (Pat) has some ideas but needs to get more information. Jake jumps back at Pat, saying, in effect, that the situation has to be resolved today.

By this time, Pat has developed a few ideas about what's causing this problem, and Jake is at the center of the issue. To resolve the immediate problem with the three potential customers, Pat suggests that he call the two key account representatives and dispatch them to the three potential customers. Pat then asks to conduct some follow-up discussions with Nancy and all of the key account representatives.

Jake seems preoccupied. He concludes the brief meeting with these words: "Pat, you write me a proposal and I'll consider it."

INSTRUCTIONS AND QUESTIONS: PART 3

1. What is your sense of Jake's closing words? Are they a kiss-off or an honest request?
2. In either case, you should find it useful to do two things:
    (a) review your analysis, from early scanning through your latest interpretations and even tentative hypotheses; and
    (b) develop a written proposal for Jake.

    Later you can compare your effort to the outline of Pat's proposal, which is detailed in Parts 4A and 4B below.

Please now return to the section in the introductory materials that is labeled "Early Analysis and Writing an OD Contract" (pp. xxv). These orienting cues will help you with both tasks.

PART 4A

Pat quickly gets his OD proposal to Jake. Basically, it identifies two alternative explanations for the problem with the key account representatives:

1. The communication lines between Jake and the key account representatives are breaking down because communications are funneled through one person, Nancy Jacobs, who is extremely busy.
2. The sales department is being "micro-managed" because the sales department does not have a middle tier of management to make day-to-day decisions, thus requiring upper management to make those decisions.

In Pat's proposal, he emphasizes the need to determine which of these two explanations is correct. To do so, he plans to collect information from the 10 key account representatives as well as Nancy. He decides to interview all 10 key account representatives over a two-day period the following week. The questions he plans to ask include these four:

1. How does information reach you from management?
2. When management has a special request for you to call on a potential customer, how long does it take for that request to get to you?
3. How is the sales department organized?
4. What type of leadership have you observed in the sales department?

INSTRUCTIONS AND QUESTIONS: PART 4A

1. Is there anything in Pat's proposal that surprises you?
2. How does Pat's proposal compare with your own?
3. Do you see opportunities for job enrichment?

PART 4B

Pat completes his interviews with the key account representatives and summarizes their responses in the following ways:

1. How does information from management reach sales reps?

Response	Frequency of Response
Through Nancy	9
Directly from Jake	1
During the semi-annual sales meetings	7
From the monthly bulletin	6
From weekly activity reports	6
From hearsay and rumors	7

2. When management has a special request for reps to call on a potential customer, how long does it take for that request to get to you?

Response	Frequency of Response
One day	1
Two days	5
Three days	3
Four days	1

3. How is the sales department organized?

Response	Frequency of Response
Flat	4
Jake and Nancy and the rest of us	2
Unclear	3
I don't know	1

4. What type of management style have sales reps observed in the sales department?

Response	Frequency of Response
Top down	8
Autocratic	9
Micro-management	10
Controlling	5

In addition, all 10 key account representatives made comments. Using quotes from the key account representatives to represent the three major types of responses, Pat develops the following frequency analysis of themes in the interviews:

Typical Comment	Frequencies of Comment
I. "You had better check with all 10 key account reps. You'll find we all have the same problems."	10
II. "Nancy is like a funnel that all information must go through to reach us.	7

Typical Comment	Frequencies of Comment
It's not her fault; it's just the way we're organized."	
III. "It's time for a change."	8

After a careful review of the above information, Pat concludes that it is necessary to carry out a second phase of data collection involving the entire sales department. Pat notifies Jake of the need for a second phase of data collection because it was not included in Pat's original proposal. Pat also must contact Nancy to arrange for her interview.

INSTRUCTIONS AND QUESTIONS: PART 4B

The evidence above begins to suggest a hypothesis that needs checking with data from all personnel in sales.

Basically, the data are "hot," and Pat's OD design provides no clear linkage to Jake's superiors. Reporting the data to Jake alone suggests the sense of having the fox in charge of the henhouse. If the present data are reported to Jake's superiors, moreover, that might risk confidentiality.

So:

1. Design a short survey to be given to all sales department employees. First, decide what you want to know and then prepare the questions and the survey.

    Second, design the distribution and collection processes you will use. Do you include all possible respondents?

2. Write yourself a note to the effect that you should never be as cavalier about upward linkages and confidentiality as you were in the original OD proposal. How would you do better?

3. Nancy will be the last person Pat interviews. Prepare the questions he will use in that interview.

Returning to the introductory materials, after you finish responding to the three instructions above, may help with the hypothesis testing to which this short survey will contribute. That introductory section is labeled "Later Scans and Hypothesis Testing" (p. xxx).

PART 5

Jake reluctantly agrees to extend the project to include his entire department. He indicates to Pat that this reluctance is due to his belief that the expanded project may disrupt the work of the sales department. He also makes this comment: "I'm not sure I want to see the results of the survey."

Jake also provides Pat with some additional information. His figures show that there are:

 3   area managers
10   key account representatives
 7   "inside" staff including Nancy
15   lead managers selected by the sales representatives in 15 districts throughout the United States
63   sales representatives
98   total people in the sales department

The company operates a bonus system anchored primarily on five of the 23 products marketed by the company. Thus, sales exceeding the sales targets for those five products yield income in addition to base salary.

Pat revises his hypotheses to include the following:

H_1 In addition to a breakdown in communication, he now believes that the bonus system may be influencing the attention being given to new accounts.

H_2 The micro-management from the top may be a function of both leadership style and organizational design.

H_3 The conflict between the management style of top management and the department structure may be causing confusion and dissatisfaction.

Pat devises a sealed questionnaire (see Exhibit III.1.1, "Sales Department Survey") and sends copies to all 98 people in the sales department, plus Jake. The questionnaire identifies each individual's position, length of time in the sales department, and age.

The results of the returned surveys are summarized in Table III.1.1, "Summary of Sales Department Survey Results."

This information must be analyzed and the results summarized. Feedback will go to Jake and, as Jake put it, to "other individuals not yet identified."

Exhibit III.1.1 Sales Department Survey

Below are questions concerning the Sales Department. Please circle the number that corresponds to your answer. DO NOT SIGN YOUR NAME.

1. How long does it take for important sales-related information to reach you?

1	2	3	4
one day	two days	three days	more than 3 days

Comments:

2. How timely is the sales-related information you receive?

1	2	3	4
always late			very timely

Comments:

3. How would you describe the type of management style by top management?

1	2	3	4
low-control			high-control

Comments:

4. How many organizational levels do you perceive there are in the Sales Department?

1	2	3	4
one level	two levels	three levels	four levels

Comments:

5. How much influence does the bonus system have on your sales efforts?

1	2	3	4
low			high

Comments:

Indicate the group in which you below:

_____	Top Management
_____	Area Managers
_____	Key Account Representatives
_____	Inside Staff
_____	Sales Representatives

If you are a Sales Representative, please indicate your district by circling the appropriate number:

1   2   3   4   5   6   7   8   9   10   11   12   13   14   15

Your Age: _____   Years of Service in the Sales Department: _____

Table III.1.1   Summary of Sales Department Survey Results—Numbers of Responses by Category

Group	Total Number	Number Returned	Time Lapse 1 day	Time Lapse 2 days	Time Lapse 3 days	Time Lapse more than 3 days	Timeliness 1	Timeliness 2	Timeliness 3	Timeliness 4	Management Style 1	Management Style 2	Management Style 3	Management Style 4	Organizational Levels 1	Organizational Levels 2	Organizational Levels 3	Organizational Levels 4	Bonus Influence 1	Bonus Influence 2	Bonus Influence 3	Bonus Influence 4
Top management	1	2		2				2				2				2	2			2		
Area managers	3	3		2			2		1			1	1	2		2	1				3	
Key account reps	10	5		5			4	1				1	1	4		4	1			1	1	4
Inside staff	7	6		5					5	1			4	2			6			3	1	
Sales reps (includes lead manager) by district																						
1	6	1		1			1				1			1	1							1
2	4	3		2			2	1					3			3				2	2	1
3	6	5		3	2		1	3	1			2	3			4	1				4	1
4	6	6		4	2		4	2				4	2			5	2		1		4	1
5	6	6		5	1		4	2				5	1			4	2		1		4	2
6	4	2		1	1		1	1					1	1		1	2					2
7	3	2		1	1			2				2			1	1				2		2
8	4	1	1					1		1					1							
9	5	3		2	1		1	2				1	2			2	1			1	2	1
10	7	2				2	2					2				2		2		2		
11	5	4		2	2		2	2				3	1			4					1	3
12	5	5	1	4			1	4				4	1			1	4			3	3	2
13	6	5	1	4	1		2	3				2	3			1	4			2	2	3
14	6	6	1	4	2		4	2				3	3			1	5			4	1	5
15	5	3		1	2		2	1				3				1	3			2	2	
Total	**99**	**70**	**5**	**40**	**21**	**3**	**8**	**29**	**30**	**3**	**1**	**26**	**33**	**10**	**1**	**33**	**34**	**2**	**0**	**10**	**33**	**26**

INSTRUCTIONS AND QUESTIONS: PART 5

The reader should take Pat's role in three particulars:

1. Analyze the data from the interviews and the survey.
2. To whom should the data be fed back?
3. What do you make of Jake's comment about not wanting to see the results of the survey?

Before you begin working, please refer to the section in the introductory materials labeled "Diagnosis, Analysis, and Alignment: Using Data to Test Hypotheses (p. xxxii)." Those summary comments and notes may provide useful cues for analyzing the data in Part 5.

PART 6

Pat now faces several choice-points concerning feedback and interventions. Thus, Pat schedules a meeting with Jake and his immediate staff—the three area managers—and Nancy. And Pat decides to format his feedback to them in terms of three major conclusions about problem areas, with the first two conclusions having two parts.

Without reservation, Jake and his three area managers accept the following descriptions of the problems:

1A "Important" information takes an average of 2½ days to reach key account and sales representatives, and when it arrives it usually is too late to be useful.
1B The bonus system, by keying in on five "high-priority products," clearly influences the efforts of key account and sales representatives. Some evidence suggests that key account representatives did not "jump at the bait" because the potential new accounts were not in the market for one of the five high-priority products.
2A A significant number of reps, staff, and managers believe that management "micro-manages" the work of the department.
2B The reps and managers perceive the organization structure to be relatively "flat," with an average of somewhat over two hierarchical levels.
3   Confusion appears to exist between the relatively flat structure of the department and the tight control exerted by management. As one rep wrote, "Why should we have area and team leaders if top management is not going to use them as an extension of management?"

Nancy fully agrees with points 2 and 3 but is very hesitant about agreeing with point 1A.

Pat's meeting with Jake and his staff turns into a discussion of how to solve these problems. Everyone appears too eager to move forward and "clear up these problems." A number of spontaneous suggestions are made, including these:

1. "Let's call everyone in and set the record straight about who's running this department."
2. "Put bonuses on five more high-priority products."
3. "Give all sales reps computers, and use e-mail to communicate with them."

After listening to this discussion and hearing members of the group get their ideas shot down by others, Pat intervenes with the following suggestions:

1. "I recommend that you feed back all of the data you have reviewed to the entire department and see if they agree with the results."
2. "If they generally agree, ask for volunteers to work along with members of management on project teams for each of the problem areas. We can define their tasks more clearly later to assure that project teams maintain their focus."
3. "The project teams can explore alternative solutions, present them to management, and gain approval for action."

The first reaction of the attendees is that Pat's proposal will be too time-consuming. However, after considerable discussion, the attendees reach full agreement to move ahead. As the meeting adjourns, attendees agree to meet on Friday at 2:00 PM to map out the plan in more detail.

INSTRUCTIONS AND QUESTIONS: PART 6

1. Compare your conclusions about the problem areas with those Pat shared with Jake's first reports. Do major similarities or differences exist? What do you make of the comparisons? Do the comparisons encourage you to change your mind?
2. Discuss whether interventions should have been designed at the feedback meeting.
3. Design an agenda for the next meeting.

4. Prepare a detailed plan for implementing the proposed project teams, including attention to:
   - number of teams. Why do you select the number you do?
   - project team objectives and tasks
   - team member roles
   - time lines
5. Prepare an answer to the following possible reaction from Jake: "Has this whole thing gotten out of hand? It looks like we started out with a small fixable problem and now look where we are. You're going to change my entire organization."

After working on these tasks, please refer to the section in the introductory materials on "Feedback and Interventions" (p. xxxiv). The comments there may help you improve your responses to the five tasks assigned above.

PART 7

Feedback to all employees was completed two months ago and, as a result, three project teams have been formed to study the five identified problems and to suggest changes:

Team	Problems	General Area
1	1A	information flow
2	1B	the bonus system
3	2A, 2B, & 3	organizations and leadership

The project teams meet with Jake, Nancy, and the three area managers to make the following recommendations:

Project Team Recommendations

1. The sales department should adopt a team-based structure, as illustrated in Figure III.1.1. Districts should be consolidated from 15 to 8. District team leaders should be selected by team members. Area managers should become area team coordinators and become part of a sales department leadership team. The plan includes details on role/job descriptions, organization missions and roles, defined accountability levels, time lines, training, and so on.
2. A computer-based system should be installed to link all district team leaders by e-mail. A "beeper" system should be provided to each sales representative for immediate access to information via the area managers. A detailed plan for implementing the recommendation is included, covering cost, schedule, training, support systems, and staffing requirements.

Figure III.1.1   Proposed Reorganization of Sales Division

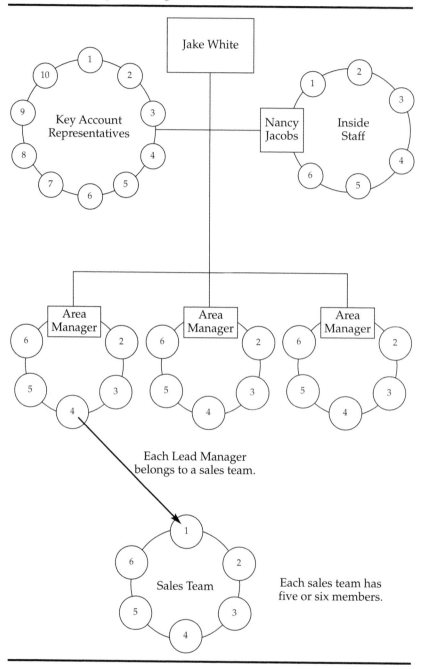

Each Lead Manager belongs to a sales team.

Each sales team has five or six members.

3. The present five-product bonus system should be dismantled and a goal-based program installed in its place. General annual goals should be set by management. Area and team leaders should work with sales teams to establish sales goals. Achievement above the goals for each product should yield a bonus that is paid annually.

INSTRUCTIONS AND QUESTIONS: PART 7

1. No effectiveness measures have yet been identified for assessing the impact of the proposed changes. Design a set of relevant effectiveness measures and a process for evaluating the effects of the changes against those measures.
2. Conduct a self-audit of your understanding of this application of OD as action research.
   Based on the seven-part analysis of the case study, identify your strengths and weaknesses, with the latter supporting a list of opportunities for improvement and the former representing the base on which to build.
3. Do you find any areas in the case study where a greater ethical and normative sensitivity seems appropriate? Consult the "Statement" in Perspective IV.

The introductory materials can help learners in this stock-taking, both retrospectively after reading, analyzing, and fine-tuning, as well as in looking forward to self-reflective experience with future OD activities. See the section on "Intervention, Implementation, and Evaluation" (p. xxxv).

PERSPECTIVE IV

A Statement of Values and Ethics by Professionals in Organization and Human Systems Development

from William Gellermann, Mark S. Frankel, and Robert F. Ladenson

Let us conclude this casebook, saving for last the most essential elements. In effect, this concluding Perspective IV provides normative guidance: a set of guidelines that apply to all OD cases, both commonplace and exotic.

Why are these guidelines necessary? To put it in a revealing way, OD is not some unguided missile, powerful but indiscriminate. Rather, OD is value-loaded in specific senses, and the Statement in Perspective IV reflects a broad (if incomplete) consensus about the overt as well as nuanced character of this value-loadedness, of this need to infuse OD approaches and techniques with specific values.

The intended use of the Statement is elemental. Typically, each case in this volume contains one or more tasks for ODers in the context of some action setting. But the most salient issues are always:

- Why OD? Or, OD for which particular purposes?
- What should ODers do, and why?

Here the Statement provides guidance—at times, specific directions; and at other times, insights about in what directions ODers should lean as they act.

IV

A Statement of Values and Ethics by Professionals in Organization and Human Systems Development*

William Gellermann,
Mark S. Frankel, and
Robert F. Ladenson

I. PREAMBLE

Organization and Human Systems Development (OD-HSD) is a professional network or community of professions whose practice is based on the applied behavioral sciences, a human systems perspective, and both human and organizational values. As OD-HSD professionals, we seek to promote and facilitate the process by which human beings and human systems live and work together for their mutual success and well-being. Our purpose is to promote a widely shared learning and discovery process dedicated to the vision of people living meaningful, productive, good lives in ways that simultaneously serve them, their organizations, their societies, and the world.

II. NATURE AND PURPOSES

For OD-HSD to exist as a profession, substantial consensus is necessary within the profession about its primary beliefs, values, and ethics. The

*Reprinted from Gellermann, W., Frankel, M. S., and Ladenson, R. F., *Values and Ethics in Organization and Human System Development: Responding to Dilemmas in Professional Life*, pp. 372–388. San Francisco: Jossey-Bass, 1990. Notes are omitted here.

process of co-creating this Statement is a means of establishing such consensus, but it is important to remember that *this Statement is not our primary objective. It is only a means to increase ethical consciousness and practice throughout our profession.*

The Statement is an *aspirational* guide, a specification of ideals toward which we strive. For a more detailed description and explanation of our professional norms, see the Annotated Statement in the book by Gellermann, Frankel, and Ladenson (1990).

The purposes of this Statement are to (1) increase our professional and ethical consciousness and our sense of ethical responsibility, (2) guide us in making more informed ethical choices, and (3) help our profession function more effectively.

We intend this Statement as a resource to help us make responsible, informed choices about our behavior by helping us to be clear about our:

Vision, since it enhances our sense of common purpose;
Beliefs, since they affect our ability to see the truth;
Values, since they are the essential element underlying our choices;
Moral rules and ideals, since they are fundamental to our being responsible members of the human community;
Ethical principles, since they provide general guidance for our choices;
Ethical guidelines, since they provide more specific guidance in the kinds of situations we encounter as OD-HSD professionals.

Using the Statement as a guide involves living consistently within its spirit and not just its words, particularly in ambiguous situations in which the good or right thing to do is not clear.

Because we view ethical practice as continuing and developmental, we encourage all OD-HSD professionals to use the Statement as a resource in (1) reflecting on their own values and ethics, ethical problems, and problem resolutions, and (2) communicating about the results of their reflection with other OD-HSD professionals, and when appropriate, with their clients.

III. BELIEFS

As OD-HSD professionals, we recognize the fundamental importance of the following beliefs, which guide our practice and provide context for our ethics. We believe that:

1. *Human beings* are
   a. Equally worthy, regardless of race, creed, age, nationality, gender, ability, socioeconomic status, or any other attribute that distorts people's perceptions of their essential equality;
   b. Rightfully entitled to equal opportunity in their lives;
   c. Interdependent economically, politically, socially, culturally, and spiritually;
   d. Rightfully responsible for taking charge of their own lives, functioning autonomously and interdependently, and for controlling and facilitating their own growth.
2. *Human systems*—including individuals, groups, organizations, communities, countries, and transnational systems—are
   a. Interdependent economically, politically, socially, culturally, and spiritually;
   b. Unique configurations of human energy—derived from needs, desires, beliefs, and values, purposes and visions, goals, talents, and resources—shaped by tensions among systems, subsystem, and macrosystem dynamics; and
   c. Open systems whose actions influence and are influenced by a variety of stakeholders.
3. *Human beings and human systems* are
   a. Interdependent and therefore positively or negatively affect one another's lives, survival, productivity, and growth;
   b. Interdependent with earth's ecosystems; and
   c. Responsible for living in harmony with all beings to ensure a sustainable future.

IV. VALUES

We acknowledge the following values or *standards of importance* as the foundation of our ethics as OD-HSD professionals:

1. Fundamental values
   a. *Life and the quest for happiness:* people respecting, appreciating, and loving the experience of their own and others' being while engaging in the search for and the process of co-creating "good" life.
   b. *Freedom, responsibility, and self-control:* people experiencing their freedom, exercising it responsibly, and being in charge of themselves.
   c. *Justice:* people living lives whose results are fair and equitable.

2. Personal and interpersonal values (may also be larger system-level values)

    a. *Human potential and empowerment:* people being healthy and aware of the fullness of their potential, realizing their power to bring that potential into being, growing into it, living it, and generally doing the best they can, both individually and collectively.

    b. *Respect, dignity, integrity, worth, and fundamental rights of individuals and other human systems:* people appreciating one another and their rights as human beings, including life, liberty, and the quest for happiness.

    c. *Authenticity, congruence, honesty and openness, understanding, and acceptance:* people being true to themselves, acting consistently with their feelings, being honest and appropriately open with one another (including expressing feelings and constructively confronting differences) and both understanding and accepting others who do the same.

    d. *Flexibility, change, and proaction:* people changing themselves on the one hand and acting assertively on the other in a continuing process whose aim is to maintain or achieve a good fit between themselves and the external reality within which they live.

3. System values (may be values at personal and interpersonal levels)

    a. *Learning, development, growth, and transformation:* people growing in ways that bring into being greater realization of their potential, individually and collectively.

    b. *Whole-win attitudes, cooperation-collaboration, trust, community, and diversity:* people caring about one another and working together to achieve results that are good for everyone (individually and collectively), experiencing the spirit of community and honoring the diversity that exists within community.

    c. *Widespread, meaningful participation in system affairs, democracy, and appropriate decision making:* people participating as fully as possible in making the decisions that affect their lives.

    d. *Effectiveness, efficiency, and alignment:* people achieving desired results with an optimal balance between results and costs, and doing so in ways that coordinate the energies of systems, subsystems, and macro systems—particularly the energies, needs, and desires of the human beings who comprise those systems.

V. ETHICS: PRINCIPLES, MORAL RULES AND IDEALS, AND JUSTIFYING VIOLATIONS

We commit ourselves to the following *standards of behavior.*

A. Fundamental Principle (Elements of a Meta-Principle Underlying All Our Ethics)

Act so that we would be willing to universalize the principles underlying our action and live with the consequences of our action if everyone were to act in accord with its underlying principles.

B. Moral Rules and Ideals

Morals (rules and ideals) are ethics aimed at minimizing harm or evil. We believe they are fundamental to living responsibly as members of the global human community.

1. *Moral rules.* Do no harm: do not kill, cause pain, disable, deprive of freedom, deprive of pleasure, deceive, cheat, break promises, disobey the law, or fail to do our duty.
2. *Moral ideals.* Prevent (or do those things that will lessen) harm suffered by anyone: prevent death, pain, disability, deprivation of freedom, deprivation of pleasure, deception, cheating, breaking of promises, disobeying of the law, and neglect of duties.

C. Justification of Moral-Ethical Violations

We recognize that violation of ethical standards (including morals) may be justified under certain conditions because such violation is required to minimize harm or to serve most fully the ideals represented by our values and ethics as a whole.

Justifying violation of morals and other ethical standards involves such considerations as: the standards violated; the harm avoided, prevented, or caused and the good promoted; the kinds of good or harm; their seriousness, duration, and probability of occurring; the number of people who will suffer or benefit; and the distribution of the benefit and suffering. In seeking to balance all of these considerations, we seek to serve the "greatest good of the whole," which includes valuing the "good of the individual" and respecting individuals' rights.

In considering possible ethics violations, we are guided by the following:

1. Do not violate moral rules without *moral* justification.
2. Do not violate moral ideals, ethical principles, or ethical guidelines without appropriate, clear, *ethical* justification.

D. Ethical Principles

1. Serve the good of the whole.
2. Do unto others as we would have them do unto us.
3. Always treat people as ends, never only as means, respect their "being" and never use them only for their ability to "do"; treat them as persons and never as objects.
4. Act so we do not increase power by more powerful stakeholders *over* the less powerful.

VI. ETHICS: GUIDELINES FOR PRACTICE

We commit ourselves to acting in accordance with the following guidelines:

I. Responsibility to Ourselves
   A. Act with integrity; be authentic and true to ourselves.
   B. Strive continually for self-knowledge and personal growth.
   C. Recognize our personal needs and desires and, when they conflict with other responsibilities, seek whole-win resolutions.
   D. Assert our own interests in ways that are fair and equitable to us as well as to our clients and their stakeholders.
II. Responsibility for Professional Development and Competence
   A. Accept responsibility for the consequences of our actions and make reasonable efforts to ensure that our services are properly used; terminate our services if they are not properly used and do what we can to see that any abuses are corrected.
   B. Develop and maintain our individual competence and establish cooperative relations with other professionals.
      1. Develop the broad range of our own competencies. These include:
         (a) Knowledge of theory and practice in
            (1) Applied behavioral science generally;
            (2) Leadership, management, administration, organizational behavior, system behavior, and organizational/system development specifically;

       (3) Labor union issues, such as collective bargaining, contracting, and quality of working life (QWL);

       (4) Multicultural issues, including issues of color and gender;

       (5) Cross-cultural issues, including issues related to our own ethnocentric tendencies and to differences and diversity within and between countries;

       (6) Values and ethics in general and how they apply to both the behavior of our client systems and our own practice;

       (7) Other fields of knowledge and practice relevant to the area(s) within OD-HSD on which we individually concentrate.

  (b) Ability to

       (1) Act effectively with individuals, groups, and large, complex systems;

       (2) Provide consultation using theory and methods of the applied behavioral sciences;

       (3) Cope with the apparent contradiction in applying behavioral science that arises when our "science" is too particular or too theoretical to be applicable or when our real approach is intuitive and not clearly grounded in science;

       (4) Articulate theory and direct its application, including creation of learning experiences for individuals; small and large groups; and large, complex systems.

2. Establish collegial and cooperative relations with other OD-HSD professionals. These include:

  (a) Using colleagues as consultants to provide ourselves with feedback or suggestions about our own development and to minimize the effects of our blind spots;

  (b) Creating partnerships with colleagues to enhance our effectiveness in serving clients whose needs are greater than we can serve alone.

C. Recognize our personal needs and desires and deal with them responsibly in the performance of our professional roles and duties.

D. Practice within the limits of our competence, culture, and experience in providing services and using techniques.

1. Neither seek nor accept assignments outside our limits without clear understanding by clients when exploration at the edge of our competence is reasonable.

    2. Refer clients to other professionals when appropriate.

    3. Consult with people who are knowledgeable about the unique conditions of clients whose activities involve specific areas in which we are inexperienced or not knowledgeable:

      (a) In special functional areas (such as marketing, engineering, or R & D);

      (b) In certain industries or institutions (such as mining, aerospace, health care, education, or government);

      (c) In multicultural settings (such as when we practice in settings in which there is significant diversity in the race, ethnicity, or gender of the people involved).

  E. Practice in cultures different from our own only with consultation from people native to or knowledgeable about those specific cultures.

III. Responsibility to Clients and Significant Others

  A. Serve the long-term well-being of our client systems and their stakeholders.

    1. Be aware of the beliefs and values relevant to serving our clients, including our own, our profession's, our culture's, and those of the people with whom we work (personal, organizational, and cultural).

    2. Be prepared to make explicit our beliefs, values, and methods as OD-HSD professionals.

    3. Avoid automatic confirmation of predetermined conclusions about the client's situation or what needs to be done by either the client or ourselves.

    4. Explore the possible implications of any OD-HSD intervention for all stakeholders likely to be significantly affected; help all stakeholders while developing and implementing OD-HSD approaches, programs, and the like, if they wish help and we are able to give it.

    5. Maintain balance in the timing, pace, and magnitude of planned change so as to support a mutually beneficial relationship between the system and its environment.

  B. Conduct any professional activity, program, or relationships in ways that are honest, responsible, and appropriately open.

    1. Inform people with whom we work about any activity or procedure in which we ask their participation.

      (a) Inform them about sponsorship, purpose and goals, our role and strategy, costs, anticipated outcomes, limitations, and risks.

      (b) Inform them in a way that supports their freedom of choice about their participation in activities initiated by us; also acknowledge that it may be appropriate for us to undertake activities initiated by recognized authorities in which participants do not have full freedom of choice.

(c) Alert them to implications and risks when they are from cultures other than our own or when we are at the edge of our competence.

(d) Ask help of the client system in making relevant cultural differences explicit.

2. Seek optimum participation by people with whom we work at every step of the process, including managers, labor unions, and workers' representatives.

3. Encourage and enable people to provide for themselves the services we provide rather than foster continued reliance on us; encourage, foster, and support self-education and self-development by individuals, groups, and all other human systems.

4. Develop, publish, and use assessment techniques that promote the welfare and best interests of clients and participants; guard against the misuse of assessment techniques and results.

5. Provide for our own accountability by evaluating and assessing the effects of our work.

(a) Make all reasonable efforts to determine if our activities have accomplished the agreed-upon goals and have not had other undesirable consequences; seek to undo any undesirable consequences, and do not attempt to cover them up; use such experiences as learning opportunities.

(b) Actively solicit and respond with an open mind to feedback regarding our work, and seek to improve our work accordingly.

6. Cease work with a client when it becomes clear that the client is not benefiting or the contract has been completed; do not accept or continue work under a contract if we cannot do so in ways consistent with the values and ethics outlined in this Statement.

C. Establish mutual agreement on a fair contract covering services and remuneration.

1. Ensure mutual understanding and agreement about the services to be performed; do not shift from that agreement without both a clearly defined professional rationale for making the shift and the informed consent of the clients and participants; withdraw from the agreement if circumstances beyond our control prevent proper fulfillment.

2. Ensure mutual understanding and agreement by putting the contract in writing to the extent feasible, yet recognize that:
   (a) The spirit of professional responsibility encompasses more than the letter of the contract.
   (b) Some contracts are necessarily incomplete because complete information is not available at the outset.
   (c) Putting the contract in writing may be neither necessary nor desirable.
3. Safeguard the best interest of the client, the professional, and the public by making sure that financial arrangements are fair and in keeping with appropriate statutes, regulations, and professional standards.

D. Deal with conflicts constructively and minimize conflicts of interest.
   1. Fully inform the client of our opinions about serving similar or competing organizations; be clear with ourselves, our clients, and other concerned stakeholders about our loyalties and responsibilities when conflicts of interest arise; keep parties informed of these conflicts; cease work with the client if the conflicts cannot be adequately resolved.
   2. Seek to act impartially when involved in conflicts among parties in the client system; help them resolve their conflicts themselves, without taking sides; if it becomes necessary to change our role from that of impartial consultant, do so explicitly; cease work with the client if necessary.
   3. Identify and respond to any major differences in professionally relevant values or ethics between ourselves and our clients; be prepared to cease work, with explanation of our reasons, if necessary.
   4. Accept differences in the expectations and interests of different stakeholders and realize that those differences cannot always be reconciled; take a whole-win approach to the resolution of differences whenever possible so that the greatest good of the whole is served, but allow for exceptions based on more fundamental principles.
   5. Work cooperatively with other internal and external consultants serving the same client systems and resolve conflicts in terms of the balanced best interests of the client system and all its stakeholders; make appropriate arrangements with other internal and external consultants about how to share responsibilities.
   6. Seek consultation and feedback from neutral third parties in cases of conflict involving ourselves, our clients, other consultants, or any of the systems' various stakeholders.

    E. Define and protect confidentiality in our client relationships.
1. Make limits of confidentiality clear to clients and participants.
2. Reveal information accepted in confidence only to appropriate or agreed-upon recipients or authorities.
3. Use information obtained during professional work in writings, lectures, or other public forums only with prior consent or when disguised so that it is impossible from our presentations alone to identify the individuals or systems with whom we have worked.
4. Make adequate provisions for maintaining confidentiality in the storage and disposal of records; make provisions for responsibly preserving records in the event of our retirement or disability.

    F. Make public statements of all kinds accurately, including promotion and advertising, and give services as advertised.
1. Base public statements providing professional opinions or information on scientifically acceptable findings and techniques as much as possible, with full recognition of the limits and uncertainties of such evidence.
2. Seek to help people make informed choices when they refer to statements we make as part of promotion or advertising.
3. Deliver services as advertised and do not shift without a clear professional rationale and the informed consent of the participants or clients.

IV. Responsibility to the OD-HSD Profession
    A. Contribute to the continuing professional development of other practitioners and of the profession as a whole.
1. Support the development of other professionals by various means, including
    (a) Mentoring with less experienced professionals;
    (b) Consulting with other colleagues;
    (c) Participating in reviews of others' practices.
2. Contribute to the body of professional knowledge and skill, including
    (a) Sharing ideas, methods, and findings about the effects of our work;
    (b) Keeping our use of copyright and trade secrets to an appropriate minimum.

    B. Promote the sharing of professional knowledge and skill.
1. Grant use of our copyrighted material as freely as possible, subject to a minimum of conditions, including a reasonable price based on professional as well as commercial values.

    2. Give credit for the ideas and products of others.

    3. Respect the rights of others in the materials they have created.

C. Work with other OD-HSD professionals in ways that exemplify what the OD-HSD profession stands for.

    1. Establish mutual understanding and agreement about our relationships, including purposes and goals, roles and responsibilities, fees, and income distribution.

    2. Avoid conflicts of interest when possible and resolve conflicts that do arise constructively (following guidelines similar to Guidelines III.D).

D. Work actively for ethical practice of individuals and organizations engaged in OD-HSD activities and, in case of questionable practice, use appropriate channels for dealing with it.

    1. Discuss directly and constructively when feasible.

    2. Use other means when necessary, including

        (a) Joint consultation and feedback (with another professional as third party);

        (b) Enforcement procedures of existing professional organizations;

        (c) Public confrontation.

E. Act in ways that bring credit to the OD-HSD profession and with due regard for colleagues in other professions.

    1. Act with sensitivity to the effects our behavior may have on the ability of colleagues to perform as professionals, individually and collectively.

    2. Act with due regard for the needs, special competencies, and obligations of colleagues in other professions.

    3. Respect the prerogatives and obligations of the institutions or organizations with which these colleagues are associated.

V. Social Responsibility

A. Accept responsibility for and act with sensitivity to the fact that our recommendations and actions may alter the lives and well-being of people within our client systems and within the larger systems of which they are subsystems.

B. Act with awareness of our own cultural filters and with sensitivity to multinational and multicultural differences and their implications.

    1. Respect the cultural orientations of the individuals, organizations, communities, countries, and other human systems

within which we work, including their customs, beliefs, values, morals, and ethics.

2. Recognize and constructively confront the counterproductive aspects of those cultures whenever feasible, but with alertness to the effects our own cultural orientation may have on our judgments.

C. Promote justice and serve the well-being of all life on earth.

1. Act assertively with our clients to promote justice and well-being, including
   (a) Constructively confronting discrimination whenever possible;
   (b) Promoting affirmative action in dealing with the effects of past discrimination;
   (c) Encouraging fairness in the distribution of the fruits of the system's productivity.

2. Contribute knowledge, skill, and other resources in support of organizations, programs, and activities that seek to improve human welfare.

3. Accept some clients who do not have sufficient resources to pay our full fees and allow them to pay reduced fees or nothing when possible.

4. Engage in self-generated or cooperative endeavors to develop means for helping across cultures.

5. Support the creation and maintenance of cultures that value freedom, responsibility, integrity, self-control, mutual respect, love, trust, openness, authenticity in relationships, empowerment, participation, and respect for fundamental human rights.

D. Withhold service from clients whose purpose(s) we consider immoral, yet recognize that such service may serve a greater good in the longer run and therefore be acceptable.

E. Act consistently with the ethics of the global scientific community of which our OD-HSD community is a part.

Finally, we recognize that accepting this Statement as a guide for our behavior involves holding ourselves to standards that may be more exacting than the laws of any countries in which we practice, the ethics of any professional associations to which we belong, or the expectations of any of our clients.

CASES IN ORGANIZATION DEVELOPMENT
Edited by Janet Tilden
Production supervision by Kim Vander Steen
Cover design by Cynthia Crampton Design, Park Ridge, Illinois
Composition by Point West, Inc., Carol Stream, Illinois
Printed and bound by The P. A. Hutchison Company, Mayfield, Pennsylvania